D1161742

The Future Makers

STIG VON BAYER

INTERNATIONAL TROUBLESHOOTER FOR PEACE

THE FUTURE MAKERS tells the history of our times through the men of our times.

THE FUTURE MAKERS is a series of books on dynamic younger men who have already contributed to the progress and development of many fields, and whose current achievements hold even greater promise for the future. Each book is biographical in structure, yet at the same time weaves into the man's life story the broader implications of what his attainments and goals are contributing to our way of life. The individual achievements and pioneering of each man in the series affects decisively current events and movements. As a maker of the future, he is a contributor to history.

The Future Makers

STIG VON BAYER

INTERNATIONAL TROUBLESHOOTER FOR PEACE

BY EDWARD HYMOFF

Introduction by The Honorable Arthur H. Dean

JAMES H. HEINEMAN, INC., NEW YORK

H

OTHER BOOKS IN THE SERIES:

SAMUEL S. STRATTON: A Story of Political Gumption
by Wilbur Cross

EUGENE H. NICKERSON: Statesman of a New Society
by Arturo Gonzalez

JOHN DIEBOLD: Breaking the Confines of the Possible
by Wilbur Cross

FIRST PRINTING 1965

The author is a member of the Society of Magazine Writers

Library of Congress Catalogue Card Number: 65–24535

For information address: James H. Heineman, Inc., 60 East 42nd Street, New York, New York, U.S.A.

Printed in the United States of America

to Kurt and Jennifer
May there always be keepers of the peace
that our children may never know war.

Preface

THE UNITED NATIONS at the age of twenty is probably Man's last chance to survive the environment he has created in this, the twentieth century. Yet, the United Nations according to the pessimists is on its last legs; optimists claim we should be happy that the UN functions at all.

Twenty years ago the hope and future of mankind was wrapped up in the success of the United Nations. There was no talk of failure on the part of war-weary nations. Twenty short years ago diplomats from 51 countries ratified—without any reservations—the United Nations Charter whose stirring preamble I wish to repeat here.

> WE THE PEOPLES OF THE UNITED NATIONS DETERMINED
> to save succeeding generations from the scourge of war, which twice in our lifetime has brought untold sorrow to mankind, and
> to reaffirm faith in fundamental human rights, in the dignity and worth of the human person, in the equal rights of men and women and of nations large and small, and
> to establish conditions under which justice and respect for

the obligations arising from treaties and other sources of international law can be maintained, and

to promote social progress and better standards of life in larger freedom,

AND FOR THESE ENDS

to practice tolerance and live together in peace with one another as good neighbors, and

to unite our strength to maintain international peace and security, and

to ensure, by the acceptance of principles and the institution of methods, that armed force shall not be used, save in the common interest, and

to employ international machinery for the promotion of the economic and social advancement of all peoples,

HAVE RESOLVED TO COMBINE OUR EFFORTS TO ACCOMPLISH THESE AIMS.

Accordingly, our respective Governments, through representatives assembled in the city of San Francisco, who have exhibited their full powers found to be in good and due form, have agreed to the present Charter of the United Nations and do hereby establish an international organization to be known as the United Nations.

There are hundreds of millions of people who have never heard of the United Nations Charter. Perhaps strident political and ideological cliches have come across louder than this preamble; perhaps memories are too short or perhaps mankind is destined to live in turmoil and, like the lemming, hurl itself to extinction.

However, I prefer to believe otherwise. When this Charter was ratified twenty years ago by fifty-one nations, none could have predicted that within this brief span of time nearly four million men from fifty-one member nations and an additional two non-member nations of the United Nations would have fought and served—and died—in the cause of peace and for a flag that belongs to the world.

As a reporter, I have covered the United Nations in peace

and in war. I have been privileged to meet military men from many lands, soldiers whom Secretary General U Thant has often referred to as the "international man . . . anybody with normal intelligence, a dedication to the principles and spirit of the United Nations and imbued with a desire to serve peace. . . ." I hope that these men of the caliber of Stig von Bayer will succeed in preserving the peace of the world.

I have tried to write about a new breed of man whose battlefield is everywhere and anywhere in the world where peace is threatened and armed forces are required. I have been able to write this book thanks to the cooperation of Captain von Bayer. I also wish to acknowledge the invaluable assistance of Dr. Ernest W. Lefever, author of *Crisis in the Congo* and his research staff at The Brookings Institute, and members of the United Nations military advisory staff.

Also, my thanks to Mr. James H. Heineman, the publisher of this book, who wanted to have this story told as a reminder that the peacekeepers have prevailed so far. Finally, my thanks to Wilbur Cross who edited this action-adventure-history, and to Frank Pape, my typist for many years, who actually put down on paper more than three million words and many days of tape-recorded interviews to make this book possible.

I hope there always will be peacekeepers to rally round the United Nations flag.

EDWARD HYMOFF

Atlantic Highlands, New Jersey
August, 1965

Table of Contents

*This book was designed by Laurence Lustig
and set in Caledonia type.*

*It was printed by letterpress on Old Forge paper,
and bound at H. Wolff Book Manufacturing Co.,
New York, New York.*

The Future Makers

STIG VON BAYER

INTERNATIONAL TROUBLESHOOTER FOR PEACE

Introduction

ONE OF THE BIGGEST problems in the formulation of disarmament plans, or in the formulation of peacekeeping activities of the United Nations, occurs in the basic question whether under Articles 36 and 42 of the United Nations Charter only the Security Council, which has "the primary responsibility for the maintenance of peace and security" with the accompanying rights of veto of its five permanent members, can authorize peacekeeping activities; or whether the General Assembly, through the "Uniting for Peace" resolution adopted on November 20, 1950, can by a two-thirds vote against the contentions of the U.S.S.R., France, or other members, recommend such activities and then induce the members to pay their pro rata share of the budgeted expenses and to otherwise cooperate in carrying out the recommendations; or to what extent the Secretary-General himself under Articles 98, 99, and 100, with the cooperation of peacekeeping units voluntarily contributed by members, but in the absence of specific authority from the appropriate body of the United Nations, may legally dispatch peacekeeping emissaries or engage in peacekeeping activities in addition to the "peace observation committees" authorized by such "Uniting for Peace" resolutions or by the Security Council itself.

In June, 1950, when the U.S.S.R. had walked out of the Security Council, the resolutions of June 25 and June 27, 1950, took the form of "requests," not directives.

The members were requested to furnish the necessary assistance to protect the Republic of Korea from aggression and to restore peace. Within three months after the initial North Korean attack sixteen nations had committed military forces for use under the United Nations flag, with the United States carrying the largest share of the burden.

Other basic questions are whether the United Nations itself should have a permanent, trained, and staffed peacekeeping unit with appropriate staff and logistical materièl and who can authorize its use, or whether the United Nations, pursuant to Article 43 of the Charter, can only call upon member nations to furnish it with national contingents from their own armies with all of the complex difficulties, timing, transportation, housing, clothing, and logistical questions this implies when men of different nationalities, religions, food-eating habits, languages, customs, training, and sympathies are supposed to be combined in an effective united UN force under a single commander and to respond to orders without debate.

In his book, *Stig von Bayer: International Troubleshooter for Peace,* Mr. Hymoff has put together a description and history of the youth and training of a young Swedish officer in the UN peacekeeping force in the Congo and later Cyprus, and in vivid narrative, attempts to portray the problems of such a force in a primitive country such as the Congo, where there are many tribes and many dialects with a long history of internecine wars and where voodoo, witchcraft, extreme tribal loyalties and hatreds, illiteracy, drugs, "dawa," "refugee camps," and gold and diamond bribery play their baffling part.

One is reminded of the descriptions in American history books of the British Army under General Braddock fighting the American Indians at the time of the French Colonial War on the North American continent. The underlying problems of men trained to fight in formation engaged on strange territory against those accustomed to fighting by stealthy, primitive methods and to using weapons as individuals would not seem to have changed a great deal.

Although possibly Mr. Hymoff underestimates the knowledge of the several diplomats of the United Nations with respect to actual tribal dialects, geographical, and logistical conditions in the Congo, his story of the training in a UN peacekeeping unit of Stig von Bayer and the officers' progress in meeting those exceptionally difficult conditions in the light of rapidly changing conditions and directives issued from afar is well told in somewhat gruesome detail.

He of course does not attempt to explain how the high command at the United Nations could have solved the problem by working out different orders for the UN peacekeeping force or to offer his recommendations for solving the equally difficult problems brought on by the authorization of wholesale firing on tribal natives before they actually attacked UN peacekeeping members.

Human beings who are fired upon and see their comrades wounded, slain, or mutilated react in pretty much the same way whether they are in national forces or in the peacekeeping uniforms of the United Nations, and the motivations of those engaged in civil war are not easy to analyze.

Mr. Hymoff attributes the failure of the League of Nations to provide security to the non-participation of the United States, but careful students of that body might think the causes more complicated. The worldwide economic collapse in the thirties accompanied by the rise in popularity of anti-democratic and nationalist doctrines and the reluctance of allies to assume the primary responsibilities for the maintenance of the peace were contributing factors.

The author also blames a number of the difficulties arising in connection with the peacekeeping operations of the United Nations forces in the Congo on the alleged actions of the Union Minière du Haut Katanga and its alleged mercenaries and upon the white mercenaries hired by Prime Minister Tshombe of Katanga and implies that the Belgian mining company should not have attempted to protect its properties or to continue its operations. While the protection of the lives of men must always come before the protection of property, the protection of lives without adequate provisions for housing, improved sanitary facilities, medical supplies, and adequate food also brings its problems, and a stable economic system would seem essential to liberty.

The situation in the Congo is still too recent for a scholarly appraisal of the actual events, and it is still too early to know whether the alleged mistakes of some of the operational UN peacekeeping officers really contributed to the peace or compounded an already difficult situation. Without attempting in any way to pass upon the accuracy of Mr. Hymoff's account I would say that his narrative certainly does point up some of the difficulties in UN peacekeeping forces and does at least raise the specter that possibly the United Nations could be wrong.

It also raises the question whether the theories expounded by many that a great power should not participate in peacekeeping activities and that all peacekeeping problems can be solved easily by using blacks against blacks or Asians against Asians really have any sound basis in actual operations.

There is no question but that both the U.S.S.R. and the Chinese Communists had involved themselves in the Congolese situation, and that the U.S.S.R., and perhaps Communist China, as well, supported Lumumba. It is easy to criticize Tshombe and his mercenaries, their treatment of the Baluba tribesmen, and the atrocities of the undisciplined Congolese Army, but the machinations of the Communists in Central Africa are hard to pinpoint, and it is difficult to know precisely what the best economic and peaceful answers are for countries such as the former Belgian Congo, Cyprus, et al. It is well to have dedicated peacekeeping officers, but someone to direct them.

NEW YORK, N.Y. ARTHUR H. DEAN
JULY 15, 1965

1

The present encounters the past

CAPTAIN STIG VON BAYER leaned from the open door of the Sikorsky helicopter and looked back. The slip stream from the spinning rotors overhead beat against his tanned features as he gripped a safety strap with one hand, while clutching his Swedish-made Karl Gustaf submachine gun in the other. He cursed the bad luck that had overtaken the other chopper. It was on the ground in a clearing half-a-mile back where it had made an emergency landing.

Ignoring the four nuns in the compartment with him, the Swedish Army officer pulled himself toward the pilot's compartment and shouted an order to the burly Norwegian at the controls.

"We must go back," he yelled. "The other copter is down."

Lieutenant Karlsen nodded and banked the white-painted helicopter in a tight 180-degree turn. Von Bayer stepped back to the open door and flicked off the safety catch on his weapon as the helicopter slowly settled to the ground. The moment that it touched down he jumped out and ran to the disabled machine where Sergeant Jeppesen, the grounded craft's Danish Army copilot, was working feverishly on the engine.

"What happened?" the Swedish captain asked.

"One of their damned blunderbusses shot up our oil line."

"Can you repair it?"

"In ten minutes if I had the parts."

The pilot and two crewmen of the disabled helicopter spread out and took up defensive positions nearby. Each man was armed and ready for an attack that might come at any moment. Somewhere in the brush the rebel tribesmen who had shot down the United Nations helicopter with their ancient muzzleloaders were racing toward the "white man's up-and-down bird."

"Let's get out of here!" von Bayer snapped. "Leave the copter. They'll be on top of us any minute now."

Faint shouting could be heard from the bush. The Swedish officer quickly ordered the three nuns to leave the disabled aircraft, calming the terrified women as he reached up to help each of the sisters to the ground.

Their white tropical habits flapping, they ran toward the other Sikorsky which squatted in the grass with its rotor slowly turning. The crew quickly assisted each of the nuns into the helicopter, unceremoniously boosting them into the passenger compartment. As soon as the last nun was inside, von Bayer called to the crew of the downed helicopter to pull back toward the second Sikorsky and board it. The shouting from the bush sounded nearer and louder.

Just as the tribesmen stormed from the underbrush, von Bayer scrambled aboard.

"Let's go!" he shouted to the blonde Norwegian at the controls. Lt. Karlsen nodded and gunned the engine, wondering to himself how the overloaded machine would rise even a single foot off the ground. The rotors flailed wildly, and the engine strained mightily. The helicopter shuddered, but didn't lift.

Howling triumphantly, the tribesmen rushed in for the kill. Von Bayer waited until the very last moment before he triggered his submachine gun. The chatter of his weapon was lost in the noise of the thundering engine. Some of the attackers fell. The helicopter lurched upward and forward, touching the ground as it settled and then bounced into the air as the rotors bit deep into the humid air and took hold with their lifting action.

A cloud of arrows sped toward the slowly rising H-19 as it staggered off. The arrows splattered against the aluminum skin of the Sikorsky, leaving slight nicks and dents where the poisoned heads struck. Unable to climb more than a hundred feet, the helicopter thundered off in the direction of Kikwit more than a hundred miles to the northwest. Von Bayer stuck his head out and watched the mob of frenzied tribesmen recede in the distance. He sorrowfully shook his head at the sight of the painted rebels brandishing ancient rifles, *panga* knives, *mukoki* spears and war clubs.

The slim, tanned Swede exhaled relief and set his weapon on the floor. Smiling reassuredly at the rescued nuns, he dug into the breast pockets of his khaki shirt and pulled out a crumpled pack of cigarettes and a five-inch holder of ornately carved elephant ivory. After carefully inserting a cigarette in the holder, he then offered the pack to the crew and thumbed the Zippo lighter engraved with his regimental crest.

The hot May sun beat down on the helicopter as it beat its way toward Leopoldville. The nuns remained silent, each with her own thoughts of the unpleasantness that might have been but for the handsome Swedish officer. The sisters had spent years in the bush attempting to spread their faith and bring civilization to a people who had been left behind by the parade of progress centuries earlier.

This was the fourth year of existence for the Republic of the Congo—four years of political turbulence and civil anarchy, violence, and chaos. The former Belgian colony was suffering from the effects of sudden, unprepared independence granted on June 30, 1960. For four years Captain Stig von Bayer had watched the Congo flounder in a morass of petty politics from within and big-power politics from without. He also had observed how the new nation had become a pawn in the East-West struggle over Africa.

These were the reasons why he was in a helicopter bearing the insignia of the United Nations. This was why he was serving under the United Nations flag; yes, he had even fought under the blue and white banner as one of a new breed of soldier —the international policeman and peacekeeper.

Adventurous, daring, and brave during many a touch-and-go situation, the twenty-seven-year-old Swedish officer was deeply stirred by the events in the new African state. When he had sprayed the attacking tribesmen with bullets, he did so reluctantly. These people were not enemies; they were not a nation of strangers as they were to most of the ninety-three thousand United Nations troops from thirty-four nations who had given their best—and in some cases their lives—to keep the peace.

The Congo was a second home to Stig von Bayer. The Congolese were a people he knew intimately. The tribesmen were people he understood; he knew their customs and he spoke their language.

For nearly four years he was the United Nations *bwana* they preferred to parley with. For forty-seven months he was the eyes and ears of the UN, and his reports were eagerly awaited by his commanders in Leopoldville and by the Secretary General and his staff in a far-off skyscraper towering over New York City's East River.

Stig von Bayer's thoughts covered a lot of years as he puffed his cigarette while the helicopter flew on. Here he was, an officer in an international peacekeeping force that in a matter of weeks was to be pulled out of the Congo because the harassed government wanted it so. Other governments also wished to see an end to the peacekeeping effort for various and sundry reasons.

The last UN troops (*les Onusiens*) were scheduled to pull out no later than June 30, 1964, and Captain Stig von Bayer, who was one of the first of the peacekeeping forces to arrive, would be one of the very last to depart. He looked forward to his departure with mixed emotions. The Congo had been his home for four years, with the exception of a month's military leave each year. Between the ages of eleven and sixteen he had lived in the Congo with his parents. He considered the Congo a second home.

Now he was preparing to take leave, and he knew that with the departure of the UN's peacekeeping forces the central African republic would be in for difficult times. It was, he thought to himself, a strange world that he lived in and one not of his own making. However, it was a world in which he shared some responsibility while serving under a flag that represented not a single all-powerful nation or leader but an idea and an ideal.

2

A far-off world

THE WORLD that Stig Erik Otto von Bayer entered in a Stockholm suburb on July 6, 1937, was a disjointed and troubled world. It was a world rushing headlong toward the greatest war in its recorded history. A generation numbering millions of young men was being armed in a futile effort to keep the peace. Other millions were being exhorted by their leaders to wage war. Despite this mad preparation, the world was also giving birth to a new generation of peacekeepers and warriors. Many would be caught up in the madness of 1939-45; they would not survive the years of conflict that would be their destiny.

The possibility of conflict was "unthinkable" when Stig von Bayer was born. The Great War of 1914-18 had taken a terrible toll in men and national treasures; it had upset a century of relative peace and gracious civilization; and it had loosed upon the world strange new ideologies that twisted the past and are still molding and shaping the present and the future. Yet, many nations blindly believed in "peace in our time," and, one by one, either succumbed to the threat of force or permitted this threat to overwhelm them.

The decade that gave birth to Stig von Bayer's generation was stormy then. War clouds loomed on the horizon, and the distant thunder of guns could be heard everywhere. The scenes and sounds of battle erupted at times in various parts of the world and jackbooted legions marched to the cadence of thundering war drums.

The events that had occurred during the decade of the young Swede's birth were only of passing historic interest by the time he was able to understand the past and relate it to the present and the future. There was one difference: these events later were to become more meaningful to him during many thoughtful interludes when he took the time to recall the past—especially the decade of his birth.

It was a decade scarred by:

The invasion of China by Japan.

A civil war that ripped the fabric of civilization from Spain.

The conquest of Ethiopia by Italy in a show of force that pitted aircraft and poison gas against spears, bows and arrows, war clubs, and shields covered with animal skins.

The appearance of Adolf Hitler and his "Thousand-Year Reich" with one aim—to conquer Europe and "tomorrow the world."

A purge of the Soviet Army officer corps by Josef Stalin who, dreaming of a Communist world, planned world revolution and the invasion of Finland.

The self-imposed isolation of the United States which ultimately wrecked the world's first international organization by refusing to become a member in the mistaken belief that the North American continent was naturally inviolate thanks to the Atlantic and Pacific Oceans.

The world of the 1930's was built of many bricks, but put together with mortar that lacked strength, cohesion, and understanding. The Nazi ideology clashed with communism. The democratic nations were torn by economic problems and shortsighted leadership. The colonial empires of the past were living on borrowed time, while the heartbeat of nationalism slowly began to throb in the breasts of the colored peoples of the world. The world of the 1930's was divided like a pie with the strongest nations receiving the biggest pieces.

The United States was a sleeping giant. The problems facing Americans were problems of the moment. Depression had shaken the North American continent—and the world—in the economic debacle of 1929. Prohibition had come to an end while criminals went on the rampage and began to organize. The labor movement finally organized and received support from the federal government which took a stronger hand in economic regulation and supervision. A "domestic corps" of that era appeared in the form of Civilian Conservation Corps camps for teen-agers and the Works Progress Administration for their elders. This was how the U.S. government made work for its people in an effort to pull itself out of the economic hole into which the nation had fallen.

The problems at home were more important than the problems elsewhere in the world. They only affected a relatively small segment of Americans with family and ethnic ties to other countries. The sleeping giant often has been described as a giant ostrich with its head in the sand. Yet there were many other nations which also could be likened to ostriches. In the world of the 1930's there was a minority, however, composed of people who hoped for the best and tried hard to make theirs a better world. It appears that they were ahead of their time.

In Geneva, Switzerland, the optimists and the idealists tried to make the League of Nations work. They failed. They experimented with one of the world's first international peacekeeping forces in December, 1934, by sending contingents of 1,500 British, 1,300 Italian, 250 Netherlands and 250 Swedish troops to the Saarland to police and keep order during the plebiscite of January 13, 1935. Amid the implied threat by the agents and secret police of one of the new ideologies 90.35 per cent of 539,541 Saarlanders who voted cast their ballots for reunion with Germany. The old Germany that had collapsed on November 11, 1918, was replaced by the Weimar Republic, then replaced by a new Reich—Nazi Germany.

The election had been administered by a plebiscite commission appointed by the Council of the League of Nations. The commission prepared voting lists and electoral machinery and an international police force maintained order. Still the League of Nations failed because its peacekeeping force had been fielded in the wrong place at the wrong time. So ended an experiment in international administration and peacekeeping.

The idea of an international military force is not as new as the United Nations or as old as the League of Nations. History records that as early as 1000 A.D., French princes of the Church discussed a willingness to wage "war against war" by intervention of allied armies led by a religious leader. The Concert of Europe did not result in an international army during the era of Metternich but national forces often acted in the name of the whole alliance.

The first modern international military force for peacekeeping purposes, commanded by a German general, succeeded in August, 1900, to bring an end to fighting in China. Although within the context of nineteenth-century imperialism, the armed forces of Germany, England, France, Russia, and the United States, were assembled into a peacekeeping force of 18,600 men to battle the Chinese Boxers, a large rebellious group of reactionary patriots who hated missionaries and all western ideas. The Boxer Rebellion, named after the Chinese rebels who called themselves the Fists of Righteous Harmony, was similar in one respect to what would occur in the Congo exactly sixty years later. The Boxers, densely ignorant, believed that magic would serve as a defense against bullets. They took to the warpath and burned bridges, killed missionaries, tore up railroad tracks, invaded the imperial capital of Peking, where resided the old Dowager Empress Tz'u Hsi, who was secretly supporting the rebels, and attacked the various foreign legations even going so far as to kill the German ambassador.

An international army, which included a regiment of U. S. Marines, marched on Peking, attacked and bombarded the city with artillery, smashed through the Boxer defenses and brought the rebels to their knees. Again, within the context of nineteenth-century imperialism, a humiliating peace was imposed and large indemnities were leveled against the imperial government of China along with a treaty stipulation that military units of the five major powers were to be stationed permanently in Peking.

History also records another effort at an international peacekeeping force immediately after World War I. However, this never reached beyond the paper-planning stage. In 1920 the League of Nations planned to establish a police force "to ensure a well-ordered and fair expression of opinion" during a plebiscite planned for Vilna occupied by a Polish army which had battled its way into Lithuania. A force of eighteen hundred soldiers provided by Belgium, Britain, Spain, France, Denmark, Norway, Sweden, and the Netherlands was to have supervised the plebiscite which was never held because Poland refused to evacuate its troops and the new Soviet government considered an international police force so close to its borders an unfriendly act and a danger to its security.

A similarly constituted international police force for plebiscite purposes was to be for another fourteen years; and the four nations which kept the peace in the Saar in 1934 were yet to have their chance. For three of these nations it would only be after their respective trials by fire in the 1939-45 war that was yet to come.

This was the world into which Stig von Bayer was born. Outwardly, Sweden during Stig's early years was a nation at peace and untroubled by the war that too few could see coming. Inwardly, the traditional neutrality of Sweden was maintained by Socialist Premier Per A. Hansson, who undertook an essential program of rearming after the meteoric rise of Nazi Germany.

Some children are born with a silver spoon in their mouths. Stig was one of those fortunate enough to be part of a wealthy landowning family. The von Bayers on his father's side were the descendants of Prussian landowners who migrated to Sweden in the late seventeenth century. The Ugglas on his maternal side of the family by tradition were officers in the

Swedish Army. This was the only difference between Stig von Bayer and his contemporaries from less affluent families.

The members of the Swedish generation into which Stig was born had one thing in common: they all were destined to one day wear a uniform and some were to serve in far off places under a flag other than the blue and gold colors of their native land.

Sweden is a peaceful country but its youth play at games of war. Stig was no different. His happiest days on the family estate at *Mônleby gård* in southwest Sweden were spent playing games where enemies were shot and killed. The cowboys chased the Indians even in Sweden. The hussars pursued the enemy. The hunters tracked their quarry.

Stig's first recollections of war were the reminiscenses of Uncle Carl ("Charlie") Uggla, a regular army officer who had taken a leave of absence to fight alongside the Finns against the Russians in the bitter winter of 1939-40. At the end of World War II Stig was eight years old. Europe lay smoking in ruins. Sweden emerged from the billowing clouds of war untouched by nothing more than a few shooting incidents during the six years of conflagration to the south, east and west.

Stig's early years briefly paralleled the final years of the League of Nations, born in 1920 to maintain the peace of the world, and dying a slow death at the hands of its own members. On the ashes of this failure rose the United Nations, an organization which Stig was to hear more of as he grew older. The United Nations began like its predecessor—as an idea. It was first expressed in the Atlantic Charter signed in 1941 by the United States and Great Britain and ultimately by other nations opposed to the Axis. Unlike United States reluctance to join the League of Nations in 1920, American leaders heartily endorsed the Atlantic Charter before the U.S. was even officially at war.

The following year the twenty-six nations fighting the Axis issued a Declaration by United Nations promising to cooperate with each other and rejecting the possibility of a separate peace. In October, 1943, the U.S., the Soviet Union, the United

Kingdom, and the Republic of China officially recognized the need for a new world organization. The Moscow declaration was signed. The United Nations was the topic of discussion at Dumbarton Oaks in Washington, D.C., in 1944 and again at Yalta in 1945.

The League of Nations had its ill-fated Covenant; the United Nations has its Charter. At San Francisco, fifty nations unanimously ratified the UN Charter and on October 24, 1945, a United Nations "with teeth" unfurled its blue and white flag.

The League of Nations was dead after twenty years. At the same age the United Nations, somewhat ailing, was still very much alive.

However, at the birth of the United Nations no one was able to foresee that by the time it reached its twentieth birthday 3,800,000 men from fifty-two nations would have served or fought as international peacekeepers under the banner inscribed with a global map encircled by the olive branches of peace.

In 1945 Stig von Bayer was of that generation of peacekeepers that was yet to serve this flag.

3

Early beginnings

As an eight-year-old boy who had everything, there were times in Stig's life that appeared to him to be of crisis proportions. Sociologists call this growing pains. The United Nations also had its growing pains during periods of crisis. Some periods of crisis were easily overcome. Others shook the very foundations of the new organization created to maintain world peace.

In 1946 Iran complained that Soviet troops stationed on her territory during World War II had not been withdrawn. The Security Council ordered the U.S.S.R. to evacuate its troops from Iranian territory. This was promptly done.

About the same time two other Middle East nations, Syria and Lebanon, requested the withdrawal of French and British troops from their respective territories. Both nations complied with the wish of the Security Council.

The peacekeeping machinery was working. It wasn't until 1948 that peacekeepers in uniform were first required. On January 1, 1948, India reported to the Security Council that tribesmen and others had been invading the state of Jammu and Kashmir and that extensive fighting was taking place. India also complained that Pakistan was assisting the tribesmen in the invasion and requested that the Security Council request that Pakistan cease and desist.

Kashmir, the area in question, is claimed both by India and Pakistan and is a territory for which both countries are willing to fight. A UN Commission for India and Pakistan (UNCIP) was formed to investigate the dispute and report its finding to the Security Council. The dispute over Kashmir centered around its eventual disposition. Formerly an Indian princedom, Kashmir borders upon both India and Pakistan. Under the scheme of partition and the Indian Independence Act of 1947, Kashmir became free to be part of either Pakistan or India in a future general election that "should be settled by a reference to the people."

Observers from several nations were quickly sent to Kashmir to negotiate and supervise a cease fire. Armed only with signal flags and arm bands reading UNITED NATIONS, these officers braved death at the hands of trigger-happy tribesmen and soldiers of both India and Pakistan. These were among the first UN peacekeepers in uniform.

Actually, the first recorded peacekeeping military team consisted of six men in uniform and three civilians in a group headed by Admiral Alan G. Kirk, a retired U. S. Navy officer who was made chairman of the mission to Greece. Still trying to recover from the wreckage of World War II, Greece was considered fair game by communist guerrillas hiding in the mountains bordering her northern neighbors. Greece was on Josef Stalin's timetable for the conquest of Europe, but the war-weary nation wouldn't succumb to the incursions by Red guerrillas. Once that first UN observer team landed in Greece and began inspecting areas where heavy attacks were mounted, this spelled *finis* to subversion that almost succeeded. The Kremlin couldn't stand the glare of notoriety when neutrals suddenly appeared on the scene and began condemning the Soviets for aggression in Greece.

With the help of vast amounts of United States economic and military aid, the embattled nation quickly regained its balance. In a few short years the Reds were ousted and Greece was firmly in the Western camp, siding with its fellow member states in high NATO councils.

Later in 1948 fighting broke out in the new nation of Israel as neighboring Arab states attacked the former British possession that had so long been an international bone of contention. By the time the shooting stopped uniformed peacekeepers from the United States, Denmark, Canada, and Sweden—each wearing a UN armband—patrolled the strife-torn nation in an effort to halt the shooting and supervise the truce.

The United Nations was growing up and so was young Stig von Bayer. In early 1949 he left Sweden on the first of his great adventures. Destination: the Belgian Congo. Stig was born into a generation of travelers. The expansion of air transportation even then had condensed the vast expanses of the world, and Stig's parents thought nothing of raising a family deep in the heart of Africa.

Stig's father Hansson, an engineer under contract to supervise the construction of roads and bridges in the African colony, presented his son with a .22 caliber rifle shortly after his arrival. The Congolese presented the son of the *kikwenda* with gifts in the form of a turtle and a parakeet. His father taught him how to shoot and the Congolese showed him how to track and hunt game, and to survive in the rain forest, in the swamp, and in the grassy *savanna.*

Stig's family lived like gypsies. As the road construction project snaked further into the interior, they would move along with the work camp. During his first six months in the Congo, Stig was tutored in educational subjects by his parents while he and the Congo and its people became better acquainted. In six months he was able to speak Swahili fluently.

Meanwhile, the bravado of a fearless twelve-year-old youngster made itself felt. Africa was new to the slim, blonde lad and his inquisitive mind reached out for knowledge that was as old as life in the Congo. Wearing nothing more than a pair of shorts and canvas rubber-soled shoes, he would disdainfully run through the sharp *savanna* grasses disregarding the many scratches and cuts that covered his bare arms, legs, and chest. Even the Congolese began to marvel at his stamina, and after six months his skin toughened to the point where the jungle flora no longer pierced or scratched his tanned limbs.

The construction route had taken the von Bayers deep into elephant country. Stig's mother, Elizabeth, a crack shot with a pistol, accepted as commonplace the incursions by groups of massive pachyderms into the vegetable gardens she tended at each new camp. Shortly after Stig's arrival he awoke with a start one night after an elephant had bellowed nearby. Frightened, he ran to the protective arms of his mother. Africa was still very strange, and the darkness hid the unknown.

In the absence of his father, she comforted and protected her son. Deliberately stepping from the *hyazi* grass hut shelter that served as home, with a pistol in one hand and a lantern in the other, she shooed away the mammoth creatures with indignant shouts emphasized by firing a few shots from the weapon. This routine soon became a family joke every time the elephants or other animals moved toward the one bit of ground that Stig's mother held most dear—her garden.

Her shooting ability with a pistol was legendary throughout the province. She and Hans would often entertain visitors with Stig's mother holding up a matchbox in her hand, and his father, from a distance of twenty-five paces, shooting it out of her hand. Elizabeth could shoot equally well. Stig's family was, indeed, a remarkably close-knit group.

During the first weeks Stig quickly became used to animals. In fact, his lack of fear on one occasion jeopardized his life. He also had been given a jungle knife by his father and delighted in killing snakes by slashing and severing the bodies of the reptiles. The Congolese were by nature, and for good reason, afraid of snakes and marveled at the *Bwana's* son who feared nothing. They called on Stig to kill whatever snakes were found, and the area through which the highway was being built abounded with reptiles of all sizes and colors.

He learned his lesson, however. One of the native workers

had been sent to the chicken pen to fetch eggs. He came screaming back to the house, one hand cupped over an eye. A cobra had suddenly reared in the pen and spat at the Congolese, striking his eye with a stream of venom. Stig's mother quickly applied first aid and the worker's eyesight was saved. The lesson had not gone unnoticed by Stig. He later chose to kill snakes with his rifle.

Africa was a new way of life for the youngster from Sweden. World events were remote for the white and black men who lived in the dark continent. The Congo was still a decade away from independence along with most of the other colonies that belonged to the historic European colonizing countries. World trouble spots were centered elsewhere and Korea was just as strange a name and a place to the Belgians and other European residents in the Congo, and to the extremely few Congolese who could read. In fact, the "Land of the Morning Calm" was as unknown to most of the peoples of Europe and the Western hemisphere as it was to the peoples of Africa.

The Congo and Korea were to later share a common experience, however. In both countries men would fight and die under the United Nations banner. Young Stig von Bayer's destiny was set in motion by the circumstances of his early life, his nationality, the times of which he was a part, and the world in which he lived.

4

From League of Nations to United Nations

THIRTY YEARS AFTER the birth and death of the impotent League of Nations, five years after the end of the greatest holocaust in history and half a decade after the birth of the United Nations, war suddenly enveloped a remote peninsula jutting from the coast of northeast Asia. At dawn on June 25, 1950, Communist North Korea—a non-member of the United Nations—attacked the two-year-old Republic of Korea—a tiny, dismal nation created by the United Nations and also not a member. In fact, Korea was a victim of the times, a nation, yet not a nation. Although the Korean peninsula is inhabited by an ancient people with a common heritage, it is an artificially divided nation.

The Allied victory of World War II freed the Korean people from nearly half a century of oppressive Japanese rule. But this victory also divided the mountainous peninsula at the Thirty-eighth Parallel. The Soviet Union following the defeat of Japan moved troops into Korea to the Thirty-eighth Parallel while the United States moved its troops into the southern half of the peninsula to this artificial demarcation line originally set up as an administrative measure. The Japanese troops on each side of the parallel were to surrender to the Allied armies north or south of the line depending upon where the defeated enemy units were stationed.

The Soviet Union refused to relinquish its control of the northern half of the Korean peninsula and quickly installed a Communist government. The United States turned over the Korean problem to the United Nations in 1947 and asked the world organization to unite Korea. Korean unification formally became a United Nations responsibility with the creation of the Temporary Commission on Korea (UNTOCK) to supervise elections. The Soviet Union boycotted the voting on the grounds that Korea was a four-power matter and the Russians refused access to North Korea when the Commission arrived in Seoul. South Korean elections were held in May, 1948, and were described by the chairman of UNTOCK as "a valid expression of the free will of the electorate in those parts of Korea which were accessible to the Commission."

On August 15, 1948, the Republic of Korea became a sovereign state, under UN sponsorship and on June 25, 1950, a victim of Communist aggression. On that same date the United States called for an emergency meeting of the UN Security Council and asked that this body consider the invasion as a threat to world peace. Under the terms of the five-year-old UN Charter the Security Council could authorize several courses of action which included economic sanctions, a blockade or collective military action.

Unless this challenge could be met, the United Nations faced the same fate as the League of Nations when its members refused to consider or take action after Japan attacked China in 1931; when Nazi troops marched into the Rhineland in 1936; or when Italy invaded Ethiopia in 1935. Two days after the shooting began in Korea a United States resolution before the Security Council calling for immediate action was passed. It included a recommendation that UN members "furnish such assistance to the Republic of Korea as may be necessary to repel the armed attack and to restore international peace and security in the area."

It was a historic day for the world. For the first time in history an international body had voted for force to meet force. Ten days later, on July 7, another Security Council resolution acknowledged that the United States military forces then fighting in Korea were acting on behalf of and as "agent" for the United Nations. The creation of a unified command was recommended and the resolution authorized the use of the United Nations flag as well as the flags of its various national contingents.

Article 43 of the Charter was invoked by the Security Council calling for "all Members of the United Nations, in order to contribute to the maintenance of international peace and security, undertake to make available to the Security Council, on its call and in accordance with a special agreement or agreements, armed forces, assistance and facilities, including rights of passage, necessary for the purpose of maintaining international peace and security."

Suffice to say, the Soviet Union at this time was boycotting the Security Council and its all-important veto power was not exacted.

The fighting in Korea was referred to as a United Nations "police action," but in the strict sense of the word the international body soon had little to do with military operations in the embattled nations. Because this was the first time that an international organization tried to be effective in a shooting situation in which peace was to be restored by force, a number of unusual situations arose during the first year of hostilities. During the first weeks of the fighting UN Secretary General Trygve Lie requested all members favoring the Security Council's actions to examine their "capacity to provide an increased volume of combat forces, particularly ground forces."

Meanwhile, the United Nations Command in Tokyo, under General Douglas MacArthur, laid down its own ground rules for participating nations. Only those nations that could provide minimum army contingents of reinforced battalion strength with supporting artillery, engineer and ordnance units were acceptable. This was a heavy burden for smaller nations. As a result there was no rush by the UN's fifty-three member governments to send armed forces to Korea. In fact, the Secretary General thought that too many nations were making only token offers and offered an alternative suggestion—one that still warrants study.

He asked if it were not feasible for the UN Command to find some way to use all able volunteers for foreign countries who might enlist in an international brigade to supplement the larger national contingents. He described a unit that might bear the United Nations name, wear its uniform, be enlisted for two or three years, and be at the disposal of the Security Council. As a practical matter, he added, it would have to be financed and organized by the United States. The U.S., however, approved of Lie's efforts to prod larger contributions out of individual states, but it was less enthusiastic about his suggestion for a brigade of volunteers. Lie later wrote in his memoirs that the U.S. received his suggestion with mixed feelings. He was told that the arming of an international brigade would require special legislation and that perhaps the job might better be left to Canada.

"They wondered what might be done with the troops if the Korean fighting ended in 1950," he wrote in his memoirs, "and I responded that they could be used for police duties there. To this they agreed; but they doubted whether volunteer forces could be moulded into combat units in time for the Korean fighting."

The United States, meantime, independently sought out additional military contingents from members of the UN once the unified command had been established in Tokyo. Twenty-two governments volunteered ground, naval or air forces. Only fifteen offers were accepted. Others either did not meet the minimum standards demanded by the UN command or were rejected for political reasons, as in the case of Nationalist China. However, countries such as India, Sweden and Italy offered medical facilities and these were accepted.

Korea became a precedent for future United Nations peace-keeping operations. During the Korean "police action," as it's still referred to in some United Nations quarters, a total of 2,323,000 men from twenty-two nations fought or served under the United Nations flag between June 25, 1950, and July 27, 1953, when the armistice agreement was signed. Since then an additional 1,400,000 men from the armed forces of the U.S. and other national military contingents including the Republic of Korea have served and are presently serving in the divided Asian peninsula beneath the United Nations banner to maintain the cease-fire and keep the peace.

Conversely, the United Nations flag became no more than a symbol in Korea as the United States took over direction of the fighting as "agent" for the UN. However, the United States had received a United Nations mandate to pursue this course of action and this authorization by the international body has remained through the subsequent truce talks and armistice signed at Panmunjom in political concurrence with the member states that provided military contingents in Korea; and later during the keeping of the peace and maintenance of the cease-fire on the UN side of the Thirty-eighth Parallel. The United Nations ultimately received progress reports and what began as a truly international effort under the international body's aegis later became no more than a charade.

On the other hand, the stage had been set for United Nations participation in future peacekeeping efforts. The world organization required experience in these matters. Korea was a test of its will. Unlike the League of Nations, the UN was not found wanting; some of its members were.

Subsequent events would strengthen its teeth, although each future crisis would follow a different pattern; and many prominent diplomats would give serious thought to the formation of an efficient international police force.

5

Boyhood in the Congo

WHILE THE FIGHTING in Korea turned into a stalemate and the United Nations command entered into lengthy truce talks with the North Koreans, backed up at the Panmunjom truce table by their Communist Chinese allies, Stig von Bayer neared manhood. The youngster quickly matured into a hardy young teen-ager who had discovered the African land in which he lived.

Kivu Province in the eastern Congo was the area he knew best, and Maniema District was his backyard where he learned about the tribal histories of the Lunda, Baluba, and Bayeke—in South Katanga—the three largest tribes in the Congo, and the Wakusu, Wasimba, and Watega tribes in his own area. The tribal histories gave young Stig an insight into the basic problems that a few short years later were to create so much havoc when the Congo finally received its independence.

At school Stig studied the Congo's history and how Leopold II, the fun-loving playboy King of Belgium, founded the Congo Free State in 1885. His exploitation of it was subjected to acutely hostile criticism, and in 1908 it became a Belgian colony. This vast central African territory, larger than Western

Europe, was a money-making plaything for the king who continuously sold trading rights and borrowed several fortunes by mortgaging portions of the territory to the international bankers of his day. The history of the Congo was wrapped up in the history of the tribes. Their basic hatreds were ingrained in the twentieth century descendants of the slaves who were taken to the Arab nations of the Middle East and to some extent to the New World. Although few among the estimated 7.5 million slaves taken captive during the four hundred years after Columbus discovered America came from the Congo, much less survived capture and transport to the New World, slave-taking in the Congo finally ended when Leopold's troops defeated Arab slavers in a pitched battle at Kasongo in 1892.

Few white men dared explore the Congo until Dr. David Livingstone disappeared deep into the Central African bush country between 1856-71 and was found by a Welshman turned American, H. M. Stanley, who penetrated the Congo for the New York *Herald.* Stanley later explored the Congo for King Leopold. But for centuries the drumbeating jungle telegraph bespoke of the slavers, the white men in their "great ships," who constantly visited the west coast of Africa for "black ivory." During these centuries few of the Congo tribesmen had ever seen a white man, but his slave-searching forays engendered a deep-seated hatred.

From his Baluba friends Stig learned of the great empire founded by King Kongolol Mukulu in the fifteenth century. The king was a despot who was later beheaded by his own people after he threatened the life of his eldest son and heir, popular with the warriors of his tribe. The Baluba empire, which was far greater in size than the low countries of Europe, lasted a mere two hundred years. In fact, the mighty Baluba empire lived, flourished, and died nearly three hundred years before Belgium became a nation.

The Lunda tribe filled the vacuum created by the demise of Baluba hegemony. Over many a campfire, Stig heard bloodcurdling tales about the Lunda tribesmen who warred against the Baluba. The tales of the great chief, M'Siri, the Bayeke tribal leader who married the daughter of the Lunda chieftain, Katanga, were not lost on the Swedish youngster. The stories of M'Siri's sadism were to Stig what ghost stories are to many youngsters from the Western world. It wasn't more than a century ago that M'Siri raised havoc with his people. He was an absolute ruler and tyrant who determined whether or not his people lived or died or were sold into slavery to the Arab slavers. He drank the blood of his victims and, as one early Belgian explorer described it from firsthand observation, "Human hearts still beating were thrown into mugs of the native *pombe* wine, which was then enjoyed by M'Siri's entire court. Men were tied to trees, and when they groaned in hunger, were given their own ears, nose, and arms to eat, and perished after devouring themselves."

At the Atheneé Royale school in Bukavu, the capital of Kivu Province, Stig also learned the Belgian version of the Congo's turbulent history. It was a history of political intrigue; of big-power designs ultimately to take over the central African region and exploit its rich mineral resources; and it also was a history of benevolent paternalism on the part of the Belgian Government's colonial administration which developed the Congo into the bastion of colonialism that Stig got to know during his youth.

The sons and grandsons of the Belgian colonizers were Stig's classmates along with a few—a very few—sons of tribal chiefs and Congolese chief clerks. It was in this boarding school that Stig learned about the two hundred tribes that inhabit the Congo in either loose alliance or deadly enmity, speaking nearly as many dialects of the four *lingua franca*—Swahili, Tshiluba, Lingala, and Kikongo.

The Belgian colonial administration brought in teachers from France and other countries who were given specific instructions not to propagandize on behalf of government colonialism. However, in Katanga where the powerful Union Minière and other industrial corporations held sway, the young, impressionable white students learned in their classes that they were fortunate to be under the benevolent protection of the companies usually lumped under one name—*la Société.*

Société Generale de Belgique is an archaic nineteenth-century corporation which once directed the destiny of the Congo from its offices in Brussels. Today it masterminds a rapidly diminishing industrial complex, as the Congolese government slowly assumes its rightful supervision of industry. But in its heyday in Katanga, *la Société* insisted that the children of its employees be made aware of the importance of the huge colonial merchant empire whose governors considered it a state and law unto itself.

"Look about you," the schoolchildren were told by their teachers in Katanga Province in the good old days of the monopoly's power, "and see the civilization that has been built by *la Société.*" Children are impressionable and the children of the whites who worked in this province of the Congo were quickly indoctrinated into the status quo.

Stig, however, was fortunate enough to have received a less indoctrinated education in Bukavu where he attended a Belgian government school. He learned that the civilization brought to the Congo was made possible from the taxes paid to the Belgian Government by *les sociétés* for building up the Congo.

Although the children of the employees of the government and *les sociétés* lived in this central African colony, most of them, unfortunately, had never lived in the bush like Stig. While many of them were able to speak the native tongues like Stig, most of them had never hunted and few of them numbered the Congolese among their friends as did Stig.

In effect, Stig von Bayer was a hero among his school chums. He had lived the type of life they only dreamed of; he had done the things that they never would, even after they were to grow to manhood and step into the role of colonialists that their fathers and grandfathers had carved for them.

The Athenée Royale was a boarding school and like boarding schools anywhere it was directed with a European discipline common in such institutions of learning. There were the usual hi-jinks by the students and the Swedish youngster was a normal lad who preferred his fun and games to studies. Stig was one student who could sneak out at night and return unobserved. He soon became the leader of a group of young teenagers who devilishly broke the strict rules of the school that forbade leaving the premises without permission, especially at night.

With his young friends, Stig would roam the streets in search of innocent adventure. The Congo was a safe place to live at the time. Lawlessness in the streets was a rarity and the violence that erupted with the birth pangs of nationalism was unheard-of at the time. It was a time for living; it was a time for youth. Stig lived through an era that will never return. It was a period of his life that he would often remember in later years when he witnessed his second homeland ravaged by violent dissension and warfare.

At the age of thirteen, Stig had killed his first leopard. The previous year he had killed a wild boar that threatened to attack him and his two Congolese companions. His semiannual visits home were pleasant enough and "home" just happened to be deep in the bush country where his father was working on a road- or bridge-building project.

There was the memorable time that Stig "disappeared" for a week on a hunting expedition and his worried father, concerned about the lengthy absence of his son, was about to notify the authorities when the youngster appeared, trailed by an entourage of tribesmen carrying meat that the young *bwana* had killed. Stig returned with a pocket full of francs which he had earned by hunting game and selling it to nearby tribes. Later he became the official hunter for the Congolese construction crews working for his father whom they called *kikwenda*, the man for whom no natural obstacle was a detour.

His sister, Francesca, was born at an American Methodist mission in the Congo and his younger brother, Goran, grew up in the jungle surrounded by houseboys and their ever-present *moke* or assistants. The living standard for Stig's family was excellent despite the many primitive areas in which they resided. Stig's mother Elizabeth, an attractive woman whose grace and breeding were apparent in any setting, was assisted by a cook and an assortment of servants. This gave her the time to tutor the two youngest children in a variety of subjects when she wasn't assisting her husband.

Among her other duties was that of nurse and doctor to the Congolese workers and their families. Each morning anywhere from twenty-five to a hundred men, women, and children lined up outside the jungle but in which the family lived awaiting treatment. Moreover, she was the chief adviser to the Congolese who often asked the wife of the *kikwenda* various questions such as when to buy a wife and from which tribe.

Once, when the *kikwenda* was ill, Stig's mother actually supervised construction work and her hard-driving efforts won her the name of *kuchamuka,* the boiling kettle whose energy and anger was something to fear when the workers did not apply themselves hard enough to their jobs.

The early maturity reached by their children became a minor problem for Hans and Elizabeth. Stig had finally reached an age where his future had to be seriously considered. However, their eldest son had his own plans for the future. He had given serious consideration to becoming a professional hunter. A friend of the family in Kenya, a prominent "great white hunter," was willing to accept Stig as an apprentice and teach him the profession of catering to the whims of the wealthy who could afford to visit Africa and engage safaris to the hunting grounds.

It was a future many a youngster would envy. Unfortunately, there were other factors that had to be considered. Stig was now sixteen. Between the ages of eighteen and twenty, all Swedish males are subject to military service. Only the physically disabled are excepted. When Stig was nearing military age, his father decided that his eldest son should complete his high school education in Sweden and then consider his future. Stig required a change of scene so that he could be in a better position to make the decisions required of young adulthood.

He returned to Sweden in 1954 and completed his high school education the following year. He reached his eighteenth birthday a month after he completed his secondary schooling. By this time he had a different goal in life; he wanted to become a professional soldier.

Sweden had watched from the sidelines during World War II, although the sentiments of her people were with the Allies rather than with the Axis. According to some social historians, Swedish soldiers will always volunteer for peacekeeping operations in an effort to (1) show the rest of the world that Swedes can and will fight for a just cause, and (2) that the Swedish tradition of non-involvement in two World Wars can best be upheld by involvement in the prevention of a third world war.

It is also claimed by some observers of Swedish affairs that Swedes have a guilt complex about their non-involvement in World War II and that having participated in major international peacekeeping operations—ten times since 1945—a national guilt complex has been mitigated.

However, these theories had no part in the decision that Stig made to enter the Swedish Army and make a career out of the profession of arms. He first donned a uniform on April 21, 1957, and was assigned to the Tenth Armored Regiment, his military alma mater and permanent unit, and began his training as a private. The Swedish Army, meanwhile, was involved in the peacekeeping operation that began as a full-fledged emergency on October 29, 1956, when the Security Council was suddenly advised that the armed forces of Israel had penetrated deeply into Egyptian territory in violation of their armistice agreement of February 24, 1949. The Israeli attack came as a surprise to the member states of the United Nations. Israel's invading spearheads were crashing across the desert wastes straight for the Suez Canal and not a single Egyptian military force was available to halt the attack. Two days after Israel launched this surprise attack French and British aircraft began bombing military targets in Egypt.

The Security Council was called into session immediately after word was received of the Israeli attack. For two days members of the Security Council could reach no agreement on the type of action to be taken and called for an emergency special session of the General Assembly, as provided in the Assembly's "Uniting for Peace" resolution. The peacekeeping machinery of the United Nations was as cumbersome in 1956 as it was in 1950. Slowly, ever so slowly, the wheels began to turn. The Assembly adopted a resolution on November 2, on the fifth day of the fighting, urging that all parties involved in hostilities in the area agree to an immediate cease-fire. The Assembly also resolved that Israel and Egypt withdraw all forces behind the armistice line established in 1949, and that other nations refrain from any acts which would delay or prevent the implementation of the resolution.

Unlike the invasion of South Korea by North Korea, both Israel and Egypt were members of the United Nations and, therefore, bound by the rules of the Charter. Within a matter of three short days the peacekeeping effort had become even more complicated as two big-power nations became involved. On the day that the General Assembly voted on the resolution that, it was hoped, would end the shooting, Israel had established control over virtually the entire Sinai Peninsula and had occupied Gaza. That same morning British and French troops landed in the Port Said area after a bombardment by elements of their respective fleets. By November 5 the situation was well in hand from a military point of view. Egypt was at the mercy of the armies of three nations. Given a bit more time, Britain, France and Israel would have completely defeated and conquered Egypt which five months earlier had suddenly proclaimed the nationalization of the Suez Canal and placed the management of the vital waterway in the hands of an Egyptian operating authority.

Both the United States and the Soviet Union, on opposite sides of the political fence, remonstrated against the trio of nations that had attacked Egypt. Something had to be done by the United Nations. Acting in concert the smaller members guided a resolution through the General Assembly establishing a United Nations Command for an emergency international force to secure and supervise a cease-fire. Overshadowing the activities of the smaller member states was the United States and the Soviet Union—the former demanding strong sanctions against the trio of invaders and the latter warning that Communist "volunteer" troops from Russia and Red China would be sent to the aid of Egypt. Although the situation was not as cut and dried as the outbreak of hostilities in Korea in 1950, the political implications were enormous. Britain, France, and Israel had attacked in concert; each nation having its own reasons. Specifically, the control of the Suez Canal had passed to Egypt by its nationalization of the important link between Europe and Asia. If Egypt could be crushed and the canal returned to the control of Britain and France, it was believed in London and Paris, many maritime states would close their eyes to the invasion. Israel, of course, had her own reasons for attacking Egypt, which included the refusal to permit Israeli ships through the canal.

The United States, closely allied to the two big powers and friendly to Israel because of America's Zionist movement, threatened to cut off its foreign aid programs. It was a threat that had to be reckoned with. Although the Soviet threat of Communist "volunteers" was impractical to carry out, Britain, France, and the United States did not want to see any Russian involvement in the Middle East.

However, something had to be done to prevent the crisis in the Middle East from escalating into a big war. In the first days of the fighting in Korea the United States, acting as executive "agent" for the United Nations, was able to take immediate military action with its own forces stationed in Japan. Six years later there was no UN "agent" to take immediate action. Instead, there was a lot of bickering by various nations as to what form of action should be taken to bring about a cease-fire. Once again statesmen began to give thought to a permanent peacekeeping force but few voiced any opinions. The 1956 Middle East crisis required a peacekeeping force "here and now."

Lester Pearson, the Prime Minister of Canada who was

then foreign minister, worked with U. S. Secretary of State John Foster Dulles to enlist the services of a small international armed force that could separate the belligerents, provide for a cooling-off period and readjust the political balance in the Middle East. Dulles was in favor of this type of UN force—what he called "a truly international peace and police force."

Meanwhile, Secretary General Dag Hammarskjold worked behind the scenes to get an emergency police forced organized. General E. L. M. Burns, a Canadian officer who headed up the United Nations Truce Supervision Organization (UNTSO) launched during the 1948-49 fighting between Israel and her Arab neighbors, was selected to head up the latest peacekeeping effort. Again, unlike Korea, a strict set of rules had to be drawn up for the peacekeeping force. Hammerskjold advised the General Assembly of the type of force he had in mind, a peacekeeping force that "obviously should have no rights other than those necessary for the execution of its function, in co-operation with local authorities. It would be more than an observer corps, but in no way a military force temporarily controlling the territory in which it is stationed. . . ."

Since two of the big powers were belligerents and the other two were threatening all sorts of action short of sending in their own troops, the official UN request for military contingents for this United Nations Emergency Force (UNEF) fell to the smaller nations. At this point came the realization that more than infantry units were required, Prime Minister Pearson recalled in 1964. The Canadian Government offered to provide a self-contained infantry battalion group. He explained:

"But after these troops had begun to move to the port of embarkation, it emerged that, of some two dozen offers of military assistance to the United Nations, most were infantry units and practically none included the supporting and technical services which the force would need—including an air component. Since the Great Powers were not participating in the force, Canada was one of the very few countries which was able, because of its military know-how and experience, to provide administrative and logistic specialists. In the end, the Canadian contingent included reconaissance, transport, maintenance, and supply units of the Canadian Army, and an observation and transport Squadron of the Royal Canadian Air Force. They were sneered at by some in the heat of partisan debate as a 'typewriter army,' but they were indispensable to the success of UNEF."

Because of the type of crisis involving a UN member nation, Egypt had something to say about the composition of the peacekeeping force. Canadian officials had committed a *faux pas.* In Egyptian eyes Canadians spoke English, wore practically the same uniform as the British invaders and, of all possible errors in judgment, the infantry battalion offered by Canada was to come from a regiment called the Queen's Own Rifles, and Egypt was reeling from the invasion by Her Majesty's fleet.

Peacekeeping efforts by the United Nations in 1956 was still regarded as something of an oddity; there was more cooperation in the decade of the fifties by member nations than at any other time during the UN's first twenty years. Twenty-four UN members offered to participate in UNEF. Offers of troop units were finally accepted from Brazil, Canada, Colombia, Denmark, Finland, India, Indonesia, Norway, Sweden, and Yugoslavia. UNEF finally fielded a total of six thousand men, who were somewhat confused by their role which, unfortunately, had not been quite spelled out because of the conflicting political situation in the General Assembly and the inability of members to reach any sort of agreement.

The question at hand voiced by UN member nations participating in UNEF boiled down to this: "When should we shoot?" General Burns was aware that the representatives of the contributing nations did not want to see UNEF become involved in any serious military action. "Nor did they like the idea of shooting at infiltrators," he added, "doubtless because they thought it would result in an outcry against UNEF similar to that which had followed the firing over the heads of a crowd in Gaza. . . .

"UNEF, however, did have the right to use force in self-defense, and this included the right to fire—that is, the commander of a UNEF post or small body of troops whose command is being attacked by armed groups or individuals had the right and duty to use any degree of force necessary to resist such attack."

Despite these limitations imposed by the contributing nations, UNEF worked to a degree. The armistice between Israel and Egypt continues in the Gaza Strip. UNEF troops wearing their distinctive UN blue helmets and patrolling the Gaza desert in white-painted vehicles and aircraft marked with the United Nations insignia are maintaining the peace between Israel and Egypt. An uneasy peace to be sure; but the soldiers of the United Nations are there. And that is the *raison d'être* for the men who serve under the United Nations flag.

If UNEF left one mark, it was in the United States. Its relative success in the Gaza Strip encouraged efforts to build on its beginnings a permanent UN police force of some kind. There was widespread American support in both official and unofficial quarters and resolutions were introduced in both houses of Congress to express legislative sentiment for the peacekeeping force.

Secretary General Hammarskjold was encouraged by the support he received from many member nations to establish the peacekeepers on a permanent basis. In his annual report in 1958 he declared:

"I shall place before the thirteenth session a summary study of the experience derived from the establishment and operation of the United Nations Emergency Force which I hope will prove useful to any consideration that may ensue of the feasibility of standby arrangements for a United Nations force. It should, of course, be clear that any such force, unless it were to be called into being by the Security Council under Chapter VII of the Charter, must constitutionally be a non-fighting force, operating on the territories of the countries concerned only with their consent and utilized only after a decision of the Security Council or General Assembly regarding a specific case, for those clearly international purposes relating to the pacific settlement of disputes which are authorized by the

Charter. UNEF has shown that such a force can, in certain circumstances, make an important contribution to the preservation of international peace."

Hammarskjold, a Swede, was concerned with maintaining the peace of the world. Private Stig von Bayer of the Swedish Army was well into his military training when the Secretary General outlined his plan.

Swedish units were an important element in the peacekeeping force entrenched in the Gaza Strip. Other nations were also represented in name as well as in numbers. But to the Israelis and the Egyptians in their respective desert outposts, there always was the presence of another "foreign" military force serving under a single banner—the blue and white UN flag that marked each of the peacekeeping observation posts.

6

Restless drumbeats

THE MILITARY LADDER to rank and privileges varies with each nation's own military tradition. In some of the newly emerging nations former sergeants in colonial forces are suddenly elevated to the ranks of colonels and generals, and become the military chiefs of their respective countries. Sweden, however, has a military heritage that goes back many centuries. Part of this heritage is written in the history of the maternal side of Stig's family; and this heritage quickly made itself apparent to Stig's superior officers. They soon discovered that he was officer material.

He had to prove it the hard way. For ten months he served as a private and then was promoted to vice-corporal. Two months later he was nominated a corporal. He discovered that the military life was for him. All thoughts of returning to Africa to undergo the training and apprenticeship leading to the exalted title of "white hunter" had long since faded away. His family was still living in the Congo, but his years of youthful adventure in Africa were now memories. Swedish volunteers were being assigned to the Middle East with UNEF, and he wanted to obtain a tour of duty in the Gaza Strip if for no other reason than that it would look good in his record. Service with the United Nations was incidental.

But there still were more rungs left in the military ladder. Unlike the majority of his countrymen, who put in their required ten months of basic military service and then return to civilian life as reservists, with time on active duty for maneuvers and availability for duty in the event of a national emergency, Stig wanted a commission. He received a nomination to warrant officer school and completed the course in six months, returning to his regiment as a sergeant and section leader. Several months with the troops turned him into a seasoned non-commissioned officer. He was now ready to enter the cadet school, a six-month course for officer candidates. After receiving a certificate which stated that he was officer caliber, he was assigned to the military school for a year—a school with varied one- to four-year courses similar to the training given at West Point, Sandhurst, and Saint Cyr.

Having entered the Swedish military academy from service in the ranks, Stig required only one year to reach the coveted rank of *fidurm* or warrant officer third class. It was March, 1960, when Stig was assigned to his final six months with the troops as a platoon leader before receiving his second lieutenant's commission. Meanwhile, the forces that were to affect his destiny and shape the future of a nation, and the world, were stirring in the Belgian Congo.

The heartbeat of Congolese nationalism began to pulsate more rapidly while Stig was preparing himself for a military career that would later flower in the former Belgian colony. The political riots in Leopoldville in January, 1959, were of more than passing interest to Stig because his family was then living in the Congo. He noted at the time that the riots by Congolese demanding independence from Belgium occurred more than twenty-three hundred miles from where his family lived.

Stig was well aware that the Congolese had not been prepared for independence. In fact, he was all but certain that they would never receive it. At least not for many many years. This failure to recognize the political forces that were stirring in the decade of the fifties were rooted in the paternalistic interpretation of Belgian responsibility. He recalled that in 1955 an official of the Institute for Colonial Studies in Antwerp proposed a thirty-year plan leading to independence. Professor A. A. J. van Bilsen was called a "radical" by the commercial and industrial administrators in the Congo and the great majority of Belgian politicians. He had dared to think of the unthinkable.

Actually, there was a ten-year plan for the Congo circulating in some quarters. The forward-looking Belgian colonial administration, unfortunately, was later lumped together in the minds of many Americans and Europeans with the archaic-thinking and conservative commercial and industrial enterprises having extensive holdings in the colony. Naturally, *les sociétés* did not want to see any change in a colonial structure that would also mean a change in the status quo. These powerful interests fought behind the scenes against any independence for the Congo.

On the other hand, similar powerful interests in the Congo also worked against independence. Try as it might, the colonial administration could not get enough Congolese to leave their tribes for the schooling and education that was required for the future leaders of an independent Congo. Tribal mores and the primitive way of life worked against the advancement of the Congolese. Chiefs forbade their tribal subjects to leave the fold—and they were obeyed.

Only a fraction of a per cent of the tribal populations had any education and it wasn't because the colonial administration didn't offer any schooling. The colonial administrators were fighting a way of life which the tribal chiefs were fighting equally hard to retain.

Later, during the chaos following independence, marauding tribesmen would go out of their way to kill educated Congolese officials no matter how slight their schooling.

However, Congo still represented Belgium's crown jewel; in some circles any discussion of independence was akin to advocating an end to Belgium's popular monarchy. Officials of the Colonial Ministry in Brussels for years believed themselves to have the Congolese situation well in hand. The Governor-General's annual reports bespoke of a mounting profit for Belgium and the nation's business interests with holdings in the Congo. The governors of the colony's six provinces—Leopoldville, Equateur, Orientale, Kasai, Kivu and Katanga—were not too concerned with the rising tide of nationalist feeling among the colony's 13.8 million black peoples whose per capita income of $88 supported one of the highest living standards in Black Africa.

Stig was in the army when the first political parties of Congolese nationalists appeared in 1957. It was somewhat difficult for him at the time to think in terms of the Congolese as politically oriented. Then came the riots of '59, bringing about an awakening for Stig and many others. His father wrote to him that the political situation was rapidly changing. Specifically after French President Charles de Gaulle shocked Belgian colonialists across the Congo River from Brazzaville in the French Congo with a declaration of immediate independence or membership in the French community. The Africans living under the French flag accepted independence; the Congolese subjects of the Belgian crown were envious. If their neighbors could have independence offered to them, why couldn't they be presented with a similar offer?

Civil unrest broke out throughout the colony. Violence was at a minimum, but the dissatisfaction was apparent to the colony's administrators. On October 16, 1959, Belgium announced that a Congolese central government would be established the following year. No date was set. Spokesmen for the Congolese were angry at the vague announcement; they also wanted to be granted immediate independence.

The granting of independence was a difficult decision partially inspired by a drop in the price of copper and the end of extensive uranium sales to the United States. In 1959 and 1960 the bottom had dropped out of the world market price of copper which the mines in Katanga had been supplying for generations. The United States began purchasing previously high-priced uranium from Canada where huge deposits had been found. No longer was this vital element for nuclear weapons a monopoly of Belgian mining interests in the Congo. Moreover, with the sudden drop in tax revenue from the Congo, Belgian officials finally and reluctantly decided that perhaps this was the time to grant independence despite the fact that the Congolese were unprepared to assume the mantle of leadership of a new and sovereign state. Of course, these were contributing factors toward the final decision to grant independence. The pressure from nationalists within the Congo also helped spur the Belgian Government to reluctantly part with their valuable central African possession.

Congolese political leaders in a matter of five short years had discovered the enormous power they wielded. They could bring mobs of their followers into the streets. They could shake the very fabric of the white society. On the other hand, they were afraid of the *Force Publique* and its white officers and Congolese troops who would go to any lengths to maintain the peace of the colony. There was no way of controlling this arm of Belgian rule and the iron-fisted strength that it represented.

In Brussels the Governor-General convened a round table conference in January, 1960, and proposed a four-year plan for a transitional period to independence. The Congolese vented strong dissent; they demanded immediate independence and threatened a "Belgian Algeria" unless this demand was met. This was the only dialogue between two peoples—Belgian colonial administrators waxing confidence in the colonial system that had been more than a century in the making; Congolese nationalists noisily threatening chaos unless their demands were met.

The colonial administrators actually believed *la Société* would retain economic control of the Congo. The Congolese nationalists just as confidently believed they could administer a new nation's governmental affairs despite the fact that their people had no training or experience in government. Both groups were never more wrong.

The Congo had virtually no effective preparation for the responsibilities of self-government, in contrast to many other new African states. All that the Belgian colony had was a legacy voiced by King Baudouin at the closing session of the 1960 round table conference. "The Belgians," he proudly declared, "were able to establish safety, peace, and all the other prerequisites of prosperity in the heart of Central Africa."

The conference ended on a note of elation for the Congolese. They were to be granted independence on June 30, 1960—less than five months away. Chaos was unavoidable. The political parties were tribally based, carrying ancient antagonisms that worked against any future cooperation in the new government. Political leaders were untrained and, in some cases, unlettered men who still utilized the services of their tribal witch doctors before making important decisions.

Perhaps a portent of the violence that was inevitable was triggered in early 1960 in a riot over the outcome of a soccer game. Angered that their team had lost to the neighboring Baluba tribe in the Belgian Congo's hinterland of Kasai Province, fierce Lulua tribesmen went berserk. Only a step removed—if that far—from cannibalism, the Lulua pounced on the usually more peaceful Baluba, noted for the art and beauty of their masks and sculpture, and set fire to a thousand of their huts. Their bodies bright with war paint, the Lulua attacked across the Kasai River in groups of three hundred armed with poisoned arrows, a few muskets and deadly *panga* machetes with which they hacked away at their ancient enemies.

Pouring into the provincial capital of Luluabourg by the thousands, terrified Baluba refugees found safety behind the hastily summoned Force Publique troops led by Belgian officers. However, hundreds of Baluba had been injured and scores killed in what had started out as a game and turned into one of the Congo's—and Africa's—worst outbreak of intertribal violence.

The most influential political leader was a tall, lanky former postal clerk with a prison record for stealing money. Goateed Patrice Lumumba also was a firebrand revolutionary who had received some political training in the Soviet Union. It was he who threatened the Belgian colonial administrators at the round table conference and panicked them into granting independence before the new nation was prepared for it. It was this new breed of Congolese political leader who would commit the new nation to its trial by fire.

It cannot be said that the new Republic of the Congo was launched without the best wishes of a great number of nations. Independence Day brought a good many ambassadors of goodwill from the rest of the world. King Baudouin was present. The United States presented a bust of Abraham Lincoln to the new government along with the offer to pay for three hundred scholarships for Congolese to study abroad.

Even the United Nations was present. Dr. Ralph J. Bunche, as a prominent Negro American political scientist, officially represented the UN in his official capacity of Undersecretary for Special Political Affairs. He brought the world organization's offer of technical assistance to the new state.

Independence Day was a day of goodwill. King Baudouin spoke of a new era of close cooperation between the new nation and Belgium. President Joseph Kasavubu replied in kind. Visiting dignitaries breathed easy. Then came the bombshell. Patrice Lumumba, speaking as the new nation's first Prime Minister, exploded into a diatribe dripping with invective. He denounced Belgium's colonial legacy as one of "atrocious sufferings." He described what he called "humiliating bondage." He bitterly recalled the "ironies, insults, blows which we had to endure morning, noon and night because we were Negroes." He then painted a picture of the new Congo of "peace, prosperity, and grandeur" that would replace the "peace of guns and bayonets" by a "peace of courage and good will."

President Kasavubu and his Western guests were shocked by the outburst which they regarded as strident, contemptuous, and ill-tempered. Patrice Lumumba indeed was a man to be watched. His leadership of the new nation could cause grave international problems.

In Sweden, Warrant Officer Stig von Bayer was busy completing his final months with the troops before accepting a commission. The letters he received from his parents described Independence Day in general terms. "I have been asked to stay on as a technical adviser," Stig's father wrote to his son. "My clerk has been promoted to project engineer and I am to work for him. He is no more qualified to be an engineer than your baby sister. I have informed the new government that either I will be in charge or I will resign."

Some nine thousand top- and middle-range administrative and technical positions were held by the Belgian majority and other Europeans when independence was granted. The new government expected these men to remain in their jobs and train Congolese to ultimately take over. However, the government expected the administrators to accept the jurisdiction of newly appointed officials who previously were nothing more than clerks.

The policy of *les sociétés* of not training Congolese for responsible positions was followed to a degree in the *Force Publique,* the colonial militia which upon independence became the *Armée Nationale Congolese*—the Congolese National Army. The *Force Publique* had combined the functions of army and national police. Its twenty-five thousand men were led by eleven hundred Europeans, mostly Belgians.

On July 5, 1960—five days after the independence ceremonies for the new nation—the army mutinied against its white officers.

Three days earlier tribal disorders had erupted in Leopoldville, Luluabourg, and Ruanda-Urundi.

These reports were headlined in Swedish newspapers. Stig feared for the life of his parents as did his brother and sister, who were living in Sweden where they were attending school. Although he had heard about the violence that occurred in the Congo's ancient tribal wars, he instinctively knew that in this, the twentieth century, the type of primitive violence in the Congo would be of a nature that would rock the civilized world.

7

"ONUC is coming!"

THE MILITARY FORCE that represented law and order in the Congo had virtually collapsed. Independence meant many things to many Congolese. Specifically, it meant to the unlettered people of the new nation having the same privileges, the same material wealth and enjoying the same type of life as the white man. After all, had not this new way of life been promised to them by the leaders of the various political parties, and their new Prime Minister—Patrice Lumumba?

The reports of the exact cause of the violence are still fragmentary and perhaps there never will be any definite answer to the question of why the tribes rebelled two days after independence was proclaimed throughout the land. The mutiny of the new Congolese National Army was something else again. The officers, mostly Belgians, were taken by surprise. They had believed that they had a prescribed role in the ANC, the role of commanders until the Congolese could be trained to assume command. Moreover, it was expected to take a number of years before this would happen. Professional soldiers take pride in the training that they undergo and the experience that they garner on the battlefields of the world. It was with some confidence that the *Force Publique* commander, Lt. Gen. Emil Jannsens, noted that his fellow Belgian officers would still be required to stay on and lead the new ANC that would change its designation from "force" to "armée."

"Before Independence—After Independence," the gray-haired Belgian officer shrugged; in any event things would still remain the same. The Belgian officer corps mainly consisted of line officers. The actual military administration was supervised by a small number of Belgian civil officials or a few officers with adjutant general backgrounds. This group of administrators was all but ignored by the new government, and the Congolese troops rebelled to everybody's surprise. The reason: the new government had overlooked a little matter of money—payment for the troops.

Under the Belgian administration the troops were always paid on time. The new government's fiscal oversight, and what later would become fiscal irresponsibility, led to the sudden outburst of violence by armed and uniformed troops who, under Belgian command and jurisdiction before independence, had been loyal to the *Force Publique* as an institution and a way of life.

It turned out that the Congolese soldier in the ANC had no loyalty to his newly independent nation. Under Belgian rule the Congolese soldier's life was carefully regulated on and off duty. Discipline was harsh, but he accepted it well because he felt that this new way of life was superior to tribal ways. He was well aware that he worked for a foreign power, symbolized by his white officers (there were no officers of his own race), and he would readily obey orders to fire on his own countrymen provided they did not belong to his own tribe. As a result, Congolese troops who policed a particular area of the Belgian colony were drawn from distant parts of the country so that tribal loyalties would not interfere with carrying out their duties.

Independence and all that it meant to the Congolese was not lost on the troops. When pay was not immediately forthcoming they demanded some of the material and psychological rewards of their civilian counterparts in the central government. When their demands were unheeded they proceeded to take what they wanted.

Prime Minister Lumumba, who was predisposed toward the Soviet bloc, had not discouraged the infiltration of Communist agents into the new nation during the five months before independence. The unexpected blowup first by the tribes outside of Leopoldville and then the mutiny of the combination police force and army rocked the nation, especially the 115,000 Belgian and European residents.

In Kasongo, Stig's father eyed the place where he had hidden some guns within easy reach if necessary.

In Sweden, Stig read with alarm the news about the troubles in the Congo.

In the capitals of the world diplomatic cables arrived one after the other. At the United Nations the history of a decade earlier—almost to the day—was about to repeat itself in a call to arms for the peacekeepers.

"The Republic of the Congo accepts without reservation the obligations stipulated in the Charter of the United Nations and undertakes to abide by the same in absolute loyalty and good faith." This message cabled to the Secretary General on July 1, 1960, was followed five days later by Belgium's wholehearted support of her former colony's request for membership in the international organization. During the interim white people and black people died.

Prime Minister Lumumba was offered the use of Belgian troops stationed at two permanent bases in the Congo to put down the mutiny and restore order. Lumumba adamantly refused. He wanted nothing to do with his former masters. From the Belgian point of view there was too much at stake in the former colony, let alone the lives of her subjects that were threatened by the riots. Patience was worn thin in Brussels. On July 9, Belgian troops were flown in from Europe without the agreement and against the wishes of the new government. Only the Congolese foreign minister, without prior consultation, agreed to the influx of Belgian troops. Leopoldville and the major cities of Elisabethville, Luluabourg and other large towns were occupied.

Patrice Lumumba called upon the UN for help. Meanwhile, he accepted advice from a large Soviet mission that had quickly been established in the new nation. The UN was asked to provide military assistance to protect the national territory of the Congo against external aggression which Lumumba declared was a "threat to international peace." Meanwhile, the independence of the Congo's richest province was proclaimed by Moise Tshombe, the president of the provincial government of Katanga, in a surprise move that further complicated affairs. The Congolese leaders in Leopoldville then requested that the UN put an end to the secession of Katanga. Lumumba accused Belgium of having fostered a colonialist conspiracy by carefully planning and preparing for the secession with a view to maintaining a hold on the Congo.

The situation was a mixed-up state of affairs. Despite his close relationship with the Soviet mission, Lumumba first asked the U.S. ambassador for help. He was referred to the UN. A week later he cabled Soviet Premier Nikita Khrushchev for assistance. Kremlin leaders knew that any Soviet interference would not be looked upon too kindly by the Western European nations who considered the dark continent "off limits" to the Communist bloc. Khrushchev offered nothing more than moral support.

During this two-week period, while the Congo's troops ran wild and Belgian military units tried to restore law and order, the great debate on what to do raged in the Security Council. Belgium was ordered to withdraw its troops. Secretary General Dag Hammarskjold was authorized by the Security Council to provide the Congolese central government with military assistance until its own "national security forces may be able, in the opinion of the Government," to restore order.

Spurred on by the Security Council's resolution of July 14, Hammarskjold set up the United Nations operation in the Congo (*Operations des Nations Unies au Congo*) and the letters ONUC became part of the local and international lexicon.

"ONUC is coming!" the Congolese people chanted during the time of troubles while they waited for the UN to act many thousands of miles away. Very few of them knew what ONUC stood for or what it looked like. Meanwhile stories about ONUC quickly circulated throughout the new nation. ONUC was a great white bird. It was a god. The Congolese eagerly watched for an army of warriors bearing gifts. ONUC was all things to all people. Specifically, it combined a civilian assistance program and a military police force. The military force, made up of units from states other than the great powers but placed under the exclusive command of the UN, was under standing orders to use force only in "self-defense" and not to intervene in the internal affairs of the Congo.

ONUC was launched with mixed feeling on the part of the Security Council members. Orders were to police the withdrawal of all Belgian troops and maintain law and order. There also were problems in the new nation that covered the constitutional crisis over the secession of Katanga. The new government insisted that it supervise the technical assistance experts who would be sent to show the Congolese how to keep the machinery of government and public affairs functioning smoothly.

Thus the Congo was a new kind of situation facing Dag Hammarskjold. He recalled that when fighting broke out in Korea it was a clear act of aggression and the United States was available to act for the United Nations. When the UN intervened during the three-pronged attack by Israel, France and Britain against Egypt the UN provided a military force to dig in between the belligerents and then police the battlefield and uphold the peace. These were the two major precedents, other than the uniformed observer teams that had patrolled other trouble spots, that Hammerskjold had to fall back on. Neither precedent was adequate. The Congo was more complex a problem; and the Secretary General wrote his own ground rules. They were accepted by the international body's membership.

Hammarskjold demanded "exclusive command" of the

peacekeeping force which would take orders only from him; the peacekeeping force would not be used as a party in "internal conflicts"; it would have "freedom of movement"; fight only in "self-defense"; the composition of the peacekeeping force would be decided only by the Secretary General with the views of the Republic of the Congo taken into account and, finally, orders would be taken only from the UN command and not from the government of the peacekeeping troops.

Hammarskjold first asked for African nations to provide troops and then, in order to get troops to the scene as quickly as possible, requested Stockholm to transfer the Swedish battalion in the Gaza Strip to the Congo. He also appealed to some of the big powers to provide aerial transportation and heavy equipment for the peacekeeping force.

Britain and the United States provided transport aircraft and crews, military equipment and supplies, and food. Canada, Sweden, and Norway were asked to provide specialized military personnel. The Soviet Union "unilaterally" joined the peacekeeping operation in its own devious way, working outside the framework of ONUC or the United Nations and thundering all the while about "Western imperialism" and "Western colonialism." Soviet transport aircraft hauled trucks and supplies and "technicians" into the Congo in what was obviously a blatant effort to infiltrate Central Africa and subvert the new nation in behalf of the Kremlin's own perverse foreign policy.

In retrospect, the Soviet Union was attempting to gain a beachhead in Africa before the agents of rival Red China did. Unknown to many Western nations at the time, the Sino-Soviet split had begun. The Kremlin wanted to entrench itself in Africa before the Chinese, who had launched an anti-white policy at the Bandung Conference of Afro-Asian nations in 1956, gained a strong foothold. Of course, the end result of any kind of Communist infiltration in the Congo would—and ultimately did—add to the chaos in the new nation.

In the General Assembly during this period the United

States delegate accused the Soviet Union of sending to the Congo ". . . hundreds of so-called technicians—whose character may be judged by the fact that only a few days ago the Congolese authorities ordered these men to leave the Congo. Meanwhile, nearly two dozen Soviet transport aircraft and one hundred Soviet trucks appeared in the Congo, not to participate in the United Nations program, not to put themselves under the United Nations authorities there, but to promote strife and bloodshed between Congolese tribes and factions."

During this hectic period other members of the United Nations accepted their responsibilities. India provided a general officer to advise Hammarskjold in military matters. African nations, in keeping with the Secretary General's request to also have regional military representation, provided troops. It was indeed an international effort, but it had taken the international organization nearly three weeks to *react* to the crisis in the Congo—and then *act*.

Wild-eyed Congolese troops in Kasongo molested Europeans during the day, beat them at night, and kept the white community in a state of fear. They fired their guns into the air and occasionally at any vehicle that white men or black dared to move.

The home of Stig's parents was searched by the ANC soldiers who haphazardly moved through the town in small groups. Orders had been issued from Leopoldville by the new government, but the ANC disregarded them. The names signed to the orders were virtually unknown to the privates and sergeants.

"Who is Major General Victor Lundula?" they asked with a shrug. "And who is Colonel Joseph Mobutu?"

During this period of chaos the troops obeyed nobody, not even their prime minister who, as acting minister of national defense, had promoted former Sergeant Major Lundula to the rank of commanding general of the ANC and ex-Sergeant Major Mobutu as his chief of staff.

The perfunctory search of the household had failed to uncover the cache of weapons. Unable to leave the town, Hannson and Elizabeth nervously waited for the right moment to depart.

From a telephone booth on the ancient military post at Strägnäs, headquarters of the Tenth Swedish Armored Regiment, Warrant Officer III Stig von Bayer phoned Stockholm after the news first broke that the Eighth Battalion at Gaza would be flown to the Congo. He volunteered his services to the Swedish Defense Department's office of UN affairs.

"Your qualifications?" asked the impersonal voice of the staff officer at the other end of the line.

Stig quickly summed up his five years residence in the Congo, and spoke of his fluency in French and Swahili.

"Oh!" the surprised voice at the other end now exclaimed, this time more personally. "You will hear from us shortly."

Stig slowly crossed the parade ground on his way back to his barracks. There had been no word from his family and concern for their safety weighed heavily. The troubles in the Congo were more personal; the role of a military peacekeeper was far from his thoughts on that warm summer day in mid-July.

8

The new lieutenant

Captain Lundquist, Stig's company commander, burst out of the orderly room and walked swiftly through his unit's area. Men snapped to attention as their commander walked by with a sheet of paper in one hand and obviously with something else in mind. At the end of one of the barracks he spotted a platoon of soldiers drilling.

"Von Bayer!" he shouted and broke into a run. Stig turned away from his platoon when his name was called. If the captain was running and calling out his name, it must be important.

"Von Bayer," the captain huffed and slowed to a walk when he neared the platoon. Stig saluted.

"The colonel wants to see you immediately!" Captain Lundquist snapped. Stig wondered to himself what he had done wrong; if the regimental commander wanted to see him right away, then he must have goofed up.

"I can't leave my platoon now, sir," Stig replied to his commanding officer. It had all happened so fast. He was flustered by the captain's sudden appearance. The fact that the regimental commander's request to see him might have something to do with his earlier telephone call to Stockholm wasn't even considered. He turned over command of the platoon to one of the noncoms and began running toward the regiment's headquarters building. A warrant officer and officer candidate does not keep his regimental commander waiting.

Nor did Colonel Virgin keep Stig waiting. He was immediately ushered into the regimental commander's office and informed that the Military Headquarters defense staff had ordered 2nd Lieutenant von Bayer to depart for the Congo and join the Swedish Battalion as a staff officer and interpreter.

"Did you say *lieutenant?*" Stig gulped. He knew that he had about two months of training left with the troops before he would receive his commission. The unexpected announcement of his promotion came as a pleasant surprise. The regimental commander wished him luck and he was dismissed.

Three days later he was aboard a white-painted Swedish Air Force aircraft flying to Africa. In Stockholm, radio newscasts and newspaper headlines from the Congo and the United Nations reported the latest developments. Chaos continued. UN troops were moving to their new stations in an effort to keep the peace in the dark continent.

Clutched in Stig's hand was a crumpled newspaper. A story datelined from Leopoldville reported the death of Europeans at the hands of mutinous ANC soldiers. Among the names of the victims was listed the von Bayer family.

The other military passengers aboard the Swedish military aircraft couldn't help but note the sorrow that etched the handsome features of the young Swedish lieutenant.

The first troops of the peacekeeping forces to land in the Congo stepped off aircraft bearing the red, white and blue bullseye circle of Britain's Royal Air Force. It was the battalion from Ghana, and the 770 troops lined up along the huge airfield near Leopoldville and in smart British Army formation, marched to their tenting area. As the huge RAF aircraft disgorged their human cargoes, a flight of noisy transports appeared on the horizon, circled the airfield and then one by one touched down with tires screeching and propellers spinning in reverse, braking the huge Lockheed C-130 Hercules aircraft to a safe taxi speed.

Rear ramps were lowered from the gigantic bodies and the first 593 troops from Tunisia walked down and formed up. Dr. Ralph Bunche, personal representative of the Secretary General (he had been in the Congo for the independence ceremonies) greeted the first contingents of the peacekeeping force and the air crews of the RAF and the U. S. Air Force who had flown the armed infantry units to the Congo from their respective homelands.

The sun beat down on the vast airport and the colorful Ghanaians and Tunisians assembled behind their own color guards. However, there was not a UN banner to be seen; none was available. The entire troop movement had occurred so quickly and without any advance preparation. At Evreux-Fauville Air Base in France, headquarters of the U. S. Air Force 322nd Air Division, the flight assignments were routine on July 14. Suddenly, the TWX in the air unit's communications center began clicking away. The message, relayed from the State Department to the Pentagon and thence to USAF Headquarters in Wiesbaden, Germany, sounded the call to quarters. It spelled out MASSIVE AIRLIFT. How massive the 322nd was not to know until a few weeks had passed, but this U. S. Air Force unit, flying for the United Nations, would provide the largest part of the aerial transportation in the greatest air-support operation since the Berlin airlift of 1948-49.

The record would state that during the first two years that the U. S. Air Force supported the United Nations peacekeeping operation in the Congo, the American transports would fly a total of 33,000 hours without a single accident.

However, the first weeks were the most hectic and it is impossible to exaggerate the conditions under which the American transports were forced to operate. Flying non-stop over uncharted areas, for distances as long as thirty-five hundred miles, the 322nd Air Division's C-130s and the C-124 Globemasters of the U. S. Military Air Transport Service carried troops and other military specialists from Tunisia, Morocco,

Sweden, Guinea, Ethiopia, Liberia, Ireland, Mali, the Sudan, India, the United Arab Republic, Canada, Pakistan, Nigeria, and Austria. The route to Leopoldville covers some of the most formidable and inaccessible terrain on earth. Navigation facilities were nonexistent, and Air Force personnel scrabbled for information and assembled it at the Evreux-Fauville base to create some semblance of operational pattern to aid the air crews.

It is one thing to talk about peacekeeping operations in the General Assembly at United Nations Headquarters in New York. It is quite another thing to watch the peacekeepers at work, especially those with the mission of transporting the police forces to the troubled area. Once the RAF and the U. S. Air Force were given the "go ahead" by their respective governments, the first phase went into operation—transporting troops and their equipment and supplies. The massive airlift called for maintenance operations at the end of the line that resembled those of a remote outfit in World War I, working with isolated and primitive facilities in combat. The mechanics and engineers of the C-130's, aided by their navigators and pilots, performed feats of near legerdemain to keep the airplanes running. They were indeed in combat—they were fighting time. Every hour that peacekeeping forces could be landed in the Congo meant that the situation could that much sooner be brought under control, and disaster averted.

Emotions were in upheaval in the Congo, but with one exception the Congolese soldiers of the ANC and the tribesmen running wild would leave the Americans alone. They knew that the giant transport planes marked by the red, white and blue bar-circle-star insignia meant that along with UN troops the aircraft were also carrying needed food, at a time when all law and order had broken down and starvation had begun to enter into the picture.

It was an emergency situation and the American air crews treated it as such. They flew twenty, thirty, and more hours without a break. Sometimes a man would grab forty winks on a stack of cargo, but all too often even this was not possible. Finally, the commander of the 322nd Air Division flew down from his headquarters in France.

When he saw many of his men with circles under their eyes and some of them so tired they were even shaking a bit, he told the crews they did *not* have to fly so many consecutive hours.

They kept flying. Then he told them he did not even think it was very smart—or safe—for them to continue in a manner that was certain to guarantee physical exhaustion and a possible accident. But they kept flying. Then he blew his top and ordered crews to limit their flights to no more than eighteen hours maximum at any one time. Nevertheless, the Americans pushed themselves to the limit of their endurance because of what they were seeing on the return flights to Europe. The pathetic refugees brought the peacekeeping operations that much closer to the Americans during the long flights in which they brought in troops and supplies and then left with transports filled with the victims of the chaos.

The refugees were the former white colonialists who had been born and raised in Africa and who knew virtually nothing else of the world except the Congo. They were literally white Africans.

"Many of the women had been beaten and raped," Jack Pruett, a Lockheed Aircraft Company representative reported at the time. "The children were beaten and abused, and we saw plenty of kids that had been maimed at the hands of the Congolese. When those Air Force crews saw things like that, they wouldn't stop working because someone had given an order or written a regulation. They flew day and night until they were ready to drop in their tracks."

Pilots and crewmen, with tears running down their faces, carrying children whose bodies had been slashed and battered mercilessly, flew their mercy missions without letup.

One American crew was attacked by sullen natives in the interior where two C-124 Globemasters had landed. That crew never took off in its own airplane, and they didn't fly for a long time afterward. Screaming Congolese attacked them with knives, sticks and rocks; they were beaten so severely that most of them were removed on stretchers and spent many weeks bedridden in a hospital. Helping to keep the peace was proving to be dangerous.

In the first few days, the C-130's began flying into the interior with supplies for UN troops who began spreading throughout the country in an effort to pacify the towns and cities where the ANC troops had mutinied.

In one incident, the latest reports from Leopoldville indicated that the UN held one airstrip. It was dusk when the Hercules flew over the air terminal outside the Congolese capital and continued on its way to the interior. Three hours later, circling over the dirt strip that passed for an airfield, the American pilot radioed for landing instructions. There were none. The tower was illuminated but silent. The pilot, who had made the same trip four days earlier, banked and lowered his flaps in order to make a short landing. Landing lights poked into the darkness and swathed the airstrip as the huge Hercules descended, touched down and then braked to a halt at the end of the runway.

The pilot spun the multi-engine aricraft around and taxied toward the tower which still remained silent. He saw that it was deserted—in fact, the entire airfield appeared deserted. Sensing that something was wrong, he rammed the throttles forward, speeding hell-for-leather down the runway and into the air just as bursts of gun fire dotted the ground below and bullets zipped through wings and fuselage. Mutinous troops had taken the airfield before the UN forces could reach their objective.

Peacekeeping operations were indeed hazardous.

Confusion reigned during the first days as troops from a dozen nations began to arrive on the scene. It was a general's nightmare, especially for Major General Carl von Horn of Sweden who had been head of the UN Truce Supervisory Organization in Jerusalem and was appointed the commanding general of the peacekeeping force. For five days he waited impatiently for a transport plane to arrive and move himself and his staff to the Congo. A U. S. Air Force transport finally brought him to Leopoldville three days after the first peacekeeping forces had arrived.

The military nightmare could be blamed on the speed of the peacekeeping operation—and the unpreparedness of the UN for an emergency of this type. Nor were the nations that offered troops prepared in any way to field peacekeeping companies, battalions, or regiments. Along with the babble of foreign tongues, the conglomeration of foreign uniforms and the different types of individual weapons that required varied sizes of ammunition, there also was the problem of feeding men with different tastes and ration preferences based on religion and national origin.

Until General von Horn's arrival, civilian representative Bunche was the military commander. A month later he commented on the problem of organizing the UN Force and admitted that there was much room for valid criticism. "It had to be quickly improvised from nothing," he explained in an official report to the Security Council. "Its military personnel has been recruited from twenty-six different countries; it has encountered internal conflicts, including serious inter-tribal warfare; and it has been dropped into the midst of a country and people who are totally unprepared by experience and psychology to understand it and to appreciate its functions and real worth."

As the peacekeeping troops poured into the chaotic country, Prime Minister Lumumba began to demand that the UN troops supplement the mutinous ANC, not replace them or disarm them. Hammarskjold refused to take orders from Lumumba; the fiery Congolese leader in turn was indignant at what he considered cavalier treatment by a white man. UN troops succeeded in disarming some ANC mutineers when the Congolese soldiers were encouraged by their own government to lay down their arms. However, these orders were not consistent. At other times the ANC was ordered not to surrender their weapons to the peacekeeping force. It appeared that Lumumba couldn't trust his own army; he ordered loyal troops to keep their arms and agreed to have the UN disarm those he thought were disloyal or whom he imagined were loyal to his political opponents.

Major General H. T. Alexander, the British commander of the Ghanaian contingent, and UN officials were caught up in the question of disarming the ANC. The British officer was all for taking away the arms of the ANC, by force if necessary. The UN staff also wanted to see the ANC disarmed but without the use of force. General Alexander had ordered his troops to disarm the ANC and in Luluabourg three thousand Congolese soldiers surrendered their weapons to the Tunisian troops. However, Dr. Bunche wanted to move slowly and carefully and pointed out that the peacekeeping army was a "peace force, not a fighting force." He underscored that the UN Force had to avoid the "extreme position of having to shoot Congolese."

The UN contingents also received clarification of the early orders issued when the peacekeepers first began to arrive on the scene. All commanders were instructed to use weapons only in "cases of great and sudden emergency and for the purpose of self-defense." Peacekeeping force officers were ordered to "ensure that the greatest care and control are used." The directive also implicitly laid down the guidelines. "Firing, even in self-defense, should be resorted to only in extreme instances," stated the orders from the Secretary General. "Any effort to disarm members of the UN Force is to be regarded as a legitimate cause for self-defense."

To disarm or not to disarm the ANC troops was the big question faced by the commanders of the various peacekeeping units by the time the first units of the Swedish battalion landed on July 24. The following day 2nd Lieutenant Stig von Bayer arrived and reported for duty.

"We've been waiting for you," one of the Swedish staff officers told the brand new lieutenant. The staff officer picked up the phone and rang up a superior.

"Our interpreter is here," he said. He listened intently as orders were given him to pass on to Lt. von Bayer. He looked up at Stig and told him to report to the Swedish company commander whose troops were patrolling one of the more explosive native quarters of Leopoldville.

"Watch out," he warned his newly arrived colleague. "That's a tough part of town you'll be in."

With hardly any time for sleep, Stig patrolled the native sections of Leopoldville. Time and again the UN troops wearing Swedish uniforms were cheered by the mercurial natives. But for no apparent reason there were other incidents when Stig recognized the growl of the mob and understood the meaning of low-pitched voices, like the rumble of a dormant volcano.

"Drive into the mob!" he ordered his frightened jeep driver. The mass of humanity parted and then converged around the white-painted jeep. The crowd waited as the thin young man stood up on his seat—"another French-speaking ONUC soldat." The humid July temperature was charged with electric tension. Stig felt it. There was only one way to ground the spark that could ignite these Congolese into a kill-crazed mass.

"Don't be stupid!" the white man bluntly spoke out in Swahili. "There's no time for destroying your country. You should be working to build it up."

The Congolese looked at each other. An ONUC who spoke their own language was unusual. The crowd suddenly dispersed. The jeep moved on, patrolling until the next mob began to form up and threaten to explode into acts of violence. When that happened, the orders from the company commander were short and to the point: "Send Lieutenant von Bayer to talk to the people!"

This period of chaos kept Stig's mind occupied. He wasn't given much time to think about his family. There was so much going on in Leopoldville during his first two days in the Congo and it seemed that his services were called for constantly. However, the political situation did not escape his alert attention. The single radio station in Leopoldville was in government hands. Prime Minister Lumumba was the star attraction, taking over the microphone every few hours to address his countrymen. It seemed to Stig that the Congolese leader would say something at seven o'clock in the evening and then two hours later broadcast opinions that were contrary to his original pronouncements.

In those two short days in Leopoldville, Stig had nothing to do with policy decisions by the high-ranking military and civilian officials of the UN. But his knowledge of Swahili gave him the edge; he understood what Patrice Lumumba was saying to his people. The Congolese leader, Stig though to himself, was mentally unbalanced, to say the least. Among Western diplomats in Leopoldville, Lumumba was considered pro-Russian and one American described the prime minister as a "most effective political organizer and rabble-rouser . . . unscrupulous and untrustworthy." Belgians, for good measure, brought out Lumumba's prison record and word spread that he was a drug addict, on the one hand, and suffered from psychological problems, on the other.

Whether or not the Congolese Prime Minister was mentally unbalanced was of no concern to Stig. Events were moving too swiftly to permit him to be concerned with anything other than carrying out his orders and doing his duty.

It was 0300 hours, the third day after Stig's arrival, when he was awakened by a phone call from Swedish headquarters, thirty minutes after falling asleep. It had been a long and trying day.

"Yes," he yawned into the mouthpiece. The voice at the other end spoke with the authority of Swedish battalion headquarters, located at the Leopoldville airport.

"Pack and be out here in two hours!" the duty officer commanded Stig. "You're going to Goma."

"Goma?" he sleepily asked, "what's in Goma?"

"The Irish!" came back the reply. The Irish! All that Stig knew about the Irish came from books and hearsay. They were a people who loved to drink, to fight and, besides, they were so stubborn that they were difficult to talk to. The young Swede had been to many places and had met many different types of people during his twenty-three years. But he had never met an Irishman; and during his service with the UN he would meet and learn to live and work with many, many more nationalities. The education of Stig von Bayer was just beginning.

"The Irish, you say?" he repeated the question, "and they're in Goma?"

The order was sudden, and Stig still was not quite awake when he had the temerity to question the staff officer at the other end of the line.

"Is that an order?"

"Yes," the officer snapped, adding sarcastically, "if you don't have any special objections."

Stig was wide-awake now. He accepted his orders, hurriedly dressed and packed his gear. A patrol jeep transported him to the airfield. At ONUC headquarters he was introduced to Commandant Adams, deputy commander of the Thirty-Second Irish Battalion. Standing in a group nearby were ten more men dressed in the British-style uniform worn by Adams. Their rifles and submachine guns were stacked against their packs lying on the floor. The men were speaking in low undertones. Stig caught the language; the brogue accent threw him, however.

Adams shoved out his hand in greeting. "We're on this same mission, m'boy," he announced to the young Swede, "and 'tis said that Goma is quite a hot spot. I hope the bloody ANC isn't spoiling for a fight. We're going in to keep the peace, y'know."

Stig nodded. This Irish officer really has a gift of gab, he thought to himself. He carefully studied the armed Irish soldiers. Each man was a broadshouldered, husky specimen and from the way they carried themselves they could handle anything. Adams had the plan of action. His troops were to be flown in the following day to Goma. But first an advance party had to land and reconnoiter the city and the airfield.

"Our troops won't fly in until headquarters receives a signal from our advance party," Adams told Stig. He spread out a map of Kivu Province.

"I've been told you know the area," the Irish officer commented. Stig nodded. "I grew up in the province," he replied.

Commandant Adams nodded. The Irish are a sentimental people, especially when it comes to discussions about home and hearth. Stig explained that seven years had passed since he was last in the Congo.

"Well, m'boy, it looks like you're due for a homecoming," the Irishman replied. "Our plane will be taking off soon. Let's get aboard."

Stig lifted his kit, slung his Karl Gustaf submachine gun over his shoulder and followed the Irish detachment to the U. S. Air Force C-124 Globemaster that loomed in the dawn's first light. It was one hell of a homecoming, he bitterly thought to himself. Try as he would, he hadn't been able to find out anything about his family.

Goma and its surprises awaited Stig's arrival.

The aircraft that Stig and his advance party of Irish troopers were in touched down to refuel at Kindu on the way to Goma. Heavily-armed Belgian Army paracommandos were stationed at the airfield and Stig stopped in at their command post, introduced himself and explained that he was searching for anybody from the Kasongo area who knew his parents. He was told that the situation was extremely serious in Kasongo; the Congolese had run amuck, killing and looting.

"A patrol has just returned from that area, however," one of the Belgian officers volunteered. He told Stig where to find the officer who had commanded the patrol. Stig rushed out of the CP and ran to the officers' quarters. Inside the barracks he shouted the Belgian officer's name and a man answered the call. Stig introduced himself and the officer informed him that a Swedish couple had joined a convoy of European refugees. The convoy was headed for Bukavu "if the damned blacks don't stop it and murder everybody," the Belgian added solemnly shaking his head.

Stig's dour features melted into a big grin. The puzzled officer wondered how come, when a man's parents were in danger, he smiled? "What kind of a son is this?" he thought to himself.

"They're alive!" Stig breathed. Sadness suddenly lifted from his shoulders. His parents were safe. He'd find some way to get to Bukavu from Goma.

"Une mille fois mercis!" Stig blurted out and grasped the Belgian officer's hand in ebullient thanks. He ran back to his Irish companions and an hour later the plane load of peace-keeping soldiers took off for Goma.

9

African reunion

THE GLOBEMASTER circled the air strip at Goma and then began to descend. Stig caught a glimpse of the ground rushing toward the aircraft and then the massive, multi-engine transport touched down and taxied to a stop. One of the members of the crew opened a hatch and lowered a ladder. Stig looked out and spotted khaki-clad ANC soldiers lying on the ground surrounding the transport. Every one of the soldiers was pointing a rifle or submachine gun at the plane. It was obvious to Stig that this was one performance he'd have to play by ear.

"Sir, have your men pack away their guns," he advised the startled Irish officer.

"What if they begin shooting at us?" Adams replied. The laughter had left his features and now he was all business.

"That's the chance we'll have to take."

Stig stepped out first. Adams followed behind. One hundred rifle and machine gun muzzles swung toward the two UN military representatives. Stig greeted the ANC troops. One of the Congolese sergeants pushed forward and demanded to know who the white men were.

"Officers of ONUC," Stig answered in Swahili. The Congolese noncom stared suspiciously at both men and then advised them that they were under arrest until the ANC could verify the identities of the two officers and the other men in the aircraft. Carrying the bags of the advance party, the ANC soldiers escorted the UN detachment to a nearby building. Stig made a speech. He announced that ONUC had arrived to protect the people of the Congo and that he and his fellow soldiers had come to Goma as friends.

"Let's pray they don't open our bags and see our weapons," Stig whispered to Commandant Adams. "These people are children; they'll believe anything they're told. If they uncover our weapons they're liable to accuse us of being Belgian paratroopers. That's who they suspect we are."

The Belgian armed forces were across the border in Rwanda. Speaking rapidly in Swahili, Stig finally convinced the spokesman for the mutinous troops that he and the Irish detachment were as they claimed—UN soldiers. That night silence descended on the town of Goma, but it was soon shattered by the sound of small arms fire. Tracer bullets sizzled from Goma toward the town of Kisiny across the lake. Answering fire came from the Belgian positions.

Commandant Adams suggested to Stig that they investigate the ruckus and see if they could bring peace to the town. The two officers were in a position to see that the mutineers had kicked off the exchange of gunfire. They demanded that the ANC cease fire, and disdainfully the two officers turned their backs on the Congolese and walked across the frontier into Belgian Army territory. Over a glass of cold beer, Stig explained to the Belgian Army commandant the purpose of the advance party's mission. The officer was all for keeping the peace, especially since a large number of Belgian civilians were still in Goma. The two UN officers parted company with the Belgian and returned across the border to Goma.

As they walked along the dark road that led from one province into the next, the chut-chut-chut of a machine gun sent bullets whistling by the two men. They didn't need further urging. Both men dived into a ditch alongside the road and began crawling in the direction of Goma. ANC troops came running out of the night.

"It's the Belgians! the Belgians!" the mutinous troops shouted hoping to place the blame for the exchange of gunfire on the Belgian doorstep. Stig had his doubts. Shortly after dawn he returned to the spot where he and Commandant Adams were fired on. All evidence pointed to the ANC; moreover, the Congolese troops had suddenly switched their stand. They wanted the UN to attack the Belgian positions.

"We will help you kill the Belgians; exterminate the Belgians," the spokesmen for the ANC declared, adding, "We're very happy that you have come here to help us kill all Belgians."

Stig raised his hand palm up, the universal sign for peace. In another country and in another era, wearing buckskin and a widebrimmed Western hat, the young Swede would have been a cavalry scout parleying with the Indians. Now he was an officer of the UN, representing the international body.

"The United Nations is the highest command," Stig deliberately and slowly intoned. "The UN needs no help; it stands alone." The parley occurred in the open between the boundaries of both provinces. Stig pointed toward the sky and warned that even now more soldiers of the UN were on their way to Goma. The U. S. Air Force transports would soon arrive, but somebody among the mutineers had other ideas. A grenade sailed out of the crowd of Congolese soldiers and civilians and landed next to the two men.

"Down!" Stig shouted to the Irish officer and shoved him sprawling into a ditch. The grenade blew up with a roar. Stig pulled himself to his feet. He was angry, but contained his emotions.

One of the Congolese noncoms announced that the Belgians were responsible. Stig refused to accept this explanation. He dressed down the ANC soldier in no uncertain terms. The Swahili words he snarled were peppered with invective. Stig held the ANC responsible and made no bones about it. But underlying the chaos he detected the fine hand of an *agent provocateur*.

The transport planes set down and the Irish troops disembarked. Commandant Adams and Stig carefully watched the UN's peacekeepers disarm the Congolese soldiers and take over all ANC positions. In the interim since July 1, and it was now July 31, the mutinous native troops had beaten up white civilians and shot up the town of Goma, looting and threatening to massacre the Europeans. Now the peacekeepers were on hand.

Stig breathed a sigh of relief. Perhaps something good would come out of this United Nations operation after all. He was overcome by a feeling of pride. It suddenly dawned on him that now he was a soldier with a purpose.

At the airfield outside the small city tucked along the shore of the northwestern corner of Lac Kivu, the Irish troopers quickly set up their headquarters. Stig informed Commandant Adams that he was going into the town itself to size up the situation. He would return in a few hours. Slinging his submachine gun on his shoulder, he left the command post.

The sunwashed town of Goma was like many others that Stig remembered from his youth. Tall shade trees lined the quiet streets and the neat European houses of whitewashed tropical stucco were empty and silent. Their owners had fled the country. The usually neat lawns were littered with debris from looted homes. The shops were shuttered although a few had obviously been broken into.

Goma, it appeared to Stig, was a dead town. Those few Europeans who had remained stayed indoors. The Congolese whom Stig passed on the street glared at him but then respectfully stood aside. The submachine gun on his shoulder was a powerful weapon, and Stig looked like a person who could and would use it.

He stopped and looked around. He had arrived at the town's principal square. Congolese went about their business, although many of them stopped when they observed the lone white soldier. The aviation-type sunglasses masked his eyes. Yet the sun was so strong that he still had to squint against the bright glare that reflected off the white buildings. At the other end of the square a lone figure slowly walked, trailed by a dog on a leash.

"It can't be!" Stig stood staring. "It can't be!" he mumbled again. "It must be the heat." But it took another few moments to sink in. The figure and the dog were no figment of his imagination. He dashed toward the other end of the square.

"Mother!" he called out. The woman with the dog turned, and shrieked joyfully when she recognized Stig running toward her. The soldier was indeed her Stig. In a virtually impossible and unbelieveable situation young Lt. Stig von Bayer was reunited with his parents.

It was a joyous reunion. Stig's father and mother were staying in a hotel. His mother was scheduled to fly back to Sweden in two days. His father, who assumed that Stig would soon arrive in the Congo with the Swedish unit, had visited the Irish CP to offer his services to the United Nations force. He had met with Commandant Adams and in the course of the conversation told the Irish officer that undoubtedly his son, who had lived part of his life in the Congo, would be arriving with the Swedish force.

"His name isn't Stig by any chance, is it?" Adams asked.

Stig's father nodded.

"Well, you just missed him. He's here with us as liaison officer and interpreter."

The Swedish engineer's eyes popped wide in disbelief. He nervously excused himself and hastily left the command post shouting, "I must return to our hotel and tell his mother this good news."

By the time he got back to the hotel, Stig and his mother were catching up on the past two months. They had been hectic and dangerous, Stig learned from his parents who related their adventures after Stig told them how he had read in a Swedish newspaper that they had been killed by the Congolese.

"Well, almost but not quite," his father commented with a wide grin.

Stig learned that during the first two weeks after the Congo received its independence, Patrice Lumumba's political followers appeared on the scene. One of them, whom his mother had met distributing propaganda leaflets told her that he and a number of other Congolese had returned just before independence from the Soviet Union where they had been going to school learning how to become propagandists. He handed her a leaflet. For those Congolese who could read, the leaflet told how every citizen of the new nation would receive a thousand francs a week without having to work any more—if he or she supported Lumumba. The goateed prime minister's followers directed physical violence against Congolese who had worked for the Belgian administration, forcing them to either join Lumumba's party or face the consequences—torture and death. This was meted out time and again.

The Belgian doctors, assisted by Congolese aides, were told that henceforth they—the doctors—would work for their aides and clean up after them. One doctor who was a friend of Stig's parents related how his assistant took over the clinic and began operating on sick Congolese.

"He was a butcher," the doctor had explained. "He was not qualified to perform surgery, or practice medicine for that matter, and when his patients died he'd just shrug his shoulders and reply that they would have died anyway."

The Congolese police visited the home of Stig's parents in Kasongo to examine their papers. Stig's father offered the police corporal a drink. One drink led to another and soon the policeman said he liked these friendly Swedes and wanted white people of their caliber to remain and help his country.

"I would like something to remember you by," the policeman told Stig's parents as he staggered to his feet and wandered outside to order his men into the house. They took all of the chairs by which to remember the Swedes.

Their cook refused to work and claimed that independence meant that he would receive money for not working. Kasongo's local Belgian police administrator, a European, was arrested by the mutinous ANC troops. Stig's father spotted him tied in the back of a small truck and succeeded in chasing and halting the vehicle.

"Where are you going with him?" he asked the soldiers.

"To the airfield," one replied.

"Why?"

"We want the white men who fly the airplanes to see that there is a white man among us. We will put *Monsieur l'Administrateur* in the middle of the airfield so that when they drop the atomic bomb he will be killed along with us."

The police administrator succeeded in escaping after a low flying UN observation plane buzzed the mob of mutinous troops and scattered them in all directions.

"These are serious times for the Congo," the Swedish engineer told his son. "These are child-like and impressionable people and no good will come of this."

"No matter," Stig grinned. "What is important is that you and mother are alive."

Two weeks after his mother departed for Sweden, his father also left Goma to return to his sprawling farm and estate at *Molneby Gard.* Stig could now get down to business. His duty in the Congo was cut out for him. He knew that the United Nations peacekeeping force had a tiger by the tail and he only hoped that his superiors were aware of this.

10

Burning fuses

TENSION LAY HEAVILY across the Congo as more troops from member nations of the UN continued to pour into the strife-torn country. Huge transport planes from the U. S. Air Force 319th Air Division touched down at bases in Ethiopia, Tunisia, Liberia, Morocco, and Sweden where, in the latter country, replacement troops were flown to Gaza to replace the troops flown earlier to the Congo.

Within a matter of weeks the U.S. had airlifted 9,213 troops and their supporting equipment, not to mention supplies of food and tentage and other types of military necessaries. Both Britain and France were against United Nations intervention in the Congo, but this didn't stop Canada or India or Ghana from providing troops in the face of criticism from the anchor of the Commonwealth.

Within a month after Stig had arrived in the Congo the uniforms that were to be seen represented the armed forces of 24 nations. There were 2,547 men from Ethiopia; Liberia, 225; Morocco, 3,250; Sudan, 390; India, 73; Canada, 164; Tunisia, 2,427; Guinea, 744; Ireland, 720; Mali, 574; Ghana, 2,389; and 628 Swedish troops. Moreover, offers of troops from Indonesia and the United Arab Republic had been accepted by the Secretary General. Two months later a total of twenty-six nations had become members of ONUC with fourteen nations providing combat troops ranging in units from 3,259 men in strength down to smaller size units numbering as little as 173 men. Twelve nations had provided military specialists. All told, ONUC represented a force of 16,082 men speaking a babel of tongues, representing a cross-section of the world's races and religions and cultures—and all contributing to the basic problems in the Congo. The basic problems that brought them to this troubled African state in the first place.

The problems that Stig faced in Goma were representative of what the forces of ONUC were faced with in other provinces of the Congo.

First, the political situation was dangerous. Left-leaning Patrice Lumumba, without rhyme or reason, ranted and raved against the United Nations presence. He demanded that the UN troops be placed under his command. This naturally was refused. His Minister of Information, Kashamura, personally broadcast inflammatory statements that only fired up the rebellious ANC troops, instead of calming them.

"What the white man owns is now yours!" the Congo's official spokesman broadcast from Leopoldville Radio. "This is the meaning of our freedom."

His voice, screaming across the ether, excited the Congolese to even greater madness. The words poured forth from Kashamura and the Congolese in the smaller towns in other provinces who heard this voice from the "boxes that speak" took their new "gospel" to heart. Those who heard the messages relayed the words from their government's spokesman, and in transmitting what was said garbled the content and meaning. The result: even greater violence.

Taking his cue from his goateed prime minister, Kasamura warned the Congolese that all the European troops arriving in the Congo were Belgian paratroopers in disguise. Sprinkled in his broadcasts were words and phrases that had originated behind the Iron Curtain. For the first time the favorite phrases of

Marxism were heard throughout the land. The enemies of the Congolese people were "capitalists," "colonialists," and "imperialists," as well as "aggressors."

Stig knew the Congolese. He had grown up with them: he spoke their language and understood their culture and mores. But he was confused. Now, they showed another face. One that he had not known existed. His thoughts he kept to himself. The more expressive Irish troops of the Thirty-third Battalion to which he was now attached aptly described the rampaging Congolese in Gaelic as *seafoideach*—"completely mad." The officers with Stig bluntly vented their opinions of the leaders of the Republic of the Congo.

"Bloody paranoids, all of 'em," one volatile soldier of Erin exploded. "Bloody" in another sense is what the Irish were to personally experience as they moved their forces into northern Katanga Province.

Meanwhile, the advance detachment of Irish troops set up headquarters in Goma and awaited reinforcements that would take up positions and act as a buffer between the mutinous Congolese Army troops and the Belgian units dug in around nearby Kisenyi in Rwanda.

The behind-the-scenes reports of intelligence officers and diplomats to their foreign ministries described the chaos in the Congo as "unusual." Terms like "sabotage," "agents," and "provocateurs" were liberally sprinkled throughout the coded cables they sent their respective governments.

Leopoldville was a hotbed of rumor and intrigue as the intelligence agencies of a number of nations worked *sub rosa* to bring about the political conditions that were most advantageous to their respective countries. Pitted against each other in the African cockpit were the CIA and KGB, the U.S. and Soviet intelligence services, respectively. Each nation was starting from scratch, as it were, in a continent that heretofore had been nothing more than a casual reference in Washington and Moscow.

The Russians took the first round in the intrigues permeating Leopoldville. Prime Minister Lumumba had secretly asked for aid from the Soviet Union. The Kremlin quickly responded. One hundred Ilyushin transport planes carrying trucks, food and "technicians" began to land at Leopoldville airport. The Soviet diplomatic mission quickly expanded in size. Soon, Russians were to be seen everywhere and the government of Prime Minister Lumumba began to sound too much like a Communist satellite in its official statements and in its actions.

To compound the confusion, Moise Tshombe, president of mineral-rich and industrialized Katanga Province, seceded from the Republic and declared that Katanga as of July 11, 1960, was an independent state. The following month, President Kalongi of Kasai Province seceded his territory. Belgian financial interests, specifically the vast Union Minière corporation, had too much to lose in Katanga and Kasai Provinces. Secession of the two provinces was preceded by promises to bolster each regime with Belgian troops and even mercenaries if necessary.

The complex political situation was met head-on by the peacekeeping soldiers of ONUC. The first explosion occurred in northern Katanga Province when Baluba tribesmen suddenly ran amuck, killing many Europeans and educated Congolese in the towns of Manono and Kabalo. Somebody or something had set off the tribesmen. Propaganda leaflets practically spelled out the pattern. In simple letters and crude pictures they depicted the white man as an enemy, Lumumba as the "liberator" and the Congo's "greatest leader."

"The white man is our enemy," the leaflets expounded to the few who could read simple words. Christianity was denounced along with priests and missionaries. Admiring adjectives describing the Soviet Union as the nation to look toward for help pointed the finger to where the chaos may have originated. The jungle telegraph reported that strangers were in the bush. It did not take much to put two and two together to add up to *agents provocateurs* stirring up the Congolese.

ONUC troops had orders to keep the peace. Other shadowy, faceless men were working round the clock to disrupt what the United Nations forces was seeking to accomplish. It was in this unique setting that the soldiers of ONUC worked in the role of peacekeepers. The forces of good were arraigned against the forces of evil.

Units of the Thirty-third Irish Battalion were deployed in northern Katanga Province to establish order. As liaison officer for the Irish Battalion, Stig saw his first action. The sight wasn't pleasant. The sleepy town of Lanorna had been looted by the rampaging Baluba and the gendarmerie had fled. A motorized UN patrol entered the burning town while the painted tribesmen were in the process of sacking it.

The troops with Stig were silent during the journey. In the distance the beat of tom-toms—the jungle telegraph—signaled the advance of ONUC forces. The trail of dust on the hot sunwashed dirt road, the insects and the uncomfortable equatorial humidity was cursed by the ONUC troops as they kept rifles and submachine guns at the ready. On the outskirts of the town the Baluba had dug holes in the road, forcing the vehicles to weave back and forth across the wide trail. Engines whining in high gear, the patrol entered the town and proceeded to the gutted administration building. Stig stepped from the lead Land Rover. He held up his right hand palm outward signaling that he had come in peace. His Karl Gustaf submachine gun was cradled in his left arm.

There was a sudden rush of bodies from out of nowhere. Screaming tribesmen brandishing swords, *panga* knives, spears, muzzle loaders, and bows and arrows rushed the lone Swede who stood his ground. Noisily chanting and shouting, they surrounded Stig and the vehicles.

"Who speaks for you?" Stig shouted as loud as he could. It seemed that a hundred voices replied. One Luba shouted that the white men were all Belgians, their hated and sworn enemies.

"Kill!" he screeched. The chant was taken up by the rest of the mob pressing around the patrol. Stig, speaking Swahili, couldn't help but notice the thick, sticky poison on the arrowheads. He wondered what he had let himself in for. Keeping the situation from getting out of hand overrode the fear that began to grip the pit of his stomach. He shouted back that ONUC had come in peace; that the soldiers of ONUC were not Belgians. He actually took the patrol off the hook by changing the subject and expressing his dismay that the tribesmen would even stoop so low as to break the law by digging holes in the road. For a moment their tempers were blunted by Stig's forensic tactics.

The town was in flames all around him. However, he instinctively kept his eyes on the Congolese instead of on the burning buildings. He berated the tribesmen for their destruction of the road and asked how food could be transported to them if they kept destroying the trails used for this purpose. Slowly, the noise subsided. The tribesmen quieted down. Stig deliberately turned his back and stepped back into the vehicle.

"We can go now," he whispered to the driver. "Slowly, take it slow. We must not show that we are afraid."

The vehicles slowly moved off, keeping pace with the lead Land Rover they were trailing. It was a frightened group of peacekeepers who sighed with relief when the burning town was well behind them. Stig slumped weakly in the front seat of the jeep. He resolved never to get so close to an unmanageable mob. He knew how close he had come to a violent death.

11

This is the custom

"BLACK AFRICANS are better equipped by virtue of race and nationality to deal with black Africans." This strategy was applied by the United Nations military headquarters during the first year of the UN presence in the Congo. The results often proved disastrous.

The soldiers of Erin had been moved into various outposts in northern Katanga Province and it took less time to acclimate to the poisonous centipedes and deadly green mamba snakes wriggling through the brush and among the palm, kola, and safu trees than it did to understand the chaotic political situation. The incessant throbbing of the tom-toms, the reports of attacks and massacres by the Baluba tribesmen kept the European troops on edge. The villages that they quickly inspected while on patrols all looked the same. There were the twisting dirt tracks that passed as roads, cracked and rutted in the dry season and impassable bogs during the rainy periods, all leading to the sandy village square sandwiched between two rows of low mud-block huts with thatched roofs.

This was the Congo. An estimated ten million Congolese lived at the end of these dirt tracks that spilled into similar villages and small towns like Manono, Nyunzu, Niemba, Kabalo, and Kabongo, which had been raided by the Baluba. Only now, the rebellious tribesmen were knowledgeably called the "Balubakat" to distinguish them from the more peaceful tribes in Katanga Province. The Balubakat (BBK) was the political party of the Baluba tribe and the rebellious warriors called themselves the *jeunesse*.

Stig led a patrol into the silent village of Kisele the day after his confrontation with the tribesmen. Bodies lay grotesquely helter-skelter in the village. White men turned even more pale and became sick at the sight of slaughter. Bodies were mutilated. Old women had been left to die after their breasts were cut off. The men who had been killed appeared to the European troops to also have been mutilated.

"No. No." Stig shook his head. His features were as pale as those of the soldiers from Erin. "Look at this."

He pointed to a body. The leg bones beneath the knee were bare. Big, black, blue-nosed flies, which the Congolese call the "black and blue devils," buzzed around the corpses and attacked the UN soldiers. They tried to brush them away, but the flies attacked again and again.

"This is not mutilation," Stig announced, softly shaking his head. "This is cannibalism. This is bad."

The soldiers were stunned. Cannibalism! The word swiftly was passed from one man to the other. The sound of safety catches being flicked to off positions and the rasp of firing bolts shoving cartridges into rifle and submachine gun chambers broke the silence.

"What do you think happened, Lieutenant Stig?" Stig looked around. He stuck his head into a nearby hut. It was obvious that the attackers had run off the goats and the young women and had killed the men, the old women, and children.

"Why?" Stig was asked. He shook his head. He had no idea why. He wondered to himself if somebody wasn't stirring up the Baluba to revolt against the Katangans. He understood one thing. He was a soldier not a diplomat. However, since his arrival in the Congo he was also being forced by events into diplomatic roles. They were bringing him face to face with other problems.

As the month of August sped by, Stig found himself involved in similar situations. After the visit to Kisele, the next incident to occur was a raid on a train between Albertville and Kabalo. Three Europeans aboard the train, Belgian workers for the railroad, and ten Congolese members of the crew had been captured by the Baluba in Niemba. The UN patrol sped to the scene. They found nothing. UN troops had not yet been detailed to ride as escort detachments aboard the trains to prevent an attack. Within a few short weeks even the patterns of attack had changed. The Baluba first appeared on the hilltops overlooking the railroad and just as quickly disappeared. Occasionally they would shoot arrows at the train, fire a muzzleloader or even hurl a spear. This, of course, was ineffective. They became more effective when they suddenly changed tactics and began removing rails by night; sometimes as much as a mile of heavy steel rail. They had discovered the railroad's weakness and began using a tactic that had been developed by Soviet partisans in their harassment of the Nazi armies that had deeply penetrated Russia during World War II.

Clearly the pro-Lumumba Baluba tribesmen were receiving some direction. But from whom?

Late in August a tall, husky Negro officer was posted to Albertville where Stig was stationed with the Irish unit. He was an Ethiopian major who spoke English and poor French. He had no knowledge of Swahili and relied on Stig to act as interpreter in his dealings with the Congolese, recognizing that insomuch as he was of the same color as the Congolese, he might have more influence as the senior ONUC military representative.

"After all," he explained to the European UN troops, "Dr. Bunche is a Negro and he seems to be getting along fine with the Congolese government leaders in Leopoldville."

Unknown to the troops in the field, however, Dr. Bunche was having one devil of a time with the Lumumba government and other Congolese leaders. A man's race or color mean nothing to the tribally fragmented Congolese.

The Ethiopian officer, an Irish officer, and an Irish sergeant joined Stig on a routine patrol to Niemba, a small town west of Albertville. This time, the patrol was to be made by train with troops atop the boxcars. Outside the town Baluba tribesmen appeared from the bush and surrounded the train. The Ethiopian jumped to the ground.

"Come with me," he called back to Stig. Swearing to himself in his native Swedish, Stig quickly jumped to the ground. "Don't go near them!" the young Swede warned the Ethiopian as he ran after the officer. The two UN officers were quickly surrounded by the Baluba.

"Translate for me!" the Ethiopian officer ordered Stig. All the young Swede could think of at the moment was what he could do to save his own and the Ethiopian's lives if the tribesmen went berserk. Fortunately, even the tribesmen were momentarily taken aback by the tall Negro officer who clearly was from another tribe. His features alone told them this. The Ethiopian officer held up his hand for silence.

"Come to me, my friends," he called out. "Come closer, we are all brothers."

Stig repeated in Swahili the Ethiopian's greeting. *He's a fool,* the young Swede told himself between the time the Ethiopian spoke out and when it was time for him to translate what was said. *He'll get us all killed.*

The tall Ethiopian announced that he was on a mission of peace, that the United Nations only wished to bring peace to the Congo so that all men could live as brothers. From the mob surrounding the two men a voice shouted that they were Belgians in disguise. Another one of the warriors shrieked an order to kill the men—the three white ones and the black one. The Baluba warriors jabbed their knives and spears at the two UN officers.

"Brothers . . ." the Ethiopian called out again for attention. The tribesmen were not having any parley. They were out for blood. From the corner of his eye, Stig spotted some of the Baluba climbing aboard the train. One of the UN soldiers hammered away with his rifle butt at the tribesmen, knocking them off the side of the train.

"Ask them about the railroad workers," shouted Stig above the din from two hundred voices. An old toothless Luba warrior shoved the muzzle of his ancient muzzleloader against Stig's chest.

"Now I will kill myself a white man," he cackled gleefully. Stig disdainfully pushed the antique flintlock aside and grasped the Ethiopian's arm.

"We have to go now!" he demanded. "These men are getting out of hand." Stig had seen what the Ethiopian had not. The tribesmen were fired up by *bangi-bangi,* the native grown hashish that left its mark on the faces of the wild-looking warriors with their wide-open, red-rimmed, and staring eyes.

The Ethiopian reluctantly permitted Stig to pull him back to the train, not out of fear but out of incomprehension. He couldn't understand why he did not get through to the tribesmen. After all, he muttered, wasn't he as black as they? Wasn't he, too, an African? He snapped out of his reverie as the train sped back to Albertville. About halfway to the city they came across a group of Congolese railroad workers.

"We must stop for these people," Stig shouted above the noise of the train which had slowed down at a curve. "They will be killed by the Baluba."

The Ethiopian, having recovered from the shock of his first meeting with the rebel tribesmen, shook his head. He ordered that the train continue back to Albertville. As far as he was concerned, the railroad workers and the tribesmen were all "brothers." Nothing would happen to them.

As soon as they returned to their headquarters, they received orders to take a mobile patrol back into Niemba. The town was considered an important communications point and a detachment would have to be left there. The following day a jeep and truck filled with UN soldiers from the Irish Battalion departed Albertville for Niemba. The Ethiopian liaison officer insisted on joining the patrol as senior officer. Word had since spread among the UN peacekeeping troops in Albertville that the countryside was being ravaged by cannibals. The ugly stories based on the massacre reports that had already been received from many points became even more gruesome with each telling. By the time the patrol reached the bridge that crossed the Niemba River and led into the town, the troops were ready for anything. The jarring ride took all of ten hours. It was late afternoon by the time the UN patrol arrived at the bridge. On the other side was massed the Baluba.

"Let's parley," Stig suggested to the Ethiopian major, adding, "We should speak to no more than two of them at a time and shoot anybody else who tries to come forward across the bridge."

The major nodded. Stig shouted for two of the tribesmen to cross the bridge. A pair of heavily painted men stalked across and the major began pleading with them to return to their villages. He said that the UN would come with food for their hungry people, that this was the only way to bring peace to their country.

While they were speaking, small groups of tribesmen began edging across the bridge.

"Major!" Stig warned, "we can't parley with them if they keep coming across."

"No! . . . no! . . . no!" the Ethiopian officer exclaimed. "Let them come. They are harmless."

Stig, a product of the Swedish military academy, lost his temper and berated his superior officer. He refused to continue interpreting for the Ethiopian if he permitted the tribesmen to cross the bridge. The Ethiopian major exploded.

"Lieutenant," he angrily barked, "I am giving the orders here!"

The parley continued as the groups of tribesmen suddenly grew into a mob of 100 men surrounding the UN patrol. The Irish troops couldn't help but notice the weapons carried by the warriors. Nervous fingers crooked around rifle and submachine gun triggers. One shot and the dusty road leading to the bridge would have exploded into a free-for-all of gunfire against clubs, bicycle chains, spears, knives and poison arrows.

The Ethiopian major's pistol and submachine gun, which he had placed on the jeep's front seat, was grabbed by one of the tribesmen. A silent tug of war ensued between the Irish soldier at the wheel of the jeep and the painted warrior. Stig was jostled by warriors who had closed in around the vehicle. Where there originally had been two tribesmen, now there were a hundred milling about.

The situation was explosive. Any moment now a warrior would reach into the truckload of soldiers parked behind the jeep and an angry Irish trooper would either strike the grasping warrior or shoot him. This would kick off a bloody massacre. No matter now many Baluba the UN soldiers might kill in self-defense, the hopped-up warriors would overwhelm the patrol and brutally murder every last man.

Suddenly, the sound of gunfire could be heard from across the bridge coming from the town of Niemba. The chut-chut of machine guns and crack of rifles echoed from the municipality. Smoke began to rise and the crackle of flames bounced in the shimmering heat from the temperature and the fires. The tribesmen froze and then scattered back into the bush. First one jeep and then a second and a third drove up to the opposite side of the bridge. Heavily armed Europeans waved and in French called out to the UN patrol that it was safe to cross the bridge and enter the town.

The men turned out to be one of the many *groupes mobiles* of sixty to eighty men, of whom approximately twenty were Europeans, which President Moise Tshombe of the new state of Katanga had placed in the field. The Katangese soldiers had saved the lives of the UN patrol by suddenly appearing on the scene and scattering the Baluba warriors. The UN patrol was invited to enter the town.

The carnage there was indescribable, including piles of human limbs and other parts of bodies. Some of the soldiers in the UN patrol who had been aboard the train the day before identified bodies of the Congolese railroad workers for whom the Ethiopian major had refused to stop the train, maintaining that they would be safe among their "brothers." These railroad workers had been crucified upside down; their stomachs had been cut open and their sexual organs were missing.

The Ethiopian officer shuddered at the sight of the carnage. Stig learned from the Belgians in the *groupe mobile* that from all of the males who had been killed by the Baluba, the berserk tribesmen had taken sexual organs as readily as a Sioux would take a white man's scalp. However, there was this one difference. The Baluba trophies were handed over to witch doctors to make "strong medicine" and, to the consternation of the UN soldiers, this medicine was believed by the *jeunesse* warriors to protect them from the bullets of ONUC.

The carnage in Niemba had to be cleared. The UN soldiers were pressed into this distasteful service by an Irish medical officer who ordered the rapidly decomposing bodies and parts of bodies burned in a common fire.

The labor that went into peacekeeping was of an ugly nature. None of the peacekeepers liked it. Least of all the Ethiopian major, who promptly requested a transfer back to Leopoldville.

12

Death near the ant hills

Stig and his Irish colleagues wearing the blue UN helmet and shoulder patch ranged north, west and south of Albertville encountering rebellious tribesmen, mutinous ANC troops and angry Belgians who supported the new state of Katanga. Simultaneously, Belgian troops had been flown into Katanga province in mid-July to maintain law and order, and protect the vast mining and industrial interests of the huge Union Minière complex. Less than two months later President Kasavubu dismissed Prime Minister Lumumba and replaced the Soviet-oriented political leader with Joseph Ileo, president of the senate. The chaos was further complicated when, on September 14, two days after Lumumba was fired, Colonel Joseph Mobutu of the ANC suspended President Kasavubu, Lumumba, and Ileo. He placed the administration of the Republic of the Congo in the hands of students to administer.

It was against this backdrop that the peacekeeping forces of ONUC tried their level best to function under the orders given them. It was a difficult situation at best. Beset by anarchy, the UN troops were forced time and again to defend themselves against political forces which defy reason and description even to this day.

The one standing order that nervous men from many nations took upon themselves to obey was: "If attacked, defend yourselves!" In early November a UN patrol was virtually wiped out. The place: Niemba. The troops: Irish. The mission: to maintain law and order. The reason for the massacre: none.

In early November, 1960, Niemba, scene of one previous massacre and later incursions by marauding Baluba tribesmen, had become a UN outpost staffed by a detachment from Company A of the Thirty-third Irish Battalion. Lieutenant Gleeson, a platoon commander, joined Stig's mobile forty-man reconnaissance patrol on a sortie ten miles south of the gutted town. Driving slowly down the sunwashed road, the patrol's vehicles dodged holes dug by the Baluba and at several points were forced to halt so that the men could remove trees that had been felled across what passed for a highway in the Congo. The men in the patrol were silent. Their eyes probed the thick underbrush in an effort to detect an ambush and they anxiously kept their upper bodies below the sides of the military vehicles. Nobody wanted to chance being hit with a poisoned arrow.

It was with a sigh of relief that the patrol returned to the fire-blackened town. Sentries were on duty, crouched behind sandbags upon which were mounted machine guns. Nobody was taking chances, least of all Lieutenant Gleeson, who had recently arrived in Niemba from Kamina Base, the ONUC staging area in central Katanga Province. The Swede and the Irish officer discussed the local situation. Gleeson admitted that he had seen some Baluba tribesmen in the distance.

"I don't think that they're very dangerous," he ventured to the Swedish officer. Stig shook his head vigorously and warned the ruddy-faced Irish officer that the Baluba were fanatics when hopped up and drugged with *bangi-bangi*. He described to the young officer what had happened to him on the few occasions he had found himself surrounded by wild-eyed tribesmen.

"Remember," Stig warned the Irish platoon commander, "if you can't defend yourself the very moment they attack you, you will be killed. Don't let them get too close to you."

Later that day Stig's patrol departed for Albertville. It was the last time he saw Gleeson alive. The date was November 7, 1960.

Early the following day two Land Rover vehicles manned by eleven Irish soldiers drove southward from Niemba. "We will return later today," Lieutenant Gleeson told the noncommissioned officer he left in charge of the outpost detachment. As a matter of course, the Niemba command post signaled ONUC headquarters in Albertville that a patrol would move south for the day and return toward nightfall. It was to be one of the many routine patrols the troops of many nations were mounting throughout the Congo. There was only one difference: Lieutenant Gleeson's patrol was not to return.

Private Thomas Kenny tied his cross-cut saw on one of the vehicles after sharpening it a few times. He was an engineer trooper in the Irish Army and the months at Kamina Base had been busy ones building quarters and other buildings for his battalion. Now, he was in a different part of the Congo although it all looked the same to him and the other men from Dublin and Counties Cork and Kerry. As the two vehicles carefully moved down the dirt road, the men rarely spoke to each other. Each man was keeping an alert eye out for the Baluba. A few miles outside of town they arrived at a native village. Lieutenant Gleeson and Sergeant Gaynor, the senior noncom, briefly spoke with some women. The two men spoke a smattering of Swahili and French, at least enough to make themselves understood.

A few miles more and they arrived at a crossing point where a stream narrowed. The wooden bridge had been partially destroyed.

"Can you fix it?" Gleeson asked Kenny. The engineer-soldier nodded.

Meanwhile, Gleeson and his platoon sergeant forded the stream and walked up the road where they suddenly halted. A low babble of voices suddenly grew to an angry roar. From either side of the thick underbrush along the road appeared a horde of painted warriors. Gleeson lifted his submachine gun and began walking backward, his platoon sergeant abreast of him.

When they came to the bridge the officer shouted that Balubas are coming down the road. "Turn the vehicles around!" he ordered. By that time it was too late. The Irish officer wanted to avoid trouble and drive off. But a group of tribesmen had cut them off. Suddenly, a huge tree crashed to the ground, blocking the retreat of the patrol's vehicles. In the excitement of the moment, there was only one thing left to do. Lieutenant Gleeson considered talking his way out of the predicament. For a moment, he thought that this would be possible. From the direction of the falling tree he spotted a mob of armed tribesmen. He knew he was in for trouble.

"Quick, lads, take cover!" he ordered and pointed to a slight rise nearby. As the men dashed for the hill a shower of arrows fell. One plunged into Gleeson's shoulder and he staggered as he ran, falling to his knees and twisting around with his weapon at the ready. Triggering off short bursts, the officer tried to cover his men as they withdrew to the knoll. But his gun became silent when the mob of warriors fell upon him with *panga* knives and clubs, battering him to a bloody pulp.

Sergeant Gaynor was the next to fall. The screaming Balubas pounced on the downed noncom and whatever cries of pain and fear that escaped from his tortured lips were quickly absorbed by the noisy mob. The crackle of rifle fire from the other soldiers failed to halt the attacking tribesmen and one by one the guns were silenced. Tom Kenny triggered off shot after shot into the mass of warriors and saw some fall, but there were others to take their place. He decided to make a break for better cover. A few feet away Private Browne was firing his submachine gun. He, too, had the same idea: to break away and run for better cover.

"Watch the anthills!" Kenny shouted to Browne. The warriors had hidden themselves in the six-foot-high insect fortresses, charging out after the running UN soldiers who dashed past.

Kenny fired off his clip and dashed from the knoll. He couldn't help but notice the bodies of Corporals Dougan and Kelly and of Privates McGuinn and Farrell sprawled where they had fallen beneath the cloud of arrows. Suddenly, a fistful of pain slammed into Kenny's back and he stumbled to his knees. An arrow had struck him. He dropped his rifle and staggered to his feet again, running past Private Fennell who, although wounded, laboriously fired his rifle.

"Get away, man!" Kenny shouted to Fennell, actually suggesting that he seek better cover.

"I'm going to die," the wounded man sobbed and continued shooting.

Kenny stumbled through the brush and a pair of hands reached up and grabbed him. It was Private Browne. His submachine gun was slung over his shoulder.

"We've got to get away from these savages," Browne gasped. "Follow me, Tom." He ran down the slope and burst through a wall of tall grasses growing from swampy ground. Kenny tried to follow. Another arrow slammed into his upper thigh and he fell on the trail broken by Browne. A third arrow slashed into the back of his neck. He was unable to rise and lay there awaiting death.

The shrieking grew louder and Kenny knew that the Baluba tribesmen had seen the trail through the swamp. The warriors came upon him and he closed his eyes and began praying for a quick death.

The tribesmen ran past. He heard their footsteps as the soft mud sucked at their running feet, splattering his head with the black muck. But some remained, chanting "*Kufa! Kufa! Kufa!*" It was the Swahili word for "kill." The sandy-haired Irish soldier lay still, all hope gone. In the distance he heard the chatter of a submachine gun. He knew that it must be Browne. Good old Browne. At least he would die taking some of the black devils with him.

A painful blow suddenly struck the back of his leg as he lay face down in the mud. Then a second blow . . . and a third . . . and fourth. He counted eighteen of the blows that slowly moved up his body. The warriors were beating him with clubs. He lost count of the blows after eighteen and the only cadence he then felt were colors as each thud of a war club exploded in a burst of black or red . . . black . . . red . . . black. He finally lost consciousness.

Trampled into the mud by hundreds of bare feet was a soggy and dirty patch of blue cloth. It was Private Kenny's blue beret with the insignia of the United Nations emblazoned in white on the crown of the headpiece. It had fallen from his pocket. Before fading back into the jungle the Baluba tribesmen had taken his helmet, his cartridge belt, and rifle.

All that remained in the area surrounding the tiny bridge south of Niemba were the silent bodies of the peacekeepers who had fallen before the fanatic tribesmen who had carried away their own dead. The peacekeepers were left where they had fallen. Late in the afternoon vultures soared high overhead, mute testimony to the death on the ground below.

13

The survivors

"LIEUTENANT VON BAYER," Commandant P. D. Hogan barked at his orderly. "Get von Bayer! Immediately!" The orderly saluted and swiftly walked out of the Irish Battalion commander's office. Nervously shuffling papers, Hogan waited for Stig to arrive. It was early evening, November 8, 1960. A scrawled message was on the table that passed for the Irish C.O.'s desk. LIEUTENANT GLEESON AND ELEVEN MAN PATROL HAVE NOT RETURNED TO NIEMBA. AWAITING INSTRUCTIONS. It was signed with the name of the sergeant in command of the detachment.

Stig burst through the door and threw a quick salute to the Irish officer. Hogan passed the message to Stig. The Swedish liaison officer suggested that a strong patrol leave Albertville that night for Niemba. Hogan said he'd request an aerial reconnaissance search at daybreak. Several hours later a strong force of Land Rovers and trucks filled with troops rumbled forth into the night toward Niemba, headlights piercing the inky blackness and flooding the dirt road ahead with bright illumination.

At the scene of the massacre the jungle fauna sniffed the

dead bodies of the soldiers of Erin, poking at some and avoiding the still form of Private Tom Kenny. A ray of life flickered in his body and the pain that wracked his cracked bones brought forth anguished sobs, indistinct delirium, and muttering.

At daybreak the white-painted aircraft from ONUC flew toward Niemba, low over the dirt road that led south from the outpost town. The pilot of one light recon plane flew over the small wood bridge that had been destroyed earlier. He spotted tire tracks, but no vehicles. Then he saw a still form wearing the light tan tropic uniform worn by the European troops of ONUC. His observer looked hard through binoculars and picked up the still form of another body and then another.

Word was radioed back to ONUC field headquarters in Albertville and relayed to the patrol enroute to Niemba. Stig, sitting in the lead Land Rover, studied the map on his lap as the field radio in the vehicle crackled and a voice from Albertville relayed the position of the lost patrol that had been radioed by the recon plane.

At the scene of the massacre Private Kenny slowly rose to his feet and staggered drunkenly deeper into the swamp. Racked with pain and delirious from fever, the soldier from Erin wandered for several hours. He fell to his knees. He crawled. He slowly got to his feet and pushed on. He had actually moved full circle.

A few hours after sunrise the mobile patrol arrived at the wrecked bridge. Irish soldiers, their blue helmets reflecting the morning sun, jumped from the trucks with their rifles held at high port. Flanking guards were posted and machine guns atop the trucks were made ready for firing. The troops fanned out.

One by one cries of dismay rang out as the soldiers discovered their buddies.

"Oh God!" one trooper moaned as he spotted the body of Sergeant Gaynor.

"Over here, it's Lieutenant Gleeson," another soldier cried out.

Stig followed the soldiers. They came across a third body and then a fourth. Within half an hour nine bodies were located. Commandant Hogan led his men deeper into the swamp. Suddenly an apparition appeared from the deep grass.

"Don't shoot!" the hoarse voice of Private Kenny called out. He recognized the blue helmets and staggered forward into the arms of Commandant Hogan. Then he pulled away, unsuccessfully raised his shattered and broken right arm in an attempt to salute.

"I'm '57 Kenny reporting, sir." Then the mass of blood and mud that resembled a man collapsed.

Overhead, a helicopter beat its way toward the wrecked bridge and set down in a cloud of dust. Colonel Burns, the southern command senior officer, debarked in time to watch the silent UN peacekeepers gently carrying the bodies of the Irish soldiers. Some of the men had been mutilated. The colonel shuddered.

The bodies were brought back to Niemba and strong motorized detachments were organized. The members of the Irish Battalion were enraged and wanted vengeance. The patrols that subsequently drove along the few roads leading from the outpost town were composed of men who would neither give nor ask any quarter if a group of Baluba warriors were spotted.

In Niemba the members of what was now a reinforced garrison were understandably nervous. Morale was low. That night, as Stig prepared to bed down, the crackle of gun fire echoed in the blackness. Two members of the Irish detachment were struck by bullets fired from the guns of their fellow soldiers. The men who had fired had thought they had seen Baluba tribesmen in the shadows.

The following morning, November 9, a patrol set out down the road. Stig accompanied the group. A few short miles outside of Niemba a haggard, hollow-eyed figure stumbled from the brush along the side of the road. A rifle was clutched in one hand. The other hand was a mass of pulpy flesh.

"FitzPatrick," he gasped to Stig and the Irish officer sitting beside him. The soldier's uniform was in tatters. He had not been struck by arrows, but the ordeal itself was a bitter one. His rifle was empty; so was his ammunition pouch.

"I killed some of the bloody beggars," he mumbled over and over again as soldiers lifted him on to one of the vehicles. The patrol turned around and headed back toward town. Later that day an old Baluba warrior, paint still marking his features, was brought in and escorted to Stig. The interrogation didn't take too long. In fact, the ONUC peacekeepers were even more confused as word spread among the troops that one of the tribesmen had explained why Lieutenant Gleeson's patrol had been attacked. His explanation reflected the chaos. ONUC soldiers shook their heads. It just did not make sense.

The old warrior obviously was still under the influence of *bangi-bangi.* Stig asked the Luba why the warriors had attacked. The old man replied that they had orders to attack and kill everybody coming along the road.

"Even ONUC?" Stig asked. The old man nodded.

"Who ordered you to attack?" Stig asked. The man shrugged his answer.

"Why did you kill everybody?"

"The witch doctor told us to. His witchcraft was strong medicine. We obeyed the witchcraft."

"Why did you not attack us yesterday?" Stig continued his interrogation.

"The ONUC soldiers looked too angry."

Stig turned to the Irish officers present and explained that the old man was telling the truth. He was too stupid to lie. The officers looked at each other. Nine lives lost because of a witch doctor.

The Gaelic equivalent of an Anglo-Saxon four letter curse rolled from the lips of Commandant Hogan. It seemed so fruitless. The Irish officer shook his head. This was the type of military situation that the staff studies and textbooks don't cover.

The diplomatic arm of ONUC, represented by civilians assigned to UN headquarters in Leopoldville, worked within a different frame of reference than the military officers. Policy was set by the civilians and carried out by the military arm of

ONUC. At the United Nations in New York, at the highest level of diplomacy, the representatives of the Western alliance, the Communist bloc and the uncommitted Asian and African nations argued the pros and cons of the methods used in the Congo to bring about law and order.

Meanwhile, the problems of maintaining law and order continued. The ONUC soldiers in the field cursed the stiff rules and regulations that went against the military grain. Soldiers of all nations were of the opinion that preventive action was the best antidote for violence. Shots fired at rebellious mobs would quickly bring an end to any trouble. The massacre of the Irish patrol, thought many commanders, could have been avoided if the small unit had immediately opened fire instead of waiting until the last moment when it was too late. They believed that the order not to fire unless actually attacked did not merit acceptance under the prevailing conditions in the Congo.

In Ireland, Parliament went into session in Dublin to debate the deaths of the nine men. Some members of the Irish Parliament believed that the price was too high for their country's involvement. They demanded that the battalion be brought home.

Other nations began to suffer casualties in small actions and their respective governments also were faced with the same questions by the loyal opposition.

To complicate matters further, some nations insisted in the UN General Assembly that deposed Prime Minister Lumumba be restored to office. This was clearly interference in the internal affairs of the Republic of the Congo. Even more so, the Soviet Union took umbrage when several of its diplomatic representatives in the Congo were beaten up by the mutinous ANC troops.

Obviously, *provocateurs* had stirred up the population, and if they were Communist bloc agents, the Soviets had reaped that which they had sown. When Colonel Mobutu had taken over the administration of the Republic and fired all of the Congo's leaders, he ordered the Soviet diplomatic mission and the Czechoslovakian legation to leave the country immediately. The Soviets, of course, were furious. At Lumumba's request they had openly defied the UN peacekeeping effort by sending a hundred transport planes loaded with trucks and food, a huge staff of "technicians," and political support for the left-leaning Prime Minister. The Western alliance, on the other hand, wanted to keep the Soviets out of Africa.

The situation in the Congo was nothing more than a diplomatic donnybrook, a forensic free-for-all. The Soviets, upon being notified that their mission was *persona non grata,* called their withdrawal "temporary" and charged that the lawful government of Prime Minister Lumumba had been unlawfully removed and a "puppet regime obedient to foreigners" installed.

Throughout all this confusion, the seceded provinces of Katanga and Kasai built up a force of mercenary soldiers to maintain law and order while disrupting the efforts of ONUC troops to solve the same problems in these new states.

It seemed that from Independence Day through the remainder of 1960, the new African country was up for grabs by any number of power blocs—large and small. In November ANC troops arrested a member of the Ghanaian Embassy in Leopoldville and charged him with meddling in Congolese affairs. Ghana's ambassador, Nathaniel A. Welbeck, strongly protested this turn of events. But then, the diminutive diplomat was protesting every move made by the ONUC command. Kwame Nkrumah, Ghana's president, had been working behind the scenes to become the leader and spokesman of Africa's newly emerging nations. Although his troops were commanded by British officers, and were nominally under the command of the United Nations, his ambassador in Leopoldville would not permit Ghana's military forces to accept the orders of ONUC unless these instructions were relayed through him. Ambassador Welbeck considered himself the supreme commander of Ghana's forces in the Congo.

This total confusion quickly sifted into the ranks of the peacekeepers. No one had foreseen so many complications. Military officers began to wonder aloud if peacekeeping was worth it.

If the peacekeepers in the field were confused, the ONUC high command in Leopoldville was even more perplexed by the course of events. During the General Assembly's fifteenth session in early autumn of 1960, highlighted by Soviet Premier Khrushchev's shoe-thumping antics as much as by the debate over the Congo, the Communist bloc attempted to thwart the Secretary-General's attempts to bring peace to the troubled African state. On October 3 Khrushchev assailed Dag Hammarskjold for carrying out UN peacekeeping policies in the Congo with behavior the Russian called "arbitrary and lawless." Khrushchev eventually went further and charged Hammarskjold with violating "the elementary principles of justice" and supporting "the colonialists." It was at this point that the pudgy Soviet leader demanded the Secretary General's resignation and the formation of a *troika* or triumvirate of leaders from the three political camps in the world's three major political camps.

This storm in New York was weathered, but the one in the Congo still hadn't blown itself out. Ghana and Guinea, two African states with peacekeeping troops in the Congo, supported the leftwing faction of Patrice Lumumba and tried to mediate the differences between the deposed prime minister and President Kasavubu. Needless to say, the efforts of both nations were rebuffed.

In Leopoldville the peacekeepers were also pressed into service as bodyguards, protecting the Congo's political leaders of all factions. Following Lumumba's dismissal, the deposed prime minister took refuge in his home and a UN Ghana guard was mounted around the building. On November 27, under what investigators still refer to as mysterious circumstances, Lumumba escaped his protectors and tried to join his supporters in Stanleyville. He was recaptured several days later at Port Francqui in Kasai Province by ANC troops under Colonel Mobutu's command and returned to Leopoldville where he was jailed. If there was any superficial hands-off policy of the Congo's internal affairs by members of the United Nations which had provided peacekeeping troops, this cloak was brushed aside by the loud protests over Lumumba's arrest. Guinea, Mali, Morocco, Indonesia, Yugoslavia, and the United Arab Republic threatened to withdraw their military forces from ONUC unless Lumumba was released.

In early December Lumumba disappeared. He was secretly taken to Katanga Province and turned over to his arch-enemy Moise Tshombe along with two of his closest followers. His whereabouts was a well-kept secret. It was not until mid-February, 1961, that the world learned through a broadcast over Katanga Radio that Lumumba had been killed in an attempt to escape. However, a report of the UN Commission organized to investigate the mysterious death of Lumumba later in 1961 reported: "Mr. Lumumba, Mr. Okito, and Mr. Mpolo were executed by a Belgian mercenary on 17 January 1961 not far from Elisabethville, and in all probability in the presence of certain members of the Government of Katanga Province, namely Mr. Tshombe, Mr. Munongo and Mr. Kibwe."

Meanwhile, rumors abounded that Lumumba and his followers had been turned over to Lunda tribesmen, bitter enemies of the Baluba with whom Lumumba was strongly aligned, and killed—and eaten. The remains of the three men were never found and Tshombe's government denied the allegations made by the UN Commission. If Lumumba's death did anything, it gave new life to his political party which required a martyr. Although his death spotlighted the political maneuvering of Tshombe and Mobutu, it also created a new regime in the Congo. Antoine Gizenga, Lumumba's chief lieutenant, was in charge of Stanleyville and, backed by a Baluba army, including tribesmen who had been members of the ANC, he declared the independence of the largest city in North Central Congo. The Communist bloc and its African supporters quickly recognized the new regime and Red China took its first step in Africa by dispatching diplomats to Gizenga's capital.

What was left of the Congolese National Army—the ANC—was spread out in four political areas of the Congo with troops belonging to nearly all of the nation's tribal spectrum. Mobutu commanded about seven thousand troops from his headquar-

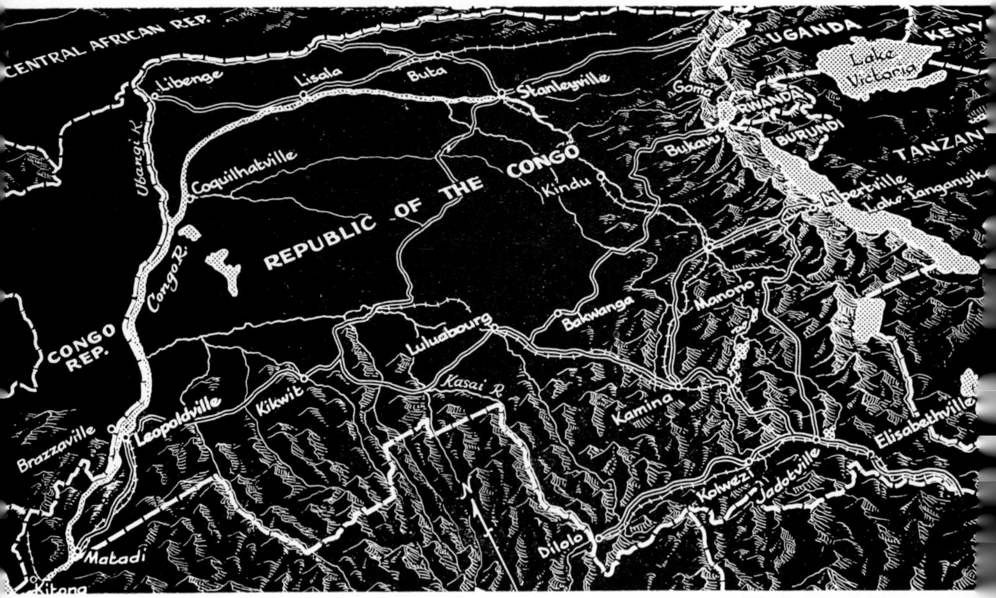

The New York Times

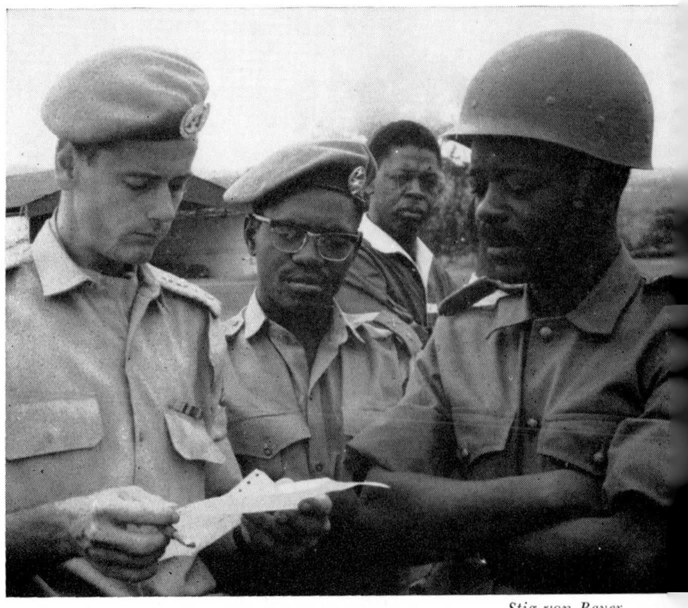

Stig von Bayer

Von Bayer conferring with military and civilian authorities.

Stig von Bayer

Von Bayer at the site of the Irish massacre.

Stig von Bayer

Honoring a fallen Irish comrade.

The inauguration of Kelubee power station.

Stig von Bayer

Stig von Bayer

"Baluba" Jeunesse.

Stig von Baye

Baluba roadblock.

Train attacked and derailed by Balubas.

Stig von Bayer

Stig von Bayer

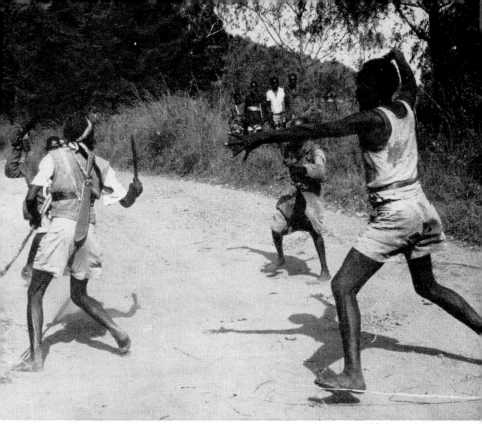

A surprise attack by tribesmen on the Jeunesse.

Stig von Bayer

Cannibalism—the aftermath of an attack.

Stig von Bayer

A tour of inspection of the 2nd Congolese Battalion under U.N. Command.

Plane shot down by ANC.

Von Bayer with ANC soldiers at wreckage.

Stig von Bayer

Stig von Bayer

Bassi tribesmen fighting the Jeunesse.

Stig von Bayer

Stig von Bayer

Von Bayer is cited for bravery.

OUTGOING TELEGRAM Department of State

INDICATE: ☐ COLLECT
☐ CHARGE TO

UNCLASSIFIED

59 7349

Origin ACTION: USUN NEW YORK 2431 March 15, 1964
SS 4:45 p.m.
Info:
G
AF
ARA
EUR
IO
P
USIA
INR

Please deliver following letter to Secretary General from President:

QUOTE

Dear Mr. Secretary General:

I know you shared my anxiety for the safety of the foreign residents threatened by the recent violence in Kwilu Province,

Would you convey my warm personal gratitude, as well as the highest appreciation of my government, to all those responsible for this operation. In particular, I would like to commend the extraordinary courage, perseverance and devotion to duty shown by the following men:

Brigadier J. A. Dextraze, Canada
Lieutenant Colonel Paul Mayer, Canada
Captain S. von Bayer, Sweden
Lieutenant T. Glantz, Sweden
Lieutenant P. Karlsen, Norway
Lieutenant E. Braga, Brazil
Lieutenant M. Narajo, Brazil
Warrant Officer S. E. Wahlund, Sweden
Warrant Officer L. Dahlgren, Sweden
Staff Sargeant J. G. Joppesen, Denmark
Sergeant Sule Adiko, Nigeria
Sergeant L. Lessard, Canada
Sergeant O. I. Johansen, Norway

The outstanding performance of this mission is worthy of the highest ideals and traditions of United ~~Nations~~ Nations peacekeeping forces.

Sincerely,

Lyndon B. Johnson

UNQUOTE

ters in Leopoldville; Tshombe in his Katangese capital of Elisabethville had about six thousand soldiers at his disposal; Albert Kalonji in South Kasai Province could count on his army of three thousand men, and Gizenga in Stanleyville had fifty-five hundred men under arms as well as the support of the Baluba in North Katanga.

A civil war was brewing and the peacekeepers were caught squarely in the middle of an explosive situation with orders to defend themselves if attacked, but only as a last resort. A new mandate was required and the Security Council on February 21 voted 9 to 0, with France and the Soviet Union abstaining, to authorize the peacekeepers to employ "force, if necessary in the last resort" in a last-ditch effort to prevent the civil war that was expected.

The six nations that had threatened to withdraw their troops from ONUC after Lumumba's escape and recapture, did so in April—a month after Nehru announced that he would provide a brigade of forty-seven hundred men to join ONUC. On the day that the Indian prime minister made his announcement a battalion of ANC troops attacked Sudanese soldiers of ONUC at the port of Matadi nearly a hundred miles up the Congo River from where this vital national lifeline flowed into the Atlantic. The port was an important supply point for the UN forces. Ships carrying supplies for ONUC docked at Matadi and unloaded their cargoes which in turn were reloaded on trains and trucks for transport further inland to Leopoldville and other cities.

The Sudanese, armed with nothing more than rifles and a few machine guns, were subjected to artillery and mortar fire. Two men were killed and a large number wounded. The attack caught the Sudanese peacekeepers completely by surprise. The garrison, completely surrounded, surrendered. It was an ignominious defeat for ONUC rivaling the massacre of the Irish patrol by the Baluba. However, both incidents occurred more than a thousand miles apart under altogether different circumstances.

Meanwhile, ONUC headquarters wasn't caught napping a

second time. When a report was received that three thousand ANC troops were moving on Kitona, the former Belgian Army base that was guarded by another force of Sudanese, four commercial airliners leased to the United Nations were each loaded with fifty-six Indonesian troops and boxes of ammunition. The pilots, American civilians, immediately took off with the reinforcements.

The base itself was under attack by the time the aircraft arrived from Leopoldville, a relatively short distance by air when one considers the total size of the Congo itself. At ONUC headquarters the attack was considered serious although there was doubt that three thousand ANC troops were deployed against the Sudanese. A brief message was sent to the Sudanese informing them to hold, that help was on the way. The situation was considered serious. If the UN lost Kitona, located at the very mouth of the Congo River on the Atlantic coast, the shipping supply line to the outside world would entirely be cut off with the exception of supply by an airlift.

The diminutive Indonesian soldiers in their oversize blue helmets—most of them paratroopers—silently sat in bucket seats along the side walls of the fuselage of each transport. For the majority of these troops from the Southwest Pacific it was the second time outside their own country they had ever flown. The first time was the flight from their homeland to the Congo. The four white-painted transports circled over the Kitona airstrip. Below, the pilots could see flashes of gunfire from the military base. The big question was: had the ANC captured the airstrip?

The pilots radioed the Kitona tower. "Come in and land quickly," came the curt voice from the tower. "We expect trouble at any minute." The transports broke their formation and banked sharply over the river, as they approached from a direction away from the shooting. As each plane touched down it taxied toward the tower. At the opposite end of the airstrip from where the planes had touched down, tiny figures could be seen running.

"It's the ANC!" exploded the air traffic controller. "Unload your men at once!"

There was no ground crew. Pilots and copilots left their cockpits. The copilots opened the wide cargo doors from the inside and shoved a ladder to the ground, while the pilots of each aircraft broke open the ammunition and grenade boxes. As each soldier passed the pilot, he would be handed a bandoleer of ammunition and four hand grenades and then the blue-helmeted peacekeeper would descend the ladder to the ground. With their shares of ammunition in their pockets or slung around their necks in a bandoleer, the Indonesians scuttled off to meet the charging enemy.

The aircraft and reinforcements had landed none too soon. The Indonesian soldiers assembled into squads and took up defensive positions about 150 feet from the four aircraft. The ANC soldiers continued to run forward. Suddenly, the rattle of rifle fire and the barking of machine guns echoed across the field. The wave of charging soldiers faltered, halted and then turned back. More than two hundred Indonesian voices began shouting and the tiny soldiers jumped to their feet and took off after the retreating Congolese. Kitona was saved. Matadi was avenged.

But perplexed ONUC soldiers in the field were frustrated. No matter from which country they came, they were professional fighting men ready to face any enemy. But in the Congo the enemy was nameless and faceless—and by whatever name he was called in whatever language used, the enemy in 1961 had also taken on the name of "frustration."

•

14

Peacekeepers without portfolio

THE NORMALLY PLACID Swedish liaison officer attached to the Irish Battalion was torn between his duty as a UN peacekeeper and his feeling for the topsy-turvy course of events. It was very simple for Stig to digest the intelligence that he was privy to by virtue of his knowledge of the Congo. But nothing seemed to make sense.

The jungle telegraph drummed incessantly in Baluba country. It became so that when the drums suddenly stopped, the ONUC soldiers stiffened and intently listened for a growling mob of tribesmen to appear and attack. The Baluba, numbering nearly half of the population of Katanga Province, attacked whites and Congolese alike. The Congolese they attacked were usually Lunda tribesmen or tribes associated with the Lunda. Moreover, Moise Tshombe was a Lunda and his lieutenant, Godefroid Munongo, was the son of a Bayeke chief allied to the Lunda. In Katanga, the civil war that the UN feared had for all practical purposes broken out in savagery which only Africans could understand and which the European troops had casually read about more in fiction than in fact.

The peacekeepers were deployed in towns along the border separating Baluba territory in northern Katanga from the areas controlled by Tshombe's troops. North Katanga, a most valuable territory in the Congo, for all practical purposes ceased to function as a productive area. In Brussels, headquarters of the industrial corporations which owned the mines in Katanga and from which huge profits had suddenly dropped, the decision was made to support Moise Tshombe with whatever he needed to remain in power and pacify his troubled province. Even more important, the Union Minière de Haute Katanga feared that its mining facilities would be destroyed. The huge company could weather the storm with its mining operations closed. On the other hand, a flooded or destroyed mining complex would ultimately and seriously hurt the company's operations.

The Katangan Government received advice and financial aid from Belgium. The advice was carried out by Tshombe. He began to hire mercenaries to bolster his own army, officered by Belgians, under a 1960 treaty. The mercenaries, soldiers of fortune and disgruntled French OAS soldiers and officers from Algeria hired in Europe and South Africa, began arriving by plane at Elisabethville. ONUC troops at the major Katangan airport couldn't help but note that some of the hard-faced men passing through customs were obviously new recruits. It was a strange sight to see the enemy arriving, knowing that they were coming to do battle with the peacekeepers and any other groups that Tshombe considered a threat to his own person and power structure.

The mercenaries were quickly deployed near the Baluba capital of Manono. The reports reaching Stig bespoke of massacres of the Baluba by white soldiers, but, as with all reports in the Congo, the tales were grossly exaggerated. Estimates of Baluba deaths could only be guessed at; figures ranging anywhere from seven thousand to a hundred thousand were impossible to establish.

The Baluba, in turn, attacked everybody whether they were

wearing the blue and white insignia of ONUC or the mottled green and tan uniforms of the mercenaries.

By the time the advance elements of the Indian Brigade arrived at ONUC's principal military base at Kamina in Western Katanga, the pattern had been set for a round of violence that was to continue until the peacekeepers were to finally leave the Congo three years later.

Swedish troops were attacked when they seized Elisabethville airport to prepare for the arrival of the reinforcements. Tshombe promptly labeled this seizure "an act of war" and incited his Conakat political party to begin a series of riots against ONUC. The Irish battalion was flown in to the airport to reinforce the beleaguered Swedes. While the riots were turning the attention of ONUC headquarters officers to civil disturbances, other activity was taking place.

Tshombe's soldiers, supported by a force of mercenaries and attacking under direct orders from the president of Katanga, drove into the town and deployed around the hotel that the Ethiopians were using as a headquarters. The ONUC soldiers from the mountain country of east Africa didn't give the Katangan military units time to complete preparations for the attack. Bayonets fixed to their American M-1 rifles, Emperor Haile Selassie's fighting men surged out from behind their barricades and attacked. Tshombe's soldiers dropped their weapons and fled. The mercenaries, taken aback by the unexpected counterattack, were captured en masse. The Ethiopians rounded up a hundred Katangese and disarmed thirty South African and two Belgian mercenaries and none too gently escorted them to what passed for a prisoner compound.

The peacekeeping efforts of ONUC slowly took hold throughout most of the Congo where blue-helmeted troops were dispatched. From every detachment outpost a UN flag fluttered. The white-painted military trucks with the UN insignia rumbled along the roads transporting ONUC civilian administrators who would assist the Congolese in governing the provinces. The mass exodus of Belgian technicians and administrators had virtually paralyzed the new nation, its economy, and essential services. Unemployment was rapidly rising in the cities, and hunger and disease loomed.

Keeping the roads and railroads open and operating was paramount. The military forces were pressed into service. Every train was ordered to travel with a detachment of blue-helmeted soldiers to guard against attack and protect the right of way against sabotage.

In late 1960, a few days after the massacre of the Irish patrol, a train rolled out of Albertville for Kabalo, formerly an important communications and commercial center in northeastern Katanga. The train was manned by an escort detachment of Irish soldiers. The metal serpent thundered across the rolling countryside into Niemba and then out of the deserted town. The detachment that had been stationed there had been pulled back to Albertville. Niemba was in the hands of the Baluba. The disciplined soldiers aboard the train, angry as they were at the Baluba, held their fire as the train passed through the railroad station and continued westward toward its destination.

Orders from ONUC headquarters had to be obeyed despite the personal feelings of the troopers and their officers.

Outside of the station a group of painted warriors waited, taunting the men aboard the train. It galled the fighting Irish when they spotted the trophies worn by some of the tribesmen. The unmistakable blue helmets were worn by some of the Baluba. One tribesman fired off a burst from a submachine gun—the weapon that a few short days before had been wrested from the dying hands of Lieutenant Gleeson.

"Steady, lads!" the detachment officer counseled. Orders were orders.

In Leopoldville ONUC officials had decided that perhaps it might be wise either to relieve the Irish troopers or to reinforce them. The high command finally decided to reinforce the European soldiers with Nigerian elements of the UN force. Perhaps it would be more logical, so the reasoning went at Leopoldville ONUC headquarters, if African soldiers rode the rails on escort mission. Perhaps the white soldiers were suspected of being Belgians. Negro troops couldn't fall under this suspicion, even by the erratic Baluba. Unfortunately, this premise proved incorrect. The Baluba proved even more of a mystery to figure out.

A truck convoy filled with Nigerians drove out of Kamina base. In Baluba country the convoy was attacked. The Nigerians were forced to fight their way through. The first train that the Nigerians escorted out of Albertville was double the usual size. Near a ravine, over which the train had to cross, the Baluba had removed rails. Then they attacked.

The African troops pulled back, retreating to a nearby hill and dug in. Throughout the night they repelled constant attacks by the jungle-wise warriors. Just before abandoning the train, the escort unit's radio operator flashed an emergency message to ONUC headquarters in Albertville. A company of Irish troops was dispatched to relieve the beleaguered Nigerians. It was a scene out of a western movie, only there was no cavalry coming to the rescue—just a company of Irish troopers spoiling for a fight.

The Baluba, now well-versed in the art of railroad sabotage, had removed the rails two miles from the abandoned train in an effort to halt the arrival of reinforcements. The troopers jumped from the rescue train and proceeded to replace the rails with backbreaking speed, hammering in bolts as fast as they could. The sabotage had been anticipated and the rescue train carried extra rails and the necessary tools for track repairs.

Stig, in his capacity of liaison officer-interpreter, carefully watched the soldiers at work. Other helmeted troopers were posted as guards. In the distance the sound of gunfire slowly dwindled as the rescue force feverishly repaired the tracks. In the bush alongside the roadbed Baluba warriors hidden in the tall grass launched occasional poison arrows into the air. Fortunately, no one was hit.

Stig suggested that a platoon of soldiers sent into the bush could flush out the hidden snipers. The Irish officer in command of the rescue force took a few minutes to think it over. The force wasn't *really* under attack. And ONUC orders were firm in outlining the conditions under which the peacekeepers could use their weapons.

"Hell," the angry Irish officer snorted, "we'll go in and get the bloody bastards." He ordered one of the lieutenants to move into the brush with his platoon.

"Fix your bayonets," he added. "A show of cold steel should give them something to think about."

Spread out and firing occasional shots into the grass, the platoon moved forward. The Baluba warriors fled.

After the track repairs were completed, the Irish company boarded the train and continued on to the scene of the battle between the African soldiers and the tribesmen. The rescue force was not a moment too soon. The Nigerians had expended all of their ammunition and were braced to fight off a final charge with their bayonet-tipped rifles. Either way it would have been a slaughter. And the peacekeeping forces of ONUC couldn't afford another massacre.

It was a case of arriving in the nick of time. Whistle howling, the engine clattered along the rails and braked to a halt on the section of track which passed by the base of the hill. Irish machine gunners opened up and sprayed the slopes where the Baluba were slowly edging toward the beleaguered Nigerians. The sight of additional blue helmets below unnerved the attacking tribesmen. They fled.

The day was saved; the Nigerians were safe.

15

Politics and patrols

THE LIFELINE of the Congo is the *Chemin de Fer du Bas-Congo au Katanga* which the soldiers of ONUC referred to as BCK, the official initials of the vital railroad that links the important cities of Katanga with each other and the outside world. The blue-helmeted soldiers depended on this railroad for supplies and reinforcements of outposts along the route. The Congolese depended on the railroad to haul food into the various tribal areas in Katanga and elsewhere in the Congo.

Union Minière operations were also dependent on the railroad. For how else would the rich copper ore and other products of the mining company be delivered to ports where ships would carry the many metal ores to various destinations throughout the world? BCK was important to the Congo and to every last man, woman, and child in the country.

Yet BCK was also hated by the soldiers of ONUC.

The railroad's right of way became a battlefield. Either the trains were under direct attack or the rails were sabotaged. One branch of the BCK* ran west from Elisabethville into Ba-

* From Albertville to Kabongo and Kindu. The railroad is the "CFL," *Chemin de Fer de Grandes Laos.*

luba, Mukulakulu, Luena, Bukama, and Kabondobianda country. During one of the early escort missions aboard the trains Stig and his Irish comrades in arms were forced to fight off attacking warriors. Three of the railroad stations along the route were manned by Moroccan soldiers. As the train slowly pulled out of the station at Mukulakulu, Moroccan sentries at their posts waved to the men in the blue helmets. The train began to pick up speed and the Irish soldiers and Stig welcomed the cool breeze of the slip stream, anticipating a pleasant trip to Kamina. The last sentry waved on the train and the men settled back.

Suddenly there was a screech of metal as the engineer hit the brake. The soldiers were hurled against one another as the engine and the boxcars behind slid to a grinding halt. Ahead, a length of track had been removed. The engine had stopped inches away from where the track ended and the emptiness of a line of wooden ties and roadbed began. If the train had not halted, its speed would have carried the engine and boxcars forward until they would have slid down the roadbed embankment and turned over, possibly with injuries or death to the soldiers.

If Irish tempers began to boil, Stig's had reached the eruption stage. He jumped from the boxcar he was in and ran back to where the lone Moroccan sentry was stationed.

"Why the hell didn't you stop the train?" Stig thundered in French to the swarthy soldier from the land of the Berbers.

The soldier just shrugged. "I don't have orders to stop trains," he replied. "I just have orders to stand guard here."

Stig stalked off muttering obscenities in his own Nordic tongue. It was obvious that there are armies and there are armies; and as the months passed Stig would be meeting up with blue-helmeted ONUC soldiers from many other nations. These meetings, he realized, would not all be pleasant.

Early in 1961, ordered to rejoin Swedish battalion headquarters, Stig reluctantly took leave of the Irish, after making one final patrol with a unit of the battalion from Erin. The patrol had reached a village on the outskirts of Balubaland. The old chief, fingering a crucifix around his neck, told Stig of a smallpox epidemic that had taken a number of lives. But the villagers regarded this as the lesser of two evils. A far greater evil was the menacing Baluba warriors who had delivered an ultimatum to the village a few hours before the patrol had arrived.

Stig nodded as the chief continued his story and the Irish soldiers listened, not understanding Swahili but somehow grasping the facts from the gestures the wizened old man made as he spoke to the Swedish officer.

"Last night the Baluba chief sent a messenger to me," the chief related. "He said my tribesmen must join the Baluba. He said we would all die if we did not join. The warriors would burn our village to the ground and take all of our possessions—including our wives."

"What did you tell him?" Stig asked.

The old chief shrugged. "What could I tell the messenger?" he asked. "I sent him away. Now we have our strongest warriors standing guard to warn us if the Baluba are coming. We will have to fight them and die."

It was a prediction made without fear, with the fatalism of centuries. Stig translated for the benefit of Commandant Hogan who was leading the patrol.

"Aye, he's a fighter after me own heart," one of the Irish soldiers said when he heard what the little old man had said. It took courage on the part of the tribesmen and their chief. The Baluba seldom made idle threats. The chief just felt that death was preferable to the allegiance which the militant Baluba demanded. First, they insisted on a payment of fifty francs—a subscription for the village if it would join the Baluba cause. Second, and most repulsive to the chief, who continued to finger the crucifix around his neck, was the vile oath of loyalty that the village tribesmen would have to take. This oath would be administered by the witch doctor and consists of partaking of *dawa,* strong medicine or magic. The oath binds initiates to the Baluba for life and those who renege are promised a horrible death. The *dawa,* as Stig well knew, consisted of a brew mainly concocted from a stew made from the genitals of mutilated enemies.

To the tribal leader nervously fingering his crucifix, this participation was unthinkable. Stig knew that the old man had converted to Christianity, and his tribe also were Christians. He understood the situation.

"A bloody protection racket!" Commandant Paddy Hogan exploded.

The UN patrol moved on. In one small town they entered the Baluba warriors were quietly present along with Shabani, one of their more important chiefs. The Irish soldiers in the trucks loudly primed their weapons in a voiceless warning that the warriors couldn't help but note. In this way the ONUC soldiers announced that at the first sign of trouble they would open fire.

Stig stepped up to the Baluba chief and nodded a greeting. Hatred flashed from the eyes of the rebellious leader who couldn't help but notice that the submachine gun crooked in Stig's arm could easily be swung in the chief's direction. Stig stared at the warrior leader and thought to himself that here was the Al Capone of the jungle. As far as Stig was concerned, Shabani was nothing more than an outright gangster backed up by a gang of murderous thugs. However, ONUC soldiers had to be diplomatic and Stig was the spokesman for the United Nations in this dusty little village. The parley with the Baluba leader consisted of small talk. It was obvious to Stig that the chief would rather see the ONUC patrol on its way. The man hated the "blue helmets." But he was wise enough to know that he could be killed if trouble suddenly erupted. Moreover, he only had a small number of warriors present. The odds were too much against attacking this group of "blue helmets."

Stig cautioned the chief against attacking any of the villages. "ONUC soldiers will track you down," Stig declared, "and even your witch doctor and his magic will not save you from the authorities." It was a threat that Stig knew the Baluba chief would not lightly dismiss. Nor was the threat an idle one.

The Lunda and Bayeke tribes in the southern part of Katanga actually directed the affairs of the secessionist province and were the mortal enemies of the Baluba.

To all of the uniformed peacekeepers of ONUC, the tribal picture was next to impossible to understand. The Baluba were instigated into revolt by *agents provocateurs* of Patrice Lumumba whom they supported. Lumumba, a member of the warlike Batatela tribe, took up the cause of the Baluba in Katanga Province seven months prior to independence by promising to install the tribe's leading chief, Jason Sendwe, in his cabinet. On the other hand, the Baluba in Kasai Province were allies to Lumumba's political enemies. Due to a quirk of the Congo's complex tribal histories, the Kasai tribe irrevocably split from the Katanga tribe when the once mighty Baluba empire collapsed in the latter half of the last century.

The Baluba in Kasai Province held the best jobs; the Baluba in Katanga were hard-working employees of the various Belgian companies. As a result, there was resentment on the part of the other tribes which banded together politically to offset the inroads made by the Baluba. Out of this conglomeration of tribes emerged the Conakat political party of Moise Tshombe and the Balubakat Cartel grouping of the tribesmen from northern Katanga.

The game of politics was new in the Congo and took on a flavor of its own with rules that circumvented the game of the same name that the European soldiers understood. The revelation that the Congo's tribes were further fragmented by politics took Stig a short while to understand. Suffice to say, he grasped the situation much more quickly than many of the UN political officers sent into the Congo from headquarters in New York. Where the soldiers of ONUC had no understanding or even comprehension of the tribal or political situation, Stig stood out as one of the very few military officers who understood the reasons behind the chaos they were trying to bring to an end. As a result of his knowledge, time and again he was asked to explain the reason why. The UN troops from Europe knew why they were in the Congo. Those from other countries, namely from African states and from Indonesia, were ordered to duty in the Congo for a variety of reasons.

It behooved Stig to explain to those who asked him what made the Congolese tick that these people were living in another century and not in the more enlightened present. All of the ONUC soldiers were told that they were in the Congo to maintain law and order because the new nation's leaders were unable to do so. They were told that the Congolese Army had mutinied, innocent people had been killed, and that the disappearance of law and order had erupted into new tribal wars that had their beginnings many centuries ago.

By the time the first six months of the UN presence had passed, thousands of Congolese had died at the hands of their tribal enemies along with hundreds of white settlers and longtime residents of the Congo. But the biggest troublemakers were the ill-disciplined Congolese National Army and the Baluba. By early 1961 a new term for terrorism became part of the ONUC lexicon. The Congo's political parties required strong-arm groups. These groups in turn assumed the role of terrorists. Since these terrorists were mainly teenagers and young men, in the beginning they took on the title of *jeunesse*—youth movement.

In the town of Manono an Irish detachment, isolated except for a radio set, huddled behind their barricades as the Baluba *jeunesse* exploded into violence against a group of their fellow tribesmen whose chief, Vincent Yangala, had defied the young militants and attended a meeting of Katanga's tribal chiefs. The *jeunesse* had warned all of the twenty-three baluba chiefs in Manono district not to attend the meeting called by Katanga's leader, Moise Tshombe. Yangala attempted to go. He was captured. A kangaroo court was held in the streets of the town and Yangala and ten of his followers were brutally killed, flayed to death with bicycle chains honed to razor sharpness and attached to sticks.

One report described how the chief's genitals were sliced off and he was burned alive with gasoline while the *jeunesse* marched through the streets of Manono behind a warrior carrying a spear upon which Yangala's penis was impaled. This ugly trophy was turned over to Yangala's bitterest rival; he would use it to make *dawa.*

The *jeunesse* were as brutal and bloodthirsty as they come. The Katangese *gendarmerie* made several half-hearted attempts to patrol the northern part of the province which the Baluba ruled with a rigid fist. One police patrol was captured by Baluba warriors and the Congolese officer who accompanied it was taken along with his men. His legs were cut off by the *jeunesse,* sticks were jammed into the stumps, and the dying man was forced to run before he was burned to death. One of the men accompanying the patrol was a Belgian soldier assigned to the police. The *jeunesse* fell upon him with *panga* knives and chopped off his legs below the knees, ripped out his anus and removed his genitals before flaying him to death and decapitating him. The other men in the patrol suffered a similar fate in Kabalo district in which ONUC soldiers from Mali were stationed and unable to thwart the Baluba terrorists.

The Irish troopers knew all about the *jeunesse* and had a better understanding of the chaotic situation during the six months that Stig was attached to the Thirty-third Battalion. The soldiers of Stig's own country were later to benefit from his kowledge, especially along the hot roadbeds of the BCK.

16

The iron lifeline

THE WORDS were of a different language, the language of the Swedes, but the tune was as American as the hot dog. The *svenska* refrain of "I've Been Workin' on the Railroad" was more fact than song. The Swedes by themselves practically kept the BCK running during the spring of 1961. Heavily armed patrols would accompany the Congolese BCK workers into Baluba country and while the railroad's laborers replaced missing rails the Swedes would mount guard against the attacking Baluba.

On one patrol between Kamina and Elisabethville a large band of *jeunesse* broke from the bush on both sides of the roadbed and charged the workers. Swedish outpost guards immediately opened fire. The railroad workers, who would only bend their backs if the Swedish soldiers worked alongside them, panicked and ran back toward the train where the other half of the sixty-man patrol were mounting guard against just such an attack. The Swedes opened fire immediately. Charging tribesmen sprawled in the tall grass obviously hit. But the warriors kept coming.

In a matter of minutes the attack was beaten off. The tracks had been replaced and the train lurched forward and slowly pulled away leaving the angry *jeunesse* behind. However, the railroad's laborers refused to do any more work. Conditions, they protested to Stig, were too dangerous. The railroad line had to be kept open. The Swedish soldiers did it, even to running the engines.

Stripped to the waist beneath an extremely hot sun, the ONUC troops from north of the fiftieth parallel sweated in that area of equatorial Africa called the Congo. Pounding in bolts to fasten rails to wooden ties and digging with all their strength to flatten out the roadbed disturbed by the destructive *jeunesse,* the Swedes worked day after day to keep the vital communications open. During another attack against a repair crew composed of Swedish soldiers, the Baluba attacked with a few modern weapons.

First, deadly arrows whooshed from the sky. "*Jeunesse!*" one of the Swedes shouted. Grabbing their rifles and submachine guns, the ONUC soldiers fell back to the train waiting for the enemy to show himself. One Swedish warrant officer climbed a nearby tree for a better look. A gun roared somewhere in the bush, blasting like a small cannon. It was one of the ancient muzzle-loaders which the *jeunesse* were using. The ball from the antique weapon struck the warrant officer's helmet and he toppled unconscious from his perch to the soft ground below.

The warrant officer now somewhat dazed, was trying to shake the cobwebs from his head. A hole one inch in diameter marred his shiny blue helmet.

Meanwhile, the Swedish patrol commander, oozing blood from three bullet wounds, angrily asked for a submachine gun. The normally placid Major Bonde had blown his top. Swearing in Swedish he shouted for one of the soldiers to give him a submachine gun.

"Now I am mad," he shouted, "I want to kill some of those bastards."

Some of the soldiers tried to restrain their commander but he was adamant. Ordering his men to attack the *jeunesse* and to follow him, he leaped from the train and ran toward the bush firing short bursts at where he thought the elusive tribesmen were hiding. Shouting soldiers followed their commander as the machine gunners on the cars laid down a curtain of covering fire. The tribesmen suddenly disappeared as quietly as they had arrived.

Two other soldiers had been wounded by Baluba guns and the casualties had to be taken to where they could receive medical treatment and be evacuated. The train rattled along the tracks to Bukama where a Moroccan company was barricaded in the railroad station. As the train approached, the Swedes could see the blue helmets of the Moroccans reflecting the bright sun. To the right of the approach to the station were a few sunwashed buildings that appeared empty until the train drew abreast of them.

The rattle of gunfire smashed into the train. The *jeunesse* opened fire from the buildings. One of the Swedish soldiers was struck in the chest and collapsed over his machine gun. Captain Kjessler, now in command of the train because the major was badly wounded, ordered the engine halted. When the train had ground noisily to a halt, the captain shouted to his soldiers to attack the buildings and then, positioning himself beside a soldier with a recoiless rifle, ordered him to fire. The bazooka, firing an explosive projectile at the buildings, pulverized the structures with the most powerful weapon that the ONUC troops had. The projectiles struck with the force of artillery shells. The buildings collapsed, burying the Baluba terrorists inside. Those who tried to run were gunned down by the angry Swedes.

Two hundred yards away the Moroccan soldiers stood and watched.

When the train finally pulled into the station, the captain stormed up to the Moroccan commander to demand an explanation of why the ONUC troops from North Africa had not come to the aid of the men aboard the train.

"What were you trying to do?" the Moroccan asked Kjessler.

"We were attacked!" he retorted, "and we opened fire to defend ourselves."

"With a recoilless rifle? Why, that's murder!"

"Not from where we were being shot at. If somebody fires at us we shoot back. Now you can go over to those buildings and count the bodies."

Barely concealing his disgust at the non-performance of the Moroccans, the Swedish officer turned on his heel and walked away. He began to question the quality of the peacekeeping soldiers that members of the United Nations were sending to the Congo. After seeing that his wounded received medical attention, Stig sent a radio message to his headquarters requesting further instructions. He was advised that a helicopter would be sent to pick up the wounded, but that he was to return to Luena where another company of Moroccan troops was stationed.

For one long month Stig and a Swedish unit remained in Luena, holed up in the railroad station and sallying forth on periodical reconnaissance patrols. At one end of the city the Moroccans were dug in. The Katangese *gendarmerie* composed of Congolese with Belgian officers was dug in at the other end of the municipality. The Swedes were virtually in the middle and before long the Baluba *jeunesse* began to take advantage of the tactical situation. Night after night the tribal warriors would send out probing patrols to test the defenses of the Swedes; and the nightly patrols sparked fire fights as the Swedish soldiers fired at the flickering shadows beneath the hot tropic moon.

One evening the Baluba attacked. The Swedes opened fire with every weapon and broke up the assault waves that came charging down the wide street that led to the railroad station. At daybreak all that could be seen were splotches of blood drying in the warming sun. The warriors had carried away their dead in an effort to confuse the Swedes into thinking that they had not destroyed the enemy. With the blood dried in the dust, clouds of devil flies buzzed over the spots where bleeding warriors had fallen.

Although the Moroccans and Swedish soldiers of the UN

were on opposite sides of the political fence from the Katangese *gendarmerie* Stig ran phone lines to each position. "We're all in the same boat," he told the Moroccan and Katangese commanders, "and if we have to fight the *jeunesse* we might as well do it together."

The Swedes still had an engine and boxcars at their disposal and several times a week they would send a patrol out of the station along the BCK right of way to examine the tracks. Less than a mile from the station the *jeunesse* had ripped up the rails. Repairing them was another matter. It took at least a hundred laborers to effect the repairs and a guard detail of a least thirty-five men. Stig and his CO had all of forty men under their command. A jeep for patrols along the roads was installed in one of the boxcars. It was effectively used to carry Stig to the *gendarmerie* and Moroccan positions.

However, Luena was a dead little city. The Europeans all had fled, and the Congolese too, in fear of the Baluba. The town was left to the dogs and the once-gentle beasts, in their search for food, banded together in killer packs. One day while Stig was driving toward the Moroccan barricades, a band of wild dogs attacked him and his jeep driver. Snarling and snapping at the men in the vehicle, the dogs chased the jeep. Once the vehicle stopped the men knew that the dogs would hurl themselves on the jeep and could literally tear the occupants to pieces. The jeep driver lifted his submachine gun and with his left hand fired off short bursts into the pack of snapping dogs while controlling the vehicle with his right hand. A trail of dead and wounded animals was left behind. The dogs that had escaped attacked their own dead and wounded, cannibalizing the bodies in an effort to satiate their empty stomachs.

With the town held by nearly five hundred troops, the *jeunesse* were at a loss. They just could not come up with a tactical solution that would crush the defenders and place the town in the hands of the thousands of tribesmen who were encamped outside Luena. However, Stig was taking no chances.

"They'll find a way," he warned the Moroccans and the Katangans. He asked that they stay alert. The Baluba finally did find a way, but it was too late. Tshombe had put together a force of nearly two thousand men spearheaded by mercenary soldiers he had been importing. The force, well armed and equipped with jeeps and trucks, moved northwest from Elisabethville in two columns crushing all Baluba opposition before them. In Luena, the commanders of the *jeunesse* finally came up with a plan. They would launch their next attack from positions between the Moroccans and *gendarmerie*. The Moroccans would shoot in the direction of the Katangans and the *gendarmerie* would fire toward the Moroccans. The Swedes in the middle would be caught in a vicious crossfire. The attack naturally had to be launched at night.

The *jeunesse* were now armed with some modern weapons stolen and captured during their many battles with the soldiers of ONUC and gendarmes of Katanga. On the night of the attack the Moroccans and the Katangese reacted as the *jeunesse* leaders predicted, opening fire at each other. Bullets whizzed over the Swedish position in the railroad station and smashed into the train in which some of Stig's men were resting. The chatter of machine gun fire and the bark of rifles along with the hooting Baluba who had launched the attack, turned the tropical city into a nightmare of sound. Swedish soldiers crouched low and ran to their positions. Stig ran to the field telephone and cranked the battery. Signal bells jangled at the other end in the Katangese and Moroccan command posts.

Stig pressed the phone to his ear waiting for somebody to answer. A Moroccan soldier finally answered followed by a Katangese police officer.

"We are under attack!" both voices shouted.

"I know that," Stig roared back. "But you are shooting at us."

"Oh, are we shooting at you?" the surprised Moroccan asked on the party line.

"We can't help shooting in your direction," the Katangan officer replied.

"Well," Stig thundered, "if you don't stop this crazy shooting we will have to defend ourselves here—with our cannon." He was referring to the recoilless rifle which both the Katangans and Moroccans had seen in action.

"Now don't fire so wildly!" Stig slammed the field phone back on its hook. A few moments later the firing from the Moroccan and Katangese positions subsided as orders were passed to the men to cut down their wild shooting.

A few days later the Katangese forces arrived to relieve the town, repairing the rails as they moved northward into the province's Baluba country. The *jeunesse* had attacked as far south as the section of electrified railroad between Elisabethville, Lubudi and Luena. In an effort to further destroy the railroad, one group of Baluba warriors obtained a length of metal cable and hurled it across the wires with the idea of pulling down the source of power for this section of the BCK. The length of cable in the hands of ten of the warriors whipped into life, crackling bolts of fire and pulsating with deadly kilowatts of energy. The tribesmen died and those in the band of *jeunesse* warriors who witnessed this strange form of death ran back into the bush crying "witchcraft! witchcraft!" Even the witch doctors traveling with the *jeunesse* marauders were impressed at the white man's deadly magic. The jungle telegraph quickly spread the word about the incident and thereafter the Baluba walked a safe distance from the electric power lines, not even daring to rip up the tracks along this section of the BCK. This was witchcraft clearly stronger than their own.

17

Problems and frustrations

WITH THE DEPARTURE of troops from the nations that sided with deposed—and executed—Patrice Lumumba, the behind-the-scenes reports of a great military scandal quickly circulated among the European soldiers of ONUC. If it was a scandal, the UN command successfully succeeded in keeping it quiet. However, several scandals were an outgrowth of the confusion that naturally prevailed when military units from twenty-six nations were banded together in a command that was multinational, multilingual, multiracial, and multireligious.

Some of the incidents were scandalous by Western military standards. Others were an outgrowth of the poor military systems from which these ONUC units had originally sprung in their own countries. Nations like Mali and Ghana had no military tradition. In Ghana's case the complete transition from British to Ghanaian officers had already taken place. The senior officers of the Ghanaian unit had been British; the junior officers were natives of their country. Mali's officers were all natives. The Indonesian troops were commanded by their own officers as were the Indians and the Egyptians. Each of these countries had no deep-rooted military tradition and, in some instances, lacked competent officers.

This peacekeeping force had one thing in common, however. This was a flag and an insignia. Each soldier wore a UN shoulder patch and the only other common items of uniform were the blue beret or field cap and the blue-painted helmet. The UN had fielded a peacekeeping army; yet, it was not quite an army. Something was lacking and many serious studies that have been made cover the broad areas rather than the fine points. As seen from the perspective of the knowledgeable soldier in the field, the fine points covered a conglomeration of sins that the experienced professional military men serving with ONUC could not help but note.

The first inkling that all was not as it should be filtered into ONUC headquarters in Leopoldville. Egyptian troops of the United Arab Republic stationed in Stanleyville, so the story goes, were busily working at smuggling gold out of the Congo. Five tons of gold ingots, registered by weight and number, had been taken from the Kilomoto gold mine, loaded aboard a Russian-made Egyptian Air Force plane and flown to Cairo where presumably the gold was sequestered. While some members of the Egyptian units assigned to ONUC were thus kept busy, others were involved in the daily peacekeeping operations. Airfields in the Congo were closed to all flights except those authorized by the UN Command in Leopoldville. The Egyptians were able to fly their staff plane back to Cairo with its load of smuggled gold. Stanleyville, at the time, was under the nominal control of Patrice Lumumba's closest confidant and deputy, Antoine Gizenga. Word quickly spread among those concerned with such matters that Gizenga had turned over the gold to the Egyptians for the express purpose of removing it from the Congo to Cairo where it was to remain until he could personally claim it. Dishonesty was to be expected and reports of wheeling and dealing and bribery were the rule rather than the exception. Influential Congolese, so the rumors spread, were open to bribes. Belgians with long experience in the Congo shrugged their shoulders. After all, had not many of the tribal chiefs accepted bribes from the Belgians to maintain peace and provide laborers for the mines?

The greatest common complaint was directed against the ineptness of the African troops serving under the UN flag. Several incidents had left a bad taste with European soldiers. One such incident occurred at Port Franqui where a unit of Ghanaian soldiers commanded by three British officers was stationed. Three Swedish soldiers were also involved. The Ghanaians were barricaded in a hotel near an ANC military camp in which rebellious Congolese soldiers were situated. Outnumbered at more than five to one, the Ghanaians lived in fear of the mutineers who, in turn, rampaged across the countryside.

The Congolese troops approached the Ghanaians on a racial basis. "We are black and we are brothers," the ANC soldiers told the Ghanaians assigned to ONUC. "Give us the white men among you and we will let you go without any trouble."

The soldiers from Ghana complied. Disarming their three British officers and the three Swedes, who were members of the ONUC movement control team, the Ghanaians turned them over to the ANC who immediately began beating the white men. Bloody and semiconscious, the men were led away one by one into the bush. Shortly after each man disappeared with his ANC escort a flurry of shots was heard. Then the next man was escorted into the jungle. Still dazed by the beating, Sergeant Aeerg, one of the Swedes, realized what was happening. The executions were for no reason other than that the mutinous Congolese troops hated all white men. As Sergeant Aeerg was led into the bush by his escort, the tall Swede suddenly broke away from two surprised ANC soldiers following behind him and tumbled headlong into the thick flora beside the death trail. Before his startled would-be executioners could react, he jumped up and began running for his life until he had escaped his pursuers. The Congolese soldiers, frightened at the fate that might befall them for letting their prisoner escape, fired off a volley of shots and returned to the larger body of mutineers—their task presumably completed.

Sergeant Aeerg succeeded in fleeing to safety and reported the incident. The Congo's rebel soldiers weren't finished with their "brother" Ghanaians. They reneged on their promise to let the Ghanaians go and instead insisted that the African soldiers serving under the UN flag should first lay down their arms, "and then we will let you go." The Ghanaians complied. The ANC soldiers gathered up the weapons and then turned them on their disarmed captives.

The message that reached ONUC headquarters in Leopoldville reported the slaughter of a total of fifty-two UN soldiers—forty-seven Africans and five whites.

Meanwhile, ONUC staff officers were faced with a problem building up among the soldiers from Mali. Assigned to Albertville during the first months of chaos in the Congo, the Mali battalion allegedly suffered a number of casualties when internal bickering in this military force erupted as Christians and Moslems battled each other. A political crisis in Mali gripped the new African state about the time its battalion was assigned to ONUC. The nation's politics were carried into its armed forces. It was not the first time that ONUC headquarters would be faced with this type of problem which rendered some of its units useless.

When Emperor Haile Selassie of Ethiopia offered a battalion of troops to bolster the UN force, he did so more out of practical politics than for any higher motive. While the emperor was on a state visit to Brazil in late 1960, an insurgent group led by his first-born son attempted to overthrow the government. Crown Prince Asfa Wassan was proclaimed emperor. But Selassie returned quickly to his revolt-torn East African country and joined loyal units of his army. After brief fighting the rebels were vanquished and those who were captured were executed or jailed. When Ethiopia's emperor was at a loss as to what to do with one of his rebellious military units, he discovered the answer: assign a unit of rebel troops to ONUC and kill two birds with one stone. His cooperation with the UN would gain favor in the international community and, at the same time, he could banish his rebel soldiers—at no cost to his treasury.

In fact, the donation of military forces to ONUC entailed little cost to the nations which supported the UN request for peacekeeping troops. Transportation was provided by the UN and the troops were even paid by the UN, although the contributing nations were assessed for peacekeeping operations the same as other members.

These were some of the many problems faced by the general staff of the multinational peacekeeping forces. But they were only part of the larger problem of logistics—the supply and maintenance of a small field army speaking in a babel of languages. The chaos in the Congo caught the UN by surprise and the plans that were made when Lumumba requested a UN armed force to restore law and order had to be implemented as expeditiously as possible. This meant that whatever instructions were issued were done so without any planning. Rajeshwar Dayal, special representative of the Secretary General, later reported to the Security Council that:

> The first units arrived within 48 hours of the Security Council decision and were immediately deployed. Such exceptional speed was warranted by the seriousness of the situation, but it also entailed considerable risks and disadvantages. The troops had to be deployed before the headquarters, logistics organization, and signal communications were even formed. Operations in local areas are still being hampered by lack of vehicles. . . . A high degree of improvisation has thus been required at all levels throughout the first stages of the operation.

What Dayal didn't cover were some of the basic nuts and bolts problems. First, there was absolutely no detailed information at UN headquarters in New York about the Congo. Maps were absolutely unavailable in Manhattan's few bookshops and map stores. However, a phone call to a Belgian company with offices on Wall Street brought forth a number of detailed maps of the former colony which, if their source were known at the time, might have provoked additional East-West debate in the UN. Other questions quickly arose. What types of weapons would the units assigned to ONUC have? Was ammunition readily available for the several different calibers of weapons? Could this ammunition be easily stored in the Congo without deterioration? Would ONUC troops be living in tents or barracks? Would tentage withstand the wear and tear of the tropical climate? The location of airstrips was of prime importance along with the types of aircraft that could land on the fields often hacked out of the jungle.

Other questions quickly arose. Specifically, what types of weapons would be most useful in the Congo? Would artillery and tanks serve any useful purpose? Should military or civilian medical facilities be utilized? Vehicles to transport troops posed additional questions such as standardization of equipment and stocks of spare parts for maintenance.

Food also became a problem. Swedish soldiers were used to eating one type of food while Indonesians favored another. Indians were limited by their religion to still other categories of food.

Finally, the communications problem was taken under discussion. What language was to be used in transmitting orders from UN headquarters to the Congo? What language should be used in the Congo to transmit instructions from ONUC headquarters to the troops in the field? Should messages be sent from New York to Leopoldville in code or in the clear, where those who might be working against the best interests of the international peacekeeping force could obtain this intelligence to thwart the UN?

These were some of the many problems that faced ONUC in the first weeks and months and even later when one crisis after another erupted in the Congo. "You might just as well have asked the New York Yankees to establish a military force there," an American military observer wryly commented.

Despite all of these problems, a UN peacekeeping army was raised and transported to the troubled country.

18

Perilous outpost

Several years prior to the outbreak in the Congo Secretary General Dag Hammarskjold was asked if it might be wise for him to have an intelligence section in the Secretariat to keep tabs on various world trouble spots. He vigorously refused to establish such a precedent or department within his headquarters. Military operations, however, even those of a peacekeeping nature, require intelligence officers and organizations. For somewhere there is an enemy and the more that a military organization—even a peacekeeping force—knows about its "enemy," the better it can function.

It was late spring 1961 when Stig was ordered to report to the Swedish battalion commander. He was given an unusual assignment—intelligence gathering.

The operations map on the wall behind the commander's desk was marked with colored pins and other bits of string and crayon lines pinpointing the current situation as it was then known to senior officers of the various peacekeeping units. The commander pointed to a small enclave in southeast Katanga that pushed into Portugese Angola.

"We suspect that Tshombe is obtaining guns and ammunition from Angola," the Swedish senior officer explained to Stig. "If he is, it's obvious that he is planning an offensive soon. We also know that mercenaries are coming into Katanga from Rhodesia to join Tshombe's *gendarmerie.*

"Also, during colonial times Belgium had an agreement with Portugal whereby sealed railroad cars could cross Angola territory and enter the Congo without being opened until they reached their destination in the colony. This treaty, we have learned, is still in effect between Katanga and Portugal.

"Lieutenant, I want you to take a few men and go to Dilolo to learn what you can. Officially, you will try to inspect the material that arrives into Katanga by train. Unofficially, see if you can learn if weapons are being shipped to Tshombe and if mercenaries are also entering Katanga by rail."

Stig saluted and left his commander's office. He required a day or two to assemble a small force of eight men, a vehicle and supplies for a week as well as the necessary weapons and a field radio. The week would stretch into a month and Stig and his eight soldiers would face a threat that only his knowledge of the Congo would finally overcome. As he began planning for the mission to Dilolo, Stig took a moment to assess the situation in the Congo. The first elements of the Indian brigade—troops of the famed Gurkha and Dogra regiments—began arriving in Katanga to replace soldiers and airmen from Indonesia, Morocco, Mali, Guinea, the United Arab Republic, and Yugoslavia. These nations, which had supported Lumumba, carried out the threat to withdraw their troops who, in turn, were replaced by the Indians. Meanwhile, relations between ONUC and Katanga's leader, Moise Tshombe, had deteriorated seriously.

Tshombe was girding for a fight and staff officers at ONUC headquarters in Leopoldville knew it. It was just a question of when Tshombe would attack. In northern Katanga, where the Baluba *jeunesse* were still running wild, Tshombe's army of mercenaries—the White Legion—spearheading his *gendarmerie* had all but completed the conquest of Balubaland in a series of bloody battles with the tribe's thousands of warriors.

At Elisabethville airport Katangese police had driven vehicles on the airstrip to prevent ONUC transport planes from landing. The Swedish unit stationed there arrested the police and removed the vehicles. Tshombe promptly declared war against the UN. After ordering all water and electricity to the Swedish camp cut off, he told a mob of six thousand of his supporters to retake the airport. The mob, armed with deadly *panga* knives, clubs, muzzleloaders, and iron bars, streamed toward the airport. Tearing down the UN flag, they cut telephone wires and smashed windows in the main building before the *gendarmerie* finally broke up the melee.

ONUC promptly flew Irish and Indian reinforcements to the airport to bolster the Swedish unit. Tshombe then retaliated in other ways. He ordered local banks to freeze UN bank accounts. He ordered his *gendarmerie* to cut all power and communications to Kamina base, the principal ONUC military camp in Katanga. And he mined a section of road over which supplies were sent to a unit of seventy Irish troopers guarding a power station.

The situation was tense. Tshombe was still holding out against returning Katanga to central government control and subjugating himself and the province he considered his nation to Prime Minister Cyrille Adoula, the Republic of the Congo's third premier. Since the previous year's political troubles in Leopoldville, Colonel Mobutu had made alliances with several other tribal and political leaders in the Congo and had installed and deposed Prime Minister Joseph Ileo, who reverted to a deputy Prime Minister's office, whereupon the military strongman appointed Adoula as prime minister. Siding with ONUC, Mobutu then threw the prestige of his office into supporting the UN and, at the same time, egging on ONUC military commanders to crush, once and for all, rebellious Moise Tshombe and return Katanga to the control of the central government.

Against this political and military backdrop, Lieutenant Stig von Bayer and eight of his Swedish soldiers drove a jeep loaded with supplies into a boxcar and settled down for the five-hundred-mile journey from Elisabethville to the tiny frontier town of Didolo deep in Tshombe country.

Stig and his small detachment of men were the first ONUC soldiers that the people in the small town had ever seen. He checked into the single hotel building with his men and the following day they began their reconnaissance of the town. The few Belgians were over-polite and the Congolese were cold but formal, like their white colleagues. Word about the troubles between Tshombe and the UN had filtered down to Dilolo. None of the Congolese made any bones about their dislike for the "blue helmets."

The radio transmitter that Stig had set up in his hotel room command post, overlooking the well laid-out park in front of the whitewashed cement building, was manned day and night. Stig wasn't taking any chances on being caught napping in what for all practical purposes was enemy territory.

The Lunda tribesmen, whose blood relations spilled over into Angola and Rhodesia, turned their backs to the "blue helmets" whenever Stig or his men walked through the dusty streets. The Tshokwe tribesmen, who originally supported Lumumba and now were pro-central government, provided Stig with the intelligence that he was looking for. The Chokla and the Lunda were enemies. But so far no outbreak of bloody violence between the majority Lunda tribe and the minority Chokla had broken out. For this Stig was thankful. There was the effective jungle telegraph and each day Stig noticed just how much more effective it was. On each successive day the Congolese population appeared more defiant toward the ONUC detachment. And each day Stig met secretly in the hotel with his Tshokwe informants, who worked as menials, and obtained the information that he had come to seek out. The sealed railroad boxcars rattling through the Dilolo station on their way north did indeed carry weapons for Tshombe's forces. However, mercenaries were entering Katanga from Rhodesia.

Two weeks after the ONUC detachment had arrived the "blue helmets" faced their first incident. They had run out of rations and for a week had been buying supplies in the local stores. Part of the ammunition that Stig had loaded up with before he left Elisabethville was a thick wallet full of Katangese currency. He radioed Elisabethville for supplies. The reply was short and to the point: Impossible! Tension between the forces of ONUC and those of Moise Tshombe had strained almost to the breaking point. ONUC had no helicopters with the five-hundred-mile range required to transport supplies to an outpost with nine men. Even if aircraft were available, there was no airstrip at Dilolo nor would the Congolese assist the hated "blue helmets" to clear a suitable landing field.

Finally, no well-armed force that could smash through the many roadblocks set up outside of Elizabethville by Tshombe's *gendarmerie* and supporters was available to come to the rescue of the nine Swedish soldiers, nor would BCK railroad officials in Elisabethville cooperate with the UN and deliver supplies to Stig. He and his men were marooned in a sea of enemies, and the Swedish soldiers of ONUC were completely on their own. Stig waited for the Katangans to show their hand. They finally did on the fourteenth day.

The rap of knuckles on the door to the hotel room in which the ONUC soldiers were living galvanized the men into action. Grabbing their rifles and submachine guns, some took up positions near the windows and others pointed their weapons at the door.

"*Entrez!*" Stig called out. The manager of the hotel stuck his head through the door.

"*Monsieur Lieutenant,*" he smugly addressed Stig in rapid French, "you and your men must leave this hotel at once."

"Why?" asked Stig.

"We do not want the blue helmets in Dilolo. Therefore, you must leave the premises today."

Stig shook his head. "*Non, non,*" he replied in rapid French to the hotel manager, "we are paying you for the use of this room and we intend to stay here until I receive orders from my headquarters to leave."

The hotel manager told Stig that the entire population in

Dilolo was up in arms over the continued presence of the blue helmets. "We don't want any ONUC people here," he reiterated, "and you had better leave today."

"Is that a threat?" the Swedish officer asked. The manager shrugged and stepped back out of the room into the corridor. As he walked away from the room Stig softly called out: "*Monsieur*, we will leave if you can find us another suitable place to stay."

This being the only hotel in the town, Stig knew that his request would be impossible to meet. The Katangans had finally come out into the open and the pressure was on. It was to be a war of wills and wits.

Shortly after the hotel manager departed one of Stig's men, manning a machine gun at a window, called him to a window. Pointing down to the street, he reported that he had spotted well armed men scurrying into positions around the hotel. Seventy members of the *gendarmerie* surrounded the hostelry. It was obvious to Stig that they had been summoned into the town from outlying districts, and they appeared mean enough to attack.

"Will they?" one of Stig's soldiers asked the officer. Stig shrugged his shoulders and admitted that they could be in for some serious trouble.

"Keep the frequency to headquarters open," Stig ordered his radio operator. Distance precluded the use of a voice radio. His operator was sending in Morse code. This was the only type of signal that could reach as far as Elisabethville. The da-dit of the transmitter's telegraph key crackled from the quiet room. Outside, the angry voices of a mob poured through the open windows. The time had come to face up to the situation. The mob wanted the nine soldiers. All that was needed was an excuse to attack. Stig was determined to make it clear to the townspeople that at the first sign of an attack, he and his men would open fire.

There was not a single European face in the throng of chanting and shuffle-dancing Congolese. The Belgians and other whites were deliberately staying out of the way. Although they, too, hated the ONUC soldiers with a passion, they felt it more expedient to allow the blacks to do any killing. Amid the roar of the people, a sharp knock sounded on the door to the room. A husky blonde man of medium height stiffly bowed from the waist, clicked his heels and then introduced himself as Monsieur Desmeth, the commanding officer of the *gendarmerie* which now had the hotel surrounded.

"You must leave at once," Desmeth ordered. "There are seventy of us to your nine."

"I have my orders," Stig replied. "We are staying!"

Stig was advised by the Belgian commander of the *gendarmerie* to look out the window. At the far end of the neatly designed courtyard and garden a mob was gathering and the buzz of voices slowly became louder.

"*Monsieur*, I must now give you an ultimatum," the Belgian policeman continued. "If you do not move out, I will be forced to let these people demonstrate against you. I know that you have been in the Congo a long time. You know what a Congolese demonstration is."

Stig knew that the Belgian official was forced by circumstances into speaking for the Congolese. Although he disliked the blue helmets as much as the natives, Commissionaire Desmeth realized that the Congolese could easily turn on him if they were thwarted by the ONUC soldiers and he, in turn, would become a victim. Stig was well aware that the Belgian officer was talking as tough as he could because this was expected of him.

"Lieutenant," Commissionaire Desmeth continued, "you do not have too long to act."

On the street below the mob of Congolese grew larger. Men dressed in skins and feathers appeared, carrying shields, spears, and bows and arrows. A few angrily shook heavy old blunderbusses at the blue helmeted figures guarding the windows.

"You understand what this means," Desmeth repeated a bit louder. Stig nodded before speaking.

"Yes, I have a good idea what they are up to," Stig confidently smiled and continued speaking in French while his men strained their ears in an effort to understand what was being said. "If the women and children get hold of me and my men, they will cut us into little pieces, cook some parts of our bodies and eat them."

"Monsieur Lieutenant, you understand the situation perfectly."

The smile left Stig's face and his cold blue eyes narrowed. He would have to bluff his way out of this predicament or face the unpleasant consequences.

"Perhaps you are not in charge here," he told the Belgian policeman. "On the other hand, you are responsible for law and order. I warn you now that if anybody comes any closer than two hundred meters to this building, he can consider himself a dead man. We will shoot the first person who dares this. Even if you send women or children, we won't care; they'll be fired on, too.

"I know that it's us or them and the deaths will be counted not by two or three or ten but by the hundreds. We have our radio transmitter here and if you attack we will tell the world about what you have done to this ONUC detachment."

Desmeth mentally took Stig's measure. He believed that the Swede was not bluffing, and instinctively knew that Stig meant what he said.

Desmeth returned to the crowd milling in the street. He spoke to the leaders of the mob and as Stig and his men watched from the windows of their room the warriors began chasing away the women and children until about five hundred men and the seventy gendarmes were left. Desmeth returned to the room.

"You now have two hours to leave," he told Stig.

"I will leave only when I receive instructions from Elisabethville," the ONUC officer replied. "We don't move anywhere without instructions and you can't get us out of here without a fight." The Belgian again departed to report the substance of his conversation to the Congolese leaders.

Meanwhile, Stig explained to his men why they could not

leave. It was not a question of stubbornness but of the realities of the situation. He told them that once they left the town in the jeep, which could not hold all nine men and enough gasoline to get through to the nearest ONUC outpost, they would certainly be attacked by Tshombe supporters. He pointed out that the demonstrators were members of Tshombe's Conakat party and, he added, "they can be as vicious as the Baluba *jeunesse.*"

Additional pressure was applied by the Belgian police officer. He ordered the water cut off and the townspeople were warned not to sell food to the Swedes. Stig met again with Desmeth who informed him of this latest move in the war of wills and wits.

"I have been expecting this," Stig acknowledged. "We have enough food for a month and water for two weeks—a month if we go on short rations." He was bluffing, of course, and it worked.

Desmeth returned to the warriors; Stig again informed his men that the detachment was in serious trouble. If the warriors lost their heads and did attack, they would by sheer force of numbers overwhelm the Swedes—and kill them all.

For twenty-four hours the warriors milled in the street, chanting and beating on their tom-toms while the Swedish soldiers nervously waited for they knew not what. Standing near one of the windows with his submachine gun ready, Stig chainsmoked while waiting for the next move in the deadly game. He and his men were resigned to death; but they were determined to go down fighting, killing as many of the attacking warriors as they could.

Every hour Stig's radio operator tapped out a message to battalion headquarters in Leopoldville. The word had quickly spread among the Swedish soldiers that a detachment of their comrades was surrounded and awaiting an imminent attack. The battalion CO kept ONUC headquarters in Leopoldville advised of the situation and deep down hoped that his men would not be attacked. He shuddered when he thought of the consequences; the horrible and violent death that awaited them. If such were the case, he hoped that death would come quickly to his men.

After twenty-four hours of sitting on tenterhooks, just waiting, Stig observed Desmeth break away from the warriors and deliberately walk toward the hotel entrance. Another threat could now be expected. Even this was a relief from the interminable waiting.

Desmeth's next threat alarmed Stig. The warriors were all set to attack under covering fire from the *gendarmerie* who were armed with modern weapons. "What do you say now?" the Belgian asked. Stig pointed to his radio transmitter and once again informed Desmeth that the world would know how the ONUC soldiers were attacked.

"I suggest that somebody had better check with President Tshombe," Stig finally interjected. A new factor was suddenly thrown into the game of wits and wills. The Belgian officer knew that Tshombe was Katanga's strongman and that the Conakat warriors would not want to defy the wishes of the man they considered their chief. He returned to the mass of men and relayed Stig's suggestion.

It was a long shot. The leaders of Tshombe's political party in Dilolo managed to get a message through to the provincial palace just at the time that Tshombe was bowing to the will of superior ONUC military force that during a two-week period had arrived in Katanga. He told his political lieutenants in Dilolo that the UN detachment should not be attacked.

A few days later a radio message from Elisabethville advised Stig that he could return. He succeeded in obtaining rail transportation for his men although the Congolese who administered BCK operations in Dilolo refused to permit the jeep to be shipped with the soldiers. Although the attack had been called off, other pressures had not. Stig was reluctant to leave any equipment behind. Conakat leaders in the town had re-asserted their order that nothing was to be sold to the blue helmets, including gasoline. Stig took this up with the Belgian police official. This was sabotage against the UN, Stig warned, and he would report this behavior to Tshombe. Desmeth passed this on to the political chiefs in the town and they relented. Tshombe's name was not taken in vain.

"Why didn't I think of Tshombe sooner?" Stig muttered to himself when the embargo was finally lifted. He placed five men aboard the train with surplus equipment and with three heavily armed Swedish soldiers accompanying him, drove nonstop back to Elisabethville in thirteen hours trailing a cloud of red dust along the pitted dirt roads. As the jeep bounced and swayed on the journey Stig could not help but recall the stories he had read as a youngster about General Custer's last stand at the battle of the Little Big Horn. Dilolo had almost become his Little Big Horn. He silently thanked Providence for deliverance.

19

Tshombe's powder kegs

CHAOTIC CONFUSION!

That was the Congo in the summer of 1961 after Stig returned to service with ONUC following a one-month leave in Sweden. He had spent nearly a year in the Congo and during this period the situation had worsened. Moise Tshombe was determined to rid Katanga of ONUC soldiers and, at the same time, maintain the independence of the province that he now considered a sovereign state. In order to do this he built up a force of between eight and ten thousand *gendarmerie* and began staffing this army with white officers and noncoms—the mercenaries that Stig had been ordered to look for during his intelligence mission to Dilolo.

ONUC headquarters estimated that some five hundred mercenaries had been recruited by Tshombe. Reports also indicated that a heavy arms buildup was in the making. Tshombe even went so far as to purchase enough aircraft to put together a small but effective air force that a U. S. Army report later described as including "'some thirty-five European pilots and mechanics operating ten piston-engine planes, five helicopters and three Fouga Magisters—two-passenger jet trainers converted into fighter-bombers. . . . Seven additional commercial planes of the Air Katanga Line could be requisitioned when needed."

However, the battle that Tshombe envisioned would be fought mainly on the ground, not in the skies over Katanga. By mid-August, 1961, Tshombe was ready. So was ONUC.

The Katangese political leader had hired mercenaries however he could and wherever he could. He had the money; Katanga was actually a Union Minière stronghold and the mining corporation's Belgian officials believed that it was to their company's best interests to keep the wealthy province free and independent of the rest of the new nation. Tshombe's agents, actually the agents of Union Minière, ranged far and wide to recruit soldiers of fortune with combat experience. One group was recruited in Belgium; others were found in France, South Africa, Rhodesia, and Nyasaland. An international company of two hundred men commanded by an Englishman who called himself "Captain Brown" included about a hundred South Africans of questionable background—social outcasts and misfits, alcoholics, fugitives from the law, and military deserters.

On the other hand, Tshombe was fortunate in obtaining the services of a hard core of experienced guerrilla fighters from a group of French officers who had seen years of service during World War II, and also had fought in Korea, Indo-China, and Algeria. These men, members of the fanatic OAS (*Organisation de l'Armée Secrète*), had escaped from North Africa after President DeGaulle had crushed the extreme rightwing secret organization. Now they were being given an opportunity to put their talents to use, although their leaders, Commandant Faulques and Colonel Tranquier, had an ulterior motive. The Congo was a French-speaking country. Katanga was supported by Belgian money and industrial interests that wanted to defend its financial stake against the so-called black tide of African nationalism.

The French proponents of OAS paralleled this Belgian philosophy and were eager to serve in the Congo if for no other reason than to build a haven for the secret army which would then plan how to make a political comeback in either France or Algeria. If the long-range ideas of these strongly motivated French mercenaries seemed unrealistic, the deadly military experience that they were bringing into the strife-torn African country was a real threat to the peacekeeping soldiers serving with ONUC.

On August 27 orders were secretly issued to all ONUC units in Katanga to implement "Operation Rumpunch" beginning at 0400 hours the following morning. The orders for the operation were issued by Brigadier K. A. S. Raja, an Indian officer commanding ONUC forces in Katanga. They were brief and explicit: round up and arrest all mercenaries!

The roundup was completed without a hitch. In an effort to keep the civilian population of Katanga from being exhorted into battling ONUC, the blue-helmeted soldiers surrounded and then captured without a fight the radio station and post office in Elisabethville along with other key installations.

During the day Swedish, Irish and Indian soldiers—in jeeps and armored cars—drove through the city arresting white men suspected of being mercenaries. Some struggled; others just gave up to the ONUC soldiers without a fight. A few of the more hot-headed mercenaries tried to battle the blue-helmeted soldiers with their bare hands. A few blows from a rifle butt quickly cooled them off. By late afternoon the peacekeepers had rounded up 338 white men.

Tshombe's plans were thwarted, temporarily, that is.

The blue-helmeted soldiers of the peacekeeping force had carried out their orders which, in turn, had been issued after extensive consultation by the civilian political staff of ONUC of which the military force was a part. The Congo basically was a political problem that required military assistance to solve. Blue-helmeted soldiers accepted their orders and carried them out as best they could. After all, the troops had unconsciously reasoned, they were serving the United Nations. And the UN could do no wrong.

If the great majority of the member nations of the international organization believed that the UN could do no wrong, the task of the peacekeeping force was naturally made that much easier. Whatever role the blue-helmeted soldiers would play in the Congo, they did not have to worry about being on the wrong side of the law, so to speak. They represented the forces of good over the forces of evil. This was the general assumption throughout most of the free world.

However, no one stopped to consider that the UN political experts in the Congo on the side of law and order could possibly err and thus give impetus to the forces of evil. Operation Rumpunch turned out to be just such an error in planning and judgment.

The arrest of the mercenaries placed in charge of Tshombe's well-armed *gendarmerie* left these Katangese troops leaderless. They ran amuck just as the central government's undisciplined ANC battalions had kicked over the traces right from the start of the African nation's independence. Once again there was chaos in the Congo on a large scale. Now, however, anarchy was rampant in industrialized Katanga. In the northern reaches of the province the *gendarmerie* attacked Europeans as well as their enemy, the Baluba.

The political planners assigned to ONUC had finally met their match in a combination of events and people that created this chaos. The civilians who had been sent to the Congo from UN headquarters in New York quickly found themselves in a nightmare situation. These political scientists, international civil servants with impressive government backgrounds, soon discovered an exasperating truth about the Congo. They were in the midst of an impossible situation.

The orderly and predictable political theories of the Western world upon which these civilians could act held no water in the Congo. It was as if these political experts had suddenly been transported to another planet inhabited by a new species. The Congo was, for all practical purposes another planet and the Congolese were, indeed, a new species, although their basic physical characteristics mirrored those of ONUC's civilians.

Confusion! Chaos! Anarchy! ONUC's civilian political experts with their European-oriented backgrounds were unable to fathom the situation in the Congo. The standards that they attempted to apply to the Congo were doomed to failure because of the chaotic state of affairs. If logic could provide solutions to the many problems in the Congo, perhaps logic might have prevailed and peacekeeping efforts easily would have borne fruit. But the Congo and its people were a primitive nation suddenly pushed and pulled into the twentieth century and unprepared to cope with their new role. Yet the tribesmen were not even aware of the sudden change in their lives.

However, there was a small group of the educated from among the Congo's primitive tribes who grasped at the opportunities: political leadership, power and its end result—wealth. Theirs was a political philosophy and a power without ethic, much less the sophistication that ONUC's civilian staff expected. On the other hand, how does a statesman representing the United Nations deal with political leaders who, in their own way, are little removed from their fellow tribesmen living in the bush? How does a statesman with a European background communicate with a Congolese political leader who is not averse to violence; who will lie, cheat, steal, and even kill; to whom human life is not sacred but the fetishism of a witch doctor is?

Arresting the mercenaries opened up a pandora's box of violence for ONUC. Rumpunch was successful but not all of the mercenaries were captured and, the intelligence that Stig was gathering, indicated that Katanga Province was still a powder keg to which a short—and burning—fuse was attached.

The Congo drama unraveled in its own strange, illogical way. Conor Cruise O'Brien, ONUC's chief political officer in Katanga and senior UN official directly representing the Secretary General, was somewhat confused by many unpredictable events that were occurring almost daily. On one occasion he requested that Tshombe dismiss his deputy and leading supporter, Godefroid Munongo, because the UN official believed that the Bayeke chieftain's son had hired a mercenary soldier to kill another UN political officer. Michel Tombelaine, a young

Frenchman who had recently arrived in the Congo from UN headquarters in New York, was the alleged victim of Munongo's wrath and at one point was arrested by Tshombe's *Sureté* —Katanga's dreaded secret police which was mostly staffed by Belgians.

Tombelaine and Stig clashed over an important issue that was to cause a bitter problem for ONUC and have far reaching repercussions. The young UN political officer was faced with a problem after the mercenaries were rounded up in the Rumpunch operation. A small party of Baluba refugees from Elisabethville suburbs had fled to the Swedish camp. This would not do. The UN was an organization that protected innocent refugees, provided succor to those unfortunates who were caught up in the backlash of battle. Tombelaine visited the Swedish battalion commander and ordered that a refugee camp be established outside the military unit's base. Stig, who was present when the order was given, advised against the plan.

"Sir, you don't know these people," the young officer explained. "Once you established a camp, within a matter of days it will be overflowing with refugees. There are thousands of Baluba who live and work here in Elisabethville. They will jump at the opportunity to get free food. They will flood any refugee camp. It is better that the Baluba remain in their own districts here in Elisabethville and in the north."

Tombelaine was adamant. The project would be completed immediately; and, as far as he was concerned, the issue was closed. In less than two weeks the refugee camp was teeming with thirty-five thousand people and a month later it would be bursting at the seams with nearly seventy thousand men, women, children, and oldsters living in filth and facing all kinds of disease.

Stig von Bayer was to become instrumental in picking up the pieces caused by Tombelaine's honest compassion for the plight of the bush country tribes, together with his impractical handling of a delicate situation. It was simply a case of one man's ignorance of a people and a country prevailing over another man's experience and knowledge of the same problem. It was also a case of ONUC's civil authorities overruling the military.

Identity cards were handed out to the Baluba entitling them to daily rations of food. Throughout Katanga the entire economy had slowed to a standstill. Starvation loomed. However, word soon spread that ONUC had brought mountains of food into Elisabethville to feed the hated Baluba. The Katangese enemies of the Baluba continued preparations for the forthcoming military showdown with ONUC if for no other reason than a hated tribe was being fed while the Lunda, Bayeka, Basongo, and other Katangese tribes starved.

Stig was dismayed by this decision to establish a refugee camp. "If you take one, you will have to take them all," he warned. "If you feed one, you will have to feed them all."

He slowly shook his head. He knew that this was only the beginning of a problem which conceivably might defy solution. It nearly did.

Although the bulk of the mercenaries were under arrest, guarded by ONUC soldiers, none of the serious military and political problems had been solved by Rumpunch. The ONUC command in attempting to bring a semblance of order to the country sided with the central government in Leopoldville in what was to become an international *cause célèbre*. The code name for the second phase of the mercenary roundup was called "Operation Morthor"—the Hindu word for "smash." While ONUC units were deployed throughout Elisabethville and other cities in Katanga, O'Brien made a last ditch effort to convince Tshombe to resolve his differences with the Central Government.

It was September 11, 1961. A company of Irish troopers had been deployed to Jadotville to protect the lives of Europeans while Operation Morthor was carried out, and to apprehend any mercenaries who happened to be in that city. At the same time the central government in Leopoldville had handed to ONUC headquarters warrants for the arrest of Tshombe and four of his top aides in the event that he turned down O'Brien's bid for a reconciliation. These arrest warrants were turned over to O'Brien. It was a delicate diplomatic situation. O'Brien's orders from UN headquarters did not give him the authority to involve himself in the Congo's affairs to the point of acting as an agent of the central government. ONUC troops could only become involved in the political turmoil if civil war broke out. In effect, if he arrested Tshombe and his colleagues in the name of the central government then he was permitting ONUC soldiers to become the instrument of the Congo's leaders in Leopoldville. At issue was the UN's role of a neutral peace-keeper.

O'Brien was in contact with Tshombe while the final plans for Morthor were being made by the ONUC military command. Tshombe, on the other hand, was not caught napping. The rumble of trucks through the streets of Elisabethville and the heavily armed truck convoys filled with troops fanning out across Katanga were reported to him by his loyal tribesmen and European civilians who supported the rebellious provincial leader. His small air force took to the skies and kept the ONUC military units under constant surveillance. While O'Brien and Tshombe played out the final moves on this diplomatic chess-board, the UN official was confident that he was in command of the situation without knowing that his adversary had prepared to counter Operation Morthor.

While the high-level planning was going on, Stig accompanied ONUC troops on patrols through Elisabethville. When it was time to go out on the patrol he'd approach the unit he'd accompany and evoke a chuckle from the men by declaring that it was time "for our daily ration of stones."

Tshombe had ordered his Conakat political captains to incite the populace against ONUC. As the patrols drove through the city's streets, young toughs would hurl stones at the blue-helmets, calling them all sorts of vile names.

After each patrol Stig would report to his immediate headquarters that "something was brewing." He was probably the only person in Elisabethville capable of measuring the mood of the Katangans. What resulted was the second largest battle in the Congo that year.

Two hours before dawn on September 12, ONUC troops moved out against the mercenaries and Tshombe and his four important ministers. Tshombe escaped the net along with three of his cabinet. Only one was taken captive. Tshombe fled to Rhodesia.

O'Brien's orders to ONUC troops in Elisabethville were to "take over the post office, the radio studio and the transmitter; to raid the *Sureté* and Ministry of Information offices; to arrest any European officials found there, and seize their files. . . ." Katangan *gendarmerie* forces had deployed themselves where the ONUC troops were to attack. The Gurkhas launched their attack against the post office building only to be hurled back by heavy machine gun and rifle fire from *gendarmerie* barricaded inside and around the structure.

While the Gurkhas attacked the post office in a fire fight that lasted throughout the morning until armored cars and recoilless rifles battered the outgunned *gendarmerie* to their knees, the Swedes swept out of their camp to nearby Radio Katanga and captured the station.

Everybody seemed to get into the act. As the ONUC troops drove through the city shuttered windows would be flung open and rifle and machine gun fire would shatter the air of quiet respectability in what were supposed to be genteel European neighborhoods. Colonel Waern, the Swedish brigade commander, wanted Stig at his side as he inspected his troops during Operation Morthor. The open-topped armored personnel carriers—four of these 1942 vintage armored cars flown to the Congo—were part of the Swedish battalion's equipment that raced through Elisabethville's streets carrying heavily armed men.

On one such patrol Stig and his C.O. ducked low as snipers opened up from rooftops and other hiding places. The colonel asked Stig who the snipers were. Stig shrugged.

"They could be anybody, sir," he finally answered. "Mercenaries. Belgians. *Gendarmerie.*" And indeed they were anybody and everybody. As they drove past a block of white stucco homes the door leading to a porch opened and one of the Belgian residents stepped out with a pistol in one hand and holding the hand of the youngest of three children with his other. His wife stood behind him. The civilian lifted the pistol and took aim at the APC.

"Duck!" somebody in the armored car shouted. The Belgian on the porch squeezed the trigger and a series of shots cracked out, some of the bullets striking the armor plate of the APC with dull thuds. The Swedish soldiers were angry, but they were a disciplined lot. The machine gunner in his turret turned his weapon toward the porch and squeezed off a burst that was deliberately aimed to strike the side of the house near the civilian without hitting his family. Startled because the blue-helmeted soldiers even *dared* fire back at him, especially with his family standing at his side, the civilian darted back indoors pushing his family off the porch. It was one hell of a "war," Stig thought to himself.

For more than a week, heavy fighting continued throughout the province. At Jadotville 158 Irish troops held out against the *gendarmerie* and tribal warriors reinforcing Tshombe's police until the blue-helmeted peacekeepers ran out of ammunition and water, at which point they were forced to surrender. This ignominious surrender was personally accepted by Katanga's Munongo. One of the two-seater jets that Tshombe had obtained for his air force bombed and strafed the embattled Irish company. After the Irish unit surrendered, ONUC headquarters ordered a maximum effort to free the prisoners. The massacre of the Irish patrol the previous November still rankled and, with the *gendarmerie* in a bitter mood it was believed by many on the ONUC military staff that the Katangans wouldn't hesitate to kill prisoners.

"Remember," Stig warned high-ranking ONUC staff officers, "these men in the *gendarmerie* are basically tribal warriors in uniform. They can and will kill as brutally as the Baluba."

Two companies of blue-helmets, one Irish and the other

Gurkha, were loaded on trucks and the convoy, escorted by two of the Swedish APCs, headed toward Jadotville nearly a hundred miles away. About halfway to the city the convoy arrived at a bridge that was heavily defended by a strong force of *gendarmerie*. Moreover, one of the jet planes strafed the convoy as the ONUC troops, battling against heavy odds in an effort to crush the defenders at the bridge, were forced to clamber back aboard their trucks and withdraw. The approach to the bridge had also been mined. Several Gurkhas were killed and a number of Irish and Gurkhas were wounded.

Meanwhile, additional confusion was compounded on top of this chaos. With more than thirty-five thousand Baluba penned in the refugee camp, the Swedes and the Irish were forced to divert badly needed troops to guarding the tribesmen. The *gendarmerie* added to the problem by sniping at the inmates of the camp, inciting the *jeunesse* to take action. Captured guns, bows and arrows, spears, and muzzleloaders, were brought out from their hiding places.

Stig was called to the refugee camp by the Baluba leaders, who wanted to parley. The hated *gendarmerie* were killing refugees, they said. They wanted to fight for the blue-helmets.

"Give us guns and ammunition to fight your enemies," Stig was asked. He vigorously shook his head, replying to the spokesman for the tribe that ONUC could fight alone without help and that the *gendarmerie* would be defeated. With that he turned away. It was obvious that the situation was now becoming extremely serious. If the Baluba broke out of the refugee camp . . . !

He instinctively knew what would happen next. The *jeunesse* would try to take command of the tribal situation. They would sneak out of the camp and attack the *gendarmerie* on their own. Even more dangerous, once free of the camp they could begin raiding in the city and kill, rob, and loot. This meant that the blue-helmeted soldiers would have another enemy to contend with. As Stig predicted, the Baluba *jeunesse* launched a series of raids in Elisabethville, sneaking away from the refugee camp at night and returning just before dawn. Behind them they left a trail of dead *gendarmerie,* civilians, and frequently European residents of the city.

The military problem was considered just that by ONUC political officers. They had originated Operation Morthor without taking into consideration the various military factors involved. ONUC intelligence, of which Stig was an important part in Katanga, knew about the arms buildup and the jets that Tshombe had purchased for his infant air force. They also knew that ONUC was outgunned and outnumbered. But it was believed that disciplined ONUC troops could defeat the undisciplined blacks who made up Tshombe's *gendarmerie.* The peacekeepers had no aircraft to match the jets, only a few helicopters and light reconnaissance aircraft.

After the attacks by the jets, ONUC grounded all transport aircraft that it could have used to reinforce various units in Katanga. There was no sense in having transports loaded with troops shot out of the sky by the wild group of mercenary pilots who were flying for Tshombe.

For six days the usually peaceful tropical days and nights in Katanga were noisy with the sound of gunfire and the crashing explosions of grenades and recoilless rifles. The bleached whitewashed buildings in Elisabethville, for example, took on the ugly facade of war. The markings of rifle and machine gun bullets and the huge gaping holes caused by the recoilless rocket rifles scarred almost every building on the tree-lined streets of Katanga's largest city. The blue-helmeted peacekeeping force did its utmost to confine the fighting to the outskirts of the city, but chasing both *gendarmerie* and the Baluba brought the armored cars and trucks filled with troops into the side streets as well as the main thoroughfares.

A company of Gurkhas from the famed Third Rifles Regiment were dug in among the anthills on the edge of the Swedish camp. Behind the camp was the overflowing refugee center. Katangese snipers and assault forces tried time and again to break past the anthills and charge into the refugee camp. In a series of constant day and night attacks, the Katangans slowly wore down the plucky Gurkhas until the company's commander asked Colonel Waern to relieve his troops. The Swedish officer replied to the request that he was unable to comply because the Swedes, too, were heavily committed. The Gurkha commander insisted that his men be relieved.

Colonel Waern, disappointed by the performance of the Gurkhas ordered his battalion commmander, Major Mide to relieve the Gurkhas. They finally rounded up twelve Swedish soldiers with minor wounds and had them marched out to the anthills.

If twelve men were to shame the Gurkhas into remaining at their positions, it didn't work. When the commander of the Gurkha company saw the group that virtually limped to the position, he exclaimed to the Swedish lieutenant heading the group: "Are you mad!"

"Yes," the Swedish officer replied, "but this is all the men we can spare."

With a machine gun and a recoilless rifle to hold the position which the Gurkhas evacuated, the Swedish officer succeeded in defending the area against attacks by both the Katangans trying to break through and the Balubas trying to break out of the refugee camp and past the ant hills.

During this outbreak of fighting, Secretary General Dag Hammarskjold had arrived in Leopoldville in a last-ditch attempt to bring the prestige of his office to bear on Tshombe and the new Central Government of Prime Minister Adoula. It was to be an exercise in personal diplomacy. He arranged for a meeting with Tshombe on September 18 to bring about a cease-fire. It was late afternoon September 17, when Hammarskjold boarded an airliner chartered by the United Nations to fly to Ndola in northern Rhodesia to personally meet with Tshombe who had obtained sanctuary in the neighboring British colony. These were Hammarskjold's last few hours on earth as the white-painted DC-6B took off with his staff of nine and a crew of five. No formal flight plan was filed and the four-engine propeller-driven aircraft took off late in the afternoon from N'Djili Airport outside of Leopoldville. From there it flew due east and then turned south to fly down Lake Tanganyika in an effort to avoid Tshombe's jets. A few minutes after midnight on the eighteenth the pilot of the UN transport checked in with the tower at Ndola airport. That was the last heard of it until sixteen hours later when search parties finally reached the charred wreckage of the transport in a jungle glade ten miles outside of the Rhodesian city. There was only one survivor; he died six days later without regaining consciousness.

For all practical purposes, the Secretary General of the United Nations was "killed in action" in an effort to bring peace to the Congo. Tshombe's infant air force had indirectly killed Dag Hammarskjold by forcing his aircraft to fly an erratic course over uncharted areas at night in an effort to evade the Fouga jets.

Perhaps the news reached the tribes faster than it reached Stig. He was attending to some paper work in his office when one of the Swedish enlisted men burst through the entrance.

"Lieutenant, Hammarskjold is dead!" the excited soldier cried out.

"Impossible!" Stig snorted, "it's another one of Tshombe's propaganda tricks."

"But it's true, sir. I just heard it on the radio."

"I don't believe it. It's Radio Katanga propaganda."

"But Lieutenant, I heard it on the BBC!"

Stig's features turned ashen. "Oh no," he muttered after the soldier told him that the news had come from the highly reputable British Broadcasting Corporation—the venerable old BBC of World War II fame known throughout the world for broadcasting the truth. He pushed back his chair and got to his feet.

"Let's go and listen," he told the soldier and followed the enlisted man into another office where a small group of silent Swedes were at that very moment crowded around a shortwave radio set listening to the news about Hammarskjold's death. It was true. Stig could read the grim news in the faces of his comrades.

The news of the Secretary General's untimely death rocked the blue-helmeted peacekeeping force. The Swedes in particular keenly felt the loss of Hammarskjold; for he, too, was a Swede.

The jungle telegraph throbbed and the drums beat out the message throughout the Congo and Katanga that the great chief of the blue-helmets was dead. Those tribes friendly to ONUC mourned the passing of Hammarskjold. The Katangan tribes loyal to Tshombe cheered the death of the chief *Onusien* and their witch doctors gloated, each claiming that his particular brand of *dawa* had crushed the hated enemy.

Throughout the world where there was a UN presence, United Nations flags limply flew at half mast.

The Hammarskjold tragedy shocked the world. His death was followed by a cease-fire, but even this silencing of the guns was tenuous at best. Sporadic violence was to continue.

20

Rations, rifles and refugees

WITH THE APPEARANCE of Tshombe's jets all ONUC transport aircraft were ordered grounded. Supply trains and truck convoys into Katanga were also halted as Tshombe's forces set up roadblocks at all of the principal rail and road intersections. ONUC troops were virtually cut off from all assistance, although radio communications between Leopoldville and Elisabethville were continued without interruption. The blue-helmeted soldiers had enough ammunition to hold out for a number of weeks. They also had enough food in Elisabethville. That is, they thought they had enough food until the *gendarmerie* assaulted the warehouses filled with rations and wrested the buildings from Indian troops.

Orders were issued to conserve food. The problem was further magnified because the food stores also consisted of the rations that ONUC was doling out to the Baluba refugees. The situation was perilous. Hunger could force the Baluba into the fray; and hungry tribesmen were even more dangerous and deadly than those fired up with *bangi bangi* hashish.

The logistics officer suggested to the C.O. that both the Irish and Swedish troops band together and launch a joint commando raid to recapture the food stores or, at best, fight their way into the warehouses and remove enough rations which could then be loaded on trucks and brought back to the military camp.

"Capital idea!" the Irish commandant exclaimed when he was approached. The plan was simple. Two platoons of troops, one Irish and one Swedish, would attack the warehouses in the early hours of September 15 and shoot their way in. They would be transported to the warehouses in armored cars which would provide covering machine gun fire. After the ONUC raiders had broken in, reinforcements would speed to the scene in trucks, set up a defense in depth, and then begin loading the trucks with supplies.

It was an imaginative plan and the commandos carried it off without a hitch. Rushing the warehouse compound, the Swedish and Irish soldiers, their faces blackened to blend with the night, burst through the *gendarmerie* sentry posts with blazing guns. The heavier caliber machine guns in the armored cars raked the area. Return fire was sporadic and then suddenly halted. The commandos ran to the storage buildings and shot the locks off the huge doors. The Swedish APCs and Irish Ferrets drove up to the buildings. An officer ran to an APC and asked for the radio's microphone.

"Objective captured," he reported to the commando's combined operations center in the military camp. "You can send the trucks. The enemy has fled."

He handed the microphone back to the driver and dashed into one of the buildings where his comrades were spreading out looking for the type of food they needed among the towering crates. What they found was a revelation—discrimination!

This commando mission nearly mushroomed into a military snarl because Stig and his Irish comrades discovered that ONUC logistics weren't what they should have been. The boxes of rations for the troops were marked EUROPEAN TROOPS or ASIAN TROOPS. It was obvious to the Irish troopers and the Swedish soldiers that they were part of an international force with different customs, eating habits and religions. But discrimination in ONUC of European and Asian peacekeepers?

"Look at what the bloody Indians are eating!" an Irish brogue as thick as a Killarney fog shouted.

"Look at what we have to eat!" a Swede hollered in his own language.

The food for the European troops consisted of dehydrated rations and other bland tinned foods that held the same flavor and evoked the same gripes as Spam did from American GIs during World War II. In fact, the European foods could be equated with Spam.

The Asian rations, on the other hand, consisted of expensive and luxuriously packaged delicacies and condiments the like of which the Irish and Swedish commandos hadn't seen since they left their own homelands. The gourmet foods earmarked for the Asian troops were irresistible. The commandos were like children let loose in a toy store. They began pulling down crates of Asian food.

"To hell with this dung!" a Swede gleefully shouted as he walked past the section marked EUROPEAN and began handing boxes of Asian food to his fellow soldiers. The trucks soon rolled into the compound and were loaded from the first warehouse the commandos had broken into and then from the nearby refrigerated warehouse which contained meat and poultry supplies, but mainly poultry which the religion of the Indian troops permitted them to eat.

The loaded trucks and the raiders returned to the military camp to report to their comrades: "Mission accomplished."

However, for a while after the cease-fire it would have been better if they had never launched their commando raid. An Indian officer controlled logistics for the UN command in Katanga. When a Swedish staff officer at ONUC headquarters in Elisabethville allowed as "how well" the Indians were eating compared to the European troops, word quickly reached the logistics officer who immediately after the fighting ended launched an investigation of the raid. Most of the stores had been looted by Katangans and their *gendarmerie* after the commando raid. However, the logistics officer wanted to hold the

Irish and Swedes responsible for the total loss, pointing out that they had "pilfered" ONUC supplies and therefore should be disciplined.

Discipline, of course, was a polite word for court martial.

The Indian logistics officer was advised by his opposite numbers from the Swedish and Irish battalions that it "appeared strange that within an international peacekeeping force of the United Nations one particular nation was provided with more expensive gourmet foods than the soldiers of other nations." Oh, it was all very diplomatically put to the Indian officer who promptly dropped any thought of preferring charges or making an issue of the commando raid.

Within the combined Irish-Swedish military camp outside of Elisabethville ONUC soldiers for the first time in many months were served with highly spiced and delectable gourmet dishes that one would never expect to find on a military mess table—especially in the heart of Africa.

"Eat well, sahibs," the mess sergeants joked as long as the captured foodstuffs lasted.

The fighting came to an end as Hammarskjold's body was flown home to Sweden. O'Brien announced that ONUC had lost seven dead and twenty-six wounded in the fighting. The peacekeeping force also temporarily lost 170 Irish troops captured in the battles at Jadotville and Elisabethville. Add to this the death of Hammarskjold and his staff and the casualty report increases to seventeen dead. An estimated two hundred Katangese were killed battling ONUC troops, five hundred wounded and a hundred taken prisoner.

This flurry of shooting had been sparked by Tshombe after he had proclaimed "total war" against ONUC and demanded that his people "fight to the last man and the last round of ammunition for Katanga's independence and freedom."

Operation Morthor ostensibly was directed against the remaining mercenaries. However, on the face of available but controversial information it appears that ONUC's civilian officials took it upon themselves to smash Tshombe's government and bring Katanga back into the central government's fold.

The very fact that O'Brien accepted the central government's arrest warrants for Tshombe and his cabinet, without informing UN headquarters in New York or ONUC military headquarters in Leopoldville of his basic plan to end Katanga's secession, obviously angered Hammarskjold when he arrived in the Congo. His untimely death, however, was followed three months later by O'Brien's resignation from UN service.

Meanwhile, Lieutenant General Sean McKeown, the Irish officer who commanded all of the peacekeeping forces in the Congo, asked for more equipment for his men and specifically demanded some artillery and tanks and jet aircraft. He received the jets—five F-86 Sabrejets from Ethiopia and five Saab jets from Sweden to build up his interceptor force, and five Canberra medium jet bombers from India. His request for artillery and tanks was turned down by the Security Council which regarded these as "offensive weapons" unbecoming a peacekeeping force.

No sooner had the ink dried on the cease-fire agreement when the central government in Leopoldville announced that it was determined to make war against Katanga "to put an end to the secession." The central government's relations with ONUC suddenly crumbled. The tension between Tshombe's government and ONUC forces in Katanga once again stretched to the breaking point and in Elisabethville *les Onusiens* were unwelcome in the bars and cabarets, restaurants, and stores. The hot and cold running war between the black and white peoples of Katanga, on the one side, and the black and white soldiers of ONUC, on the other, once again was beginning to heat up as 1961 rolled into its final months.

As for the mercenaries, the men who ostensibly were at the core of the fighting and the reason for the whole shooting match, they quickly faded from sight. After shedding their uniforms they disappeared within the giant industrial complex of Union Minière, taking positions as employes of the mining company while preparing for another round of fighting that was to break out in December.

In the center of this imbroglio stood Stig and his blue-helmeted comrades. Theirs was not to reason why. Then again, the question was asked over and over by the peacekeeping troops: could reason prevail?

The refugee problem after the September cease-fire snowballed into nearly unmanageable proportions. The Swedish units were on one end of the vast camp and Irish units were on the other. Depending upon which way the wind blew on any particular day, the stench from the refugee camp was unbearable. The Baluba were crammed together, living as they did in their small villages without the sanitary facilities that a larger establishment required. Moreover, fourteen Baluba sub-tribes were living together in unnatural circumstances and the camp was threatened by the rivalries of the tribal units whose mutual bond was fear of the Kantangese *gendarmerie.* The Balubakat *jeunesse* quickly organized itself into a political police force without rhyme or reason other than to extend brutal power and leadership.

Michel Tombelaine, the ONUC official who had ordered the refugee program established, saw what had been thought to be a civilian and humanitarian problem quickly become both a political and a military problem.

The camp was set up near Elisabethville's botanical gardens. The *jeunesse,* Stig later learned, forced the tribesmen and their families to move into the refugee camp from various native quarters in Elisabethville. Refusal to comply meant death. The *jeunesse* set many similarly ugly examples in an effort to control the Baluba. Many of the Baluba worked in Elisabethville. The *jeunesse* leaders reasoned that if ONUC was foolish enough to grant a haven to the Baluba, this was the time to pull the tribes together thus giving the youth movement leaders even stronger political control of their tribe. The *jeunesse* leaders felt that if the Baluba suddenly stopped working the economy of Elisabethville—and Katanga—would collapse. So what if the Baluba were out of work? ONUC would feed them. After all, had not Tombelaine declared that the Baluba were a persecuted people who required help?

As it turned out, Tombelaine played right into the hands of the *jeunesse.* Once he had publicly offered political sanctuary to the refugees, the population of the camp expanded along with the sprawling city of bedlam. While additional tribesmen and their families arrived at the camp every day, more and more Belgians who owned homes near the refugee camp moved away. The Baluba were like locusts. Empty houses weren't just lived in; they were dismantled and carried away piece by piece. Wood, glass and bricks would reappear in the refugee camp as small jerry-built shacks.

Stig and his comrades watched an entire block of homes deserted by the Belgians who had fled disappear somewhere in the camp during the night. Nor was the distribution of food a simple matter. The first daily food ration handouts resulted in thundering stampedes and danger to the ONUC soldiers who had the responsibility of doling out supplies for meals. After one particular mobbing Stig ordered a bottle-shaped food ration distribution area set up to control the amount of people who could approach the supply trucks at any one time.

The daily distribution of rations was something that the blue-helmeted soldiers didn't relish. Each day a detachment of men would be driven to the food distribution points for duty. This meant that each peacekeeper assigned to this dangerous duty would have to stand on guard to protect the men who handed out the rations. Rifles with fixed bayonets were the order of the day, as if the thought of cold steel would prevent the refugees from rushing the men whose job it was to hand out food.

A small number of war dogs were rushed to Katanga to assist the peacekeepers in their various guard duties. The dogs were pressed into service at the food points after a wild mob of Baluba stampeded through the area, knocking down the soldiers while disregarding their bayonet-tipped rifles and swarming all over the stores of food like locusts until not even one empty cardboard carton was left.

Once the soldiers fired their guns in the air to halt a wild mob attacking the food distributors. The war dogs were useless. Like a thundering herd of frightened steers, the Baluba overwhelmed the soldiers, trampling over the men after they were hurled to the ground and stamping out the lives of the dogs who tried to hold the mob back with bared fangs.

During one of these mob scenes a Swedish soldier fired in the air, but was knocked down at the same time his rifle cracked out. A bullet ricocheted and killed a Luba woman. The refugee camp commander, a Swedish officer, stormed into Stig's office and demanded that the soldier be courtmartialed.

"Sir," Stig explained to the angry major, "I don't think that we can blame the soldier. This was an accident. And even if it were not, the fault lies with both of us. We are responsible for seeing that the refugees do not mob soldiers. These men are threatened by sure death and we haven't issued any definitive instructions as to how they should defend themselves.

"If anybody is unfortunately killed, well. . . ."

Stig shrugged his shoulders after voicing his feelings in the matter. He explained that as far as he was concerned, the ONUC political advisers had not been made aware of the danger the troops faced while engaged in humanitarian acts.

"Our men should have the right to defend themselves when their lives are in danger," he added.

The refugee camp commander slowly calmed down. Stig's explanation made sense. The only problem he now had was explaining in a lengthy report how an ONUC soldier accidentally killed a woman.

"You know these ONUC civilians," he grimaced as he left Stig's office in the military camp headquarters building. "They only can see one side of this bloody picture. And it's certainly not our side."

Stig also entered the refugee camp several times each day in an effort to measure the temper of the Baluba and discover what the *jeunesse* were up to. During the fighting in September Stig was faced with two problems. One was military; it involved Operation Morthor. The other was political; it concerned the refugee camp. Stig knew that if the Baluba warriors within the refugee camp made a concerted effort to escape and enter the battle raging between ONUC forces and Katangese *gendarmerie,* an extremely bloody mess would result. One that would have grave international repercussions. If the Baluba *jeunesse* once tasted blood in the streets of Elisabethville, they would massacre at random, attacking and killing ONUC troops as well as mercenaries, Belgian and other European civilians and the Katangese *gendarmerie* not to mention members of the provincial tribes that were allied to Tshombe and supported his Conakat party.

Stig conscientiously advised his immediate superiors about the latent threat within the refugee camp. They, in turn, passed this information to ONUC, but with a virtual vest-pocket shooting war reverberating throughout Katanga the top-ranking military commanders were more concerned with the battle that was taking place than with one that had not yet erupted.

Once the cease-fire became effective Stig turned all of his attention to the refugee camp. Two weeks after a tenuous peace had returned to Katanga, Stig had left ONUC Brigade headquarters and was walking toward Swedish Battalion headquarters about half a mile away when the sharp report of gunfire crackled through the air. Breaking into a run, he dashed back to the Swedish camp and then, crouching low, ran into the headquarters building. Bullets plunged past him as he ran into the battalion C.O.'s office.

"Am I glad to see you!" Major Ulf Mide exclaimed. "What the hell is going on out there? I almost got killed." He pointed to the bullet holes in the walls of his office and told Stig that an armored car was waiting outside for the major.

"I think I know what's happening," Stig replied. For two weeks tension had been building up in the camp as the Baluba *jeunesse* took advantage of the cease-fire in order to sneak out from the camp to kill and loot in Elisabethville suburbs.

"Then get going," the major replied. "There should be a detail of men in the APC waiting for you." Stig saluted and dashed out to the armored car. He directed the driver to pour on the gas and head for a small hill overlooking the refugee camp. If he was correct in his assumption, anti-Baluba tribesmen were firing into the refugee quarters.

"Hurry! Hurry!" Stig ordered the driver. The armored vehicle careened through dusty streets before breaking out into an open road leading toward a low, rolling hill. Up ahead Stig spotted the culprits.

"Damn!" he muttered as he turned to the soldiers sitting in back. "It's the Katangese police."

The APC bounced off the road and along the slope between the local police and the refugee camp. Stig bounded out of the vehicle and ran along the line of men shouting for them to stop shooting. "Where is your commander?" he thundered, assuming the tone of voice and manner that the *gendarmerie* expected from white men. A police officer *commissaire* wearing a major's rank came forward.

"What the hell are you doing?" Stig asked the officer.

"We are going to finish off the Baluba,'" he replied.

"Why?"

"They killed ten of our policemen and twenty civilians. They say that they are starving and we know they have killed these people to eat them. Now we are going to kill all of the Baluba."

"Impossible!" Stig snapped. The Katangese officer was taken aback by Stig's approach to the problem. "You are not killing the Baluba refugees from this hill. You are firing in the wrong direction. You are shooting up *our* camp. Do you realize what we will do if you kill one *Onusien*?"

"*Pardon. Pardon.* Please excuse us for this error. We did not know. Please move *les Onusiens* to another place and we will get on with our duty."

Stig shook his head vigorously. Behind him the Swedish soldiers stood, their submachine guns at the ready. The machine gunners manning the heavier weapons on the armored car also waited for Stig's command to fire. The Katangese major got the message and turned to his men and ordered them to return to their barracks. Stig slowly exhaled. It had been a close one. Too close.

Suddenly the wild yelping of charging warriors rent the silence. Running up the slope were armed Baluba tribesmen flourishing muskets, bows, spears and the inevitable clubs to which the deadly bicycle chains were attached. Some of them, clad in skins and feathers with their bodies decorated with war paint, led the more conventionally dressed tribesmen. Terror-stricken by the mob's sudden appearance, the Katangese police dropped their rifles and fled before the sudden invasion. There were hundreds of tribesmen; they were a noisy wave of attackers, and all scented blood.

"Follow me!" Stig ordered. The Swedish soldiers raced after their lieutenant as he ran toward the tribesmen instead of in the other direction.

"Don't get too close!" Stig shouted. "Watch those bicycle chains!"

Spotting the blue-helmeted soldiers, the wave of warriors halted. Stig stopped running and ordered his men to spread out. Then, slowly and carefully walking toward the tribesmen, he demanded to speak to their leader. A group of young men belligerently pushed forward, shouldering aside those who stood in their way. "*Jeunesse!*" Stig muttered to himself. He must be careful with these fanatics.

"Go back to your homes in the camp and put away your weapons!" the young Swedish officer declared speaking in the language the Baluba understood—their own. Staring down the *jeunesse* leaders, Stig stood his ground. He was poised and confident on the surface, but inside he was frightened as any man would be. He knew what kind of a horrible death awaited his detachment and himself if the warriors wanted to fight. No matter how many the Swedish soldiers killed, they'd be mobbed and overwhelmed by hundreds of bodies whose grasping, clutching hands would tear apart the peacekeepers.

Reluctantly, the *jeunesse* leaders turned and lost themselves in the crowd. Stig moved forward with his men, pushing a bit to hurry the warriors along. The Swedish soldiers relaxed. It was all over. The peacekeepers fell back and watched the tribesmen continue down the slope back toward the refugee camp. They had come upon a number of giant anthills. Stig ordered his men to wait and not move forward among the anthills. It was fortunate that he did. The sudden whoosh of arrows singing through the air and the thud and clatter of the primitive airborne weapons was followed by a series of war whoops. From behind the anthills the Baluba came charging, swinging their razor-sharp bicycle chains, clutching spears and other weapons.

Stig had no alternative but to order his men to stand and defend themselves. "Fire! But for hell, don't miss!" he shouted as he squeezed off short bursts from his submachine gun. For five minutes the men accompanying Stig fired into the mob, watching them fall by the dozens. The advancing waves of attackers faltered, halted, and then turned and ran, dropping their weapons as they fled among the mounds of anthills and on down the slope to the refugee camp. Suddenly it ended. There was silence, with not even the moans of the wounded and the dying.

From another direction an armored car and trucks filled with a company of Swedes noisily pulled up to the road overlooking the blue-helmeted soldiers standing down the slope. The soldiers in the trucks jumped out and began running toward Stig, led by Major Mide.

"What the hell is going on here?" the Swedish battalion commander, obviously angry, shouted as he drew near to the detachment. He spotted bodies scattered across the slope and looking at it from his own position, wondered how he'd be able to explain why his troops were forced to kill Baluba refugees. Stig explained what had taken place. The major grunted. If it had happened to any one of his other officers, there would probably be the devil to pay and an investigation by ONUC political advisers. Anyway, what would ONUC civilians know about danger. His men had to defend themselves. And Stig, who knew the blacks better than any one else in the Swedish battalion, obviously couldn't help himself. He did what he had to do. The major was satisfied and quickly cooled off.

"I'd better get into the camp," Stig suggested to the major

who told him to take some men, adding: "Be careful. These beggars may be out to get you."

Stig turned away and with his eleven men following walked down the slope and into the camp. The Baluba who had been killed and wounded during the battle a short time before had disappeared. The soldiers with Stig gaped in awe as they walked through the insect village of anthills. There was not a single body in the grass.

"I know I hit at least twenty of them," a soldier commented.

"I got at least the same number," another one said.

"Where are they, Lieutenant?" a third Swedish soldier asked Stig who just shook his head and shrugged his shoulders. Their guess was as good as his. Inside the camp they discovered a truck filled with the bodies of Katangans and in another spot they uncovered the bodies of the ten missing members of the *gendarmerie.* All of the bodies bore the same mutilations—missing sexual organs. The Swedish soldiers sickened at the sight. It was only the beginning.

When Stig returned to his headquarters he suggested that on the following day the Swedish and Irish companies begin a large-scale search of the camp. "I think we may uncover a number of new problems which the civilian administration of ONUC doesn't suspect," he added.

Some six thousand Baluba tribesmen in the refugee camp continued to hold down their jobs in Elisabethville. Despite the apparent hatred of the Baluba by the Katangans, the money that the tribesmen from the northern part of the province had to spend was welcomed by the merchants in the city. Meantime, the *jeunesse* had strengthened their hold over the refugees. Those among the Baluba who worked in the city were forced to turn over part of their wages to the *jeunesse.* It was nothing more than outright piracy although the *jeunesse* leaders referred to it as a tax. Each day when rations were distributed by ONUC at a point near the camp, the *jeunesse* were at the gates waiting to confiscate their levy or share of the food.

21

Witch doctor vs. blue helmet

At the end of September, when the tropical rains began, Stig suggested to ONUC that the refugees be moved a few miles further away to a new camp laid out with some sanitation facilities and permitting more efficient control of the Baluba by the peacekeeping force. There was, of course, a personal motive. The Irish and Swedish troops were forced to put up with the horrible stench that emanated from the refugees. The very fact that disease did not run rampant was due to luck and the UN and Red Cross public health specialists who worked ceaselessly against overwhelming conditions.

The refugee camp had grown like a formless amoeba and by early October the Irish and Swedish military camps were virtually surrounded by the Baluba and the ugly odors that sickened the European soldiers. There no longer was any question from which direction the wind blew the essence of filth. The odor from the camp permeated everything. The ONUC soldiers welcomed patrol duty in Elisabethville. In fact, they even would have welcomed the most dangerous of combat assignments. Anything to escape the "stinking" Baluba camp.

Meanwhile, ONUC political advisers continued to receive

the spokesmen for the refugees and conducted almost daily conferences under the assumption that as long as talks were going on, there wouldn't be any trouble. This is the philosophy of civilized men: to keep open a dialogue from which men of goodwill can solve their disputes. Amongst the tribesmen there was only a primitive ethic and differences were settled with the aid of a witch doctor's *dawa* or by tribal warfare. The peace table, as ONUC political advisers were slow to learn, settled nothing. There really could be no dialogue between primitive man and civilized man, between tribal leaders who envisioned nothing beyond the scope of their ancestral lands and the UN's international men who regarded the flare-up in the Congo as a seriously troublesome sore spot on the face of the world.

"These people only respect strength," Stig often told his superior officers. However, he qualified his statement by explaining that force combined with knowledge of these unpredictable primitives usually could solve what appeared to be insurmountable problems. A week after ONUC announced to the refugees that their camp would be moved, Stig was given the opportunity to practice what he preached.

Stig was placed in command of the moving operation with an admonition from Colonel Waern to, "Please see that there are no shooting situations for I do not want to have to answer politically for one more incident." Stig nodded and assured his commander that he would do his utmost to prevent any violence.

On a cloudy morning during the second week of October, 1961, the Swedish soldiers began moving the tribesmen and their families. Trucks rumbled into the refugee camp and Stig ordered one vehicle to follow his jeep as he slowly led it to a jerry-built building which was a shade smaller than a witch doctor's house. The building belonged to an important chief.

Stig entered and addressed the Luba chief.

"This is the day you are to move," he crisply announced in Swahili. The chief stolidly remained silent.

"These are the orders of ONUC," the slim young Swedish

officer continued. The chief shook his head. Nobody could make him move, not even the blue-helmets.

"You may kill us so that we all rot here," the chief continued once he got started, "but never will we move . . . never!"

Stig nodded. He understood perfectly. He stepped out of the building and ordered his troops to line up. Then he selected a platoon of men and ordered them to begin tearing down the building in which the chief was holding court with his tribesmen and load it aboard a truck.

"Pull it down around his head if you have to," he told his men.

The chief and his people saw that Stig wasn't going to take no for an answer. The tribe living in that section of the refugee camp began packing up their belongings. Day by day the camp grew smaller as the Baluba moved to their new camp.

Meanwhile, the Irish were having problems. The Irish battalion commander had heard of Stig's success. He wanted Lieutenant von Bayer's advice. The tribes in that section of the camp under control of the Irish were as stubborn "as an Irishman" in their determination to stay.

"Just do what we did," he explained to the officers in the Irish battalion.

Once these ONUC troops got the hang of it, their section of the camp quickly contracted as the Baluba quietly moved to their new location. Force tempered with knowledge successfully solved this sticky problem.

"Just how can we cope with these savages?"

One of the Malayan enlisted men assigned to ONUC battalion headquarters had just brought in a disturbing report. Drunken soldiers of the ANC loyal to Antoine Gizenga, Lumumba's leftwing vice-premier who had established himself in Stanleyville, Orientale Province, had gone on a rampage. Gizenga, who claimed to head the legitimate Congolese government, had set up a capital city in the African nation's northeast province and surrounded himself with several thousand ANC soldiers who swore loyalty to him.

However, the shocking news was not about the mutinous soldiers who were raiding and looting and killing. It was about the men they had killed. ONUC had stationed a company of Malayan soldiers at Kindu, in Kivu Province, which shared its northern border with Orientale Province's southern frontier. The mutinous ANC troops had surged across the common border and captured thirteen Italian airmen who were stationed at the Kivu airstrip. They were forcibly dragged through the streets of Kindu and finally died horrribly when the rebellious soldiers hacked them to pieces with panga knives. Then to add horror to this vile deed, some of the dead Italians were eaten by the members of the ANC's undisciplined Twentieth battalion while the remains of the others were thrown into the Lualaba River.

The fate of these unfortunate airmen shocked ONUC. The peacekeepers tried to discover the reasons for this brutal crime that occurred on November 14, 1961. Teams of investigators were sent to Kivu. The ONUC troops stationed at Kindu reportedly were unable to do anything to curb future atrocities that might occur. They were outnumbered nine to one by the mutineers who believed themselves indestructible by virtue of witch doctor magic.

The only explanation that Colonel Pakassa, the commander of the two thousand-man Kindu garrison could give for the atrocity was, "soldiers will be soldiers."

It wasn't until July, 1964, that Major Constantin Malongi, second in command, was sentenced to death in Leopoldville for sabotage. Colonel Pakassa fled into exile. However, the damage was irreparable and the untrustworthiness of the ANC once again was brought to the fore. As far as the soldiers of ONUC were concerned, *every* Congolese in uniform was a potential enemy.

The answer to why the Congolese, no matter what tribe or tribal group they belonged to, went berserk could be found in the refugee camp in Elisabethville. In fact, Stig tried to explain just how much hold the witch doctors had over their tribesmen. But the twentieth-century diplomats, ONUC's political officers from civilized countries, still couldn't seem to understand why the witch doctors were as strong as they turned out to be.

Following the attack by the refugees against the Katangese police and civilians, Stig was permitted to search the camp thoroughly the following day. It was during this search that he made his point about witch doctors: they were, indeed, all-powerful.

Inside the massive compound, Stig led a detail of soldiers directly to the habitat of the most important witch doctor. "Look for the biggest houses," Stig advised the Irish and Swedish officers leading their troops in the search for Baluba wounded during the previous day's clash.

One might expect that the tribal chiefs would have the biggest houses but, as Stig explained, most Congolese no matter what their tribal affiliation, groveled low before the most powerful man in their village—the witch doctor or *ju ju* man.

Stig led one detachment of soldiers to the biggest house he could spot in the area that the Swedes were searching. The ramshackle building, made from parts of Belgian houses that the Baluba had torn down, housed another grisly find. There were small holes in the ground from which was heard the low moaning of agonized humans. Stig ordered the soldiers to carefully dig around each hole. As the holes were widened the soldiers discovered an arm, then a leg and finally a body covered with damp earth. There were ten people buried alive. The soldiers pulled them out of these graves and had the unfortunates, all of whom had been wounded in the attack against Stig the previous day, sent to the refugee camp hospital.

The soldiers continued their search of the building. The witch doctor apparently was making his rounds and was not present while Stig was going about his thorough investigation of the premises.

"Lieutenant, look at this!" one soldier shouted with an audible shiver of disgust.

In a cauldron were the mutilated parts from the bodies discovered the day before in the camp. Stig also uncovered a cache of *bangi bangi*. A short time later the witch doctor, a wizened old man, returned and was arrested by the soldiers of ONUC. Outside of the witch doctor's hut a mob of tribesmen gathered, muttering dangerously as the soldiers mounted guard and held the Baluba at bay with their bayonets.

Stig explained to one of his fellow officers that the witch doctor should be summarily executed on the spot if for no other reason than to make an example of him before his people. "We should show them that his magic won't stop bullets," he explained grimly. "This man will undoubtedly prove even a greater threat in the future."

No matter how Stig felt personally about witch doctors he knew they had to be turned over to the ONUC provost marshal authorities. Most of the witch doctors were rounded up and imprisoned in a military stockade. However, the damage had been done by these powerful men with their roots, barks, herbs, bits and pieces of animals and humans, rattles, and bones. They held their tribes in a powerful, all-encompassing grip that even the most brutal of modern dictators backed by an efficient secret police and propaganda machinery could never hope to match. The witch doctors, as Stig explained in his reports, cared not for political power. They lived in comparative luxury. Tribesmen either feared them or were beholden to them because of their *dawa* or magical powers. Their services were available for a fee. Whether it was paid in money or in cattle was immaterial. Whatever represented wealth was demanded, and received, by the witch doctors for their services. They would prepare an evil spell for a tribesman on one day, if he paid for this type of service to vanquish an enemy. The next day the victim might die out of sheer fright when finding the signs of evil magic at his door. Or, the victim might pay the witch doctor a higher fee to lift the spell.

The highest bidder, Stig reported, always managed to buy a witch doctor's services. Even the fanatic *jeunesse* strongly believed in the powers of their witch doctors. And while their followers believed, the *jeunesse* chiefs also knew that they, too, could buy the support of these jungle charlatans who have been practicing their own strange ethic since time immemorial.

The Baluba *jeunesse,* as similar youth groups in other tribes would later follow suit, paid their *ju ju* men to give them the strength to vanquish all enemies. Specifically, as ONUC soldiers would later learn, marauding *jeunesse* tribal bands would attack the peacekeepers under the mistaken impression that the bullets of *les Onusiens* would turn to water. They would attack and they would die, and even in death some of them would not be stopped.

The peacekeepers had failed to bring peace to the troubled Congo. Whatever was done in the name of the United Nations was damned from a number of quarters. In fact, the most apt description of the blue-helmeted ONUC force at the time was that it was damned if it did, and damned if it didn't. The central government in Leopoldville damned ONUC almost as often as Tshombe did from his capital in Elisabethville. At one point, the central government even tried to bring Katanga to its knees by invading the province with ANC troops. They were hurled back by the well-led Katangese *gendarmerie.* The ANC was nothing more than an ill-disciplined rabble who cared not a whit about obeying its officers. The *gendarmerie,* on the other hand, fought hard and successfully to hurl back the invaders. It was apparent that the mercenaries had returned.

ONUC intelligence estimated that more than three hundred mercenaries were in Tshombe's army. Tshombe, for his part, launched a propaganda tirade against ONUC. At a private dinner held in Elisabethville late in November for visiting U. S. Senator Thomas Dodd, a staunch Tshombe supporter, members of the *gendarmerie* posted nearby took little notice of the automobiles that drove up with members of the diplomatic colony. Finally, just before the U. S. consular vehicle carrying Dodd arrived an ONUC staff car pulled up. Out stepped the civilian chief of ONUC in Elisabethville and his aide. The *gendarmerie* attacked both men. A brutal beating was administered to Brian Urquhart, who had recently arrived in the Congo from New York, and his assistant, George Ivan Smith. Urquhart, suffering from the pain of cracked ribs and a broken nose, was hustled off to a *gendarmerie* camp and placed under detention.

An American consular official immediately contacted Tshombe and members of his cabinet and insisted that ONUC's chief be released. Meanwhile, the news of Urquhart's beating and kidnapping was received at ONUC military headquarters. Patrols were sent out to find the missing official. One jeep with a Gurkha driver and a Sikh officer from the Indian brigade disappeared during the search; the bodies of the men were never found. Three hours after Urquhart was beaten and abducted, Tshombe ordered his release. It was now late November and the tense situation in Katanga was rapidly coming to a boil.

"U Thant will launch a war on our territory," Tshombe broadcast to his people in Katanga. "Tomorrow or the day after tomorrow, there will be a trial of strength. When the time comes, let Katanga fighters arise in every street, on every path, on every highway, in every village. You cannot all have automatic weapons or rifles. But we still have our poisoned arrows, our spears, our axes for cutting down trees, our picks for digging ditches, our hearts to beat with courage. Not a road must remain passable, not one United Nations mercenary must feel safe in any place whatever. . . ."

In the first days of December tension mounted. *Gendarmerie* set up road blocks in Elisabethville directed against the movement of ONUC. The peacekeeping soldiers stationed at the airport were under sporadic rifle fire from snipers. This was the showdown between Katanga and ONUC. The Secretary General authorized ONUC to take "all counter-action—ground and aerial—deemed necessary" to remove roadblocks established in an effort to impede UN movement and operations. Indian soldiers forcibly removed a roadblock between ONUC headquarters and the airport. Shortly afterwards, on the afternoon of December 5, Katanga's forces launched an attack against ONUC with mortars, machine guns, and rifles. The attack was well-coordinated. It wasn't directed by Katangese *gendarmerie* officers but by mercenaries—the men with combat experience. That night Katanga's Fouga jets bombed the airport. This time, however, ONUC was ready with its own jets which strafed Katangan positions and later escorted the U. S. Air Force transports carrying blue-helmeted reinforcements and supplies from Leopoldville.

ONUC finally was on the offensive. Brigadier Raja, the ONUC commander in Katanga, was given wider latitude than any previous senior military officer. This was war; no longer were the civilian political officers calling the shots. Military operations required military knowhow. The blue-helmeted soldiers were heavily committed. Until reinforcements arrived they were outnumbered and in some cases outgunned by the mercenary-led *gendarmerie*. This was to be no simple roundup of mercenaries but an all-out offensive aimed at crushing the *gendarmerie* and ultimately forcing Tshombe to return Katanga to the central government.

The political intricacies meant nothing to the Swedes, Irish, Indians, and Ethiopian troops thrown into the battle. Now it was a simple matter of survival in combat. The first days of battle saw ONUC's jets in the air, sweeping into Katanga from another province to strike at Katangese truck convoys and Tshombe's air force at Kolweizi. Most of the mercenary air force was destroyed on the ground. Aerial supremacy practically guaranteed an ONUC victory.

Meanwhile, officers from four different nations staffed ONUC headquarters at the airport. The predominant language was English and the precisely clipped voices of Indian officers mingled with the accents of the Swedes and the Irish who also staffed the command post. Although instructions at headquarters were in English, orders were issued to the battalion commanders in the field in their own language. The Swedes, for example, ran a secure radio network; none of the Katangese forces understood the language. The Gurkhas rattled on in Nepalese and the Dogras in Hindi. The Katangan forces, on the other hand, relied on Swahili to convey instructions. But now there were enough ONUC interpreters available to eavesdrop on the radio bands used by Tshombe's forces. This was all part of the combat intelligence techniques used by modern armies.

The UN, which at the highest level had deplored the very mention of the term "intelligence gathering," was forced to utilize battlefield eavesdropping by use of radio intercept techniques.

The military staff at this point cared not one whit about the feelings of the top-level civilians at UN headquarters in New York. This was war and finally the peacekeepers were given an opportunity to bring about peace in their own way—by fighting for it.

Stig was smack in the middle of all the action right from the time he received the first report of Swedish casualties. A jeep with three Swedish ONUC soldiers had been fired on by *gendarmerie* manning a roadblock. Out of control, the vehicle careened down the street with a dead soldier at the wheel and two others severely wounded. It jumped a sidewalk in one of Elisabethville's residential areas inhabited by upper middle-class Belgians and slammed into a wall. A woman came out of her house and ran toward the vehicle. When she saw that the jeep and men were from ONUC, she spat at them as they lay bleeding, their lives ebbing away. "Dirty *Onusien!*" she shrieked and returned to her home.

The day-by-day fighting was confined to the outskirts of the city although mortar shells whooshed in among the buildings and exploded with all of the destruction that is possible in war. Early in December ONUC was outnumbered. Brigadier Raja radioed to Leopoldville for reinforcements and twenty-one U. S. Air Force transports began airlifting a second Swedish battalion to join the one fighting in Elisabethville, another Irish battalion, a second Ethiopian battalion, and additional armored cars for the Swedes.

Gendarmerie opposition stiffened from the very beginning as the Katangans fielded for the first time a paracommando battalion that had secretly been organized and trained by the elusive General Norbert Moke, Katanga force commander who in reality was thin, ascetic Major Rene Faulques, an OAS officer who had received the Legion of Honor medal for combat actions in Indo-China and Algeria. The heavily armed paracommandos surged out from their bases within the sprawling Union

Minière complex and began hammering away at the blue-helmeted troops who sought to hold their strategic positions on the outskirts of the city.

Stig's intelligence assessment of the Union Minière participation was later voiced by Secretary General U Thant in a reply to protests by Belgian Foreign Minister Paul Henri Spaak that the mining company's holdings were *not* being used by the mercenaries or the *gendarmerie*. "You must be aware of the extent of the assistance the Union Minière has given to secessionists in Katanga," the Secretary General cabled. "According to unimpeachable sources, officials of the Union Minière have proudly admitted the manufacture of *gendarmerie* armoured cars and of bombs which have been dropped on the airport and ONUC Headquarters in Elisabethville. It is also a well-known fact that Union Minière has never denied having made it possible for mercenaries to go underground by putting them nominally on their payroll."

Brigadier Raja managed to contain the fighting to the outskirts although it was obvious that the Katangese leaders were trying to turn the course of battle in another direction. Specifically, a guerrilla-type war whereby the *gendarmerie* would fight a series of house-to-house delayed actions within the city, thus blunting the effectiveness of ONUC forces. It also meant that civilians would wittingly or unwittingly be exposed to gunfire.

For several days the fighting consisted of hit-and-run actions by the mobile paracommandos. The peacekeepers launched probing attacks and as the fighting began to settle into a pattern it became apparent that the Katangese forces held three key points—an underpass leading into Elisabethville over which the BCK railroad passed: Camp Massart, a strongly defended military base; and the Union Minière complex.

Stig, in his role of battalion intelligence officer, was ordered to accompany an assault against the tunnel, as the underpass was called. The *gendarmerie* were strongly dug in along the approaches to the underpass. As the Swedish soldiers approached behind their armored cars, the Katangans opened fire with everything they had. Geysers of red dust erupted all around the APCs from the mortar shells that kept falling. Shrapnel from the exploding shells hammered against the vehicles as the machine gunner in the turret of each APC laid down covering fire from his twin machine guns. An unusually heavy thud shook the APC Stig was commanding. One of the soldiers leaned out and spotted a tear-shaped shell that had lodged in one of the firing ports.

"Lieutenant, there's an unexploded mortar shell jammed here," he informed Stig. "What shall I do with it?" Stig hurriedly poked his head out, looked over the side, and immediately ducked for cover. It wasn't a mortar shell, but a recoilless rifle rocket—a bazooka projectile.

"Driver, let's get out of here!" Stig shouted. There was immediate danger facing the APCs. One hit by a recoilless rifle and its armor-piercing rocket would knock out the armored car and kill or wound the men inside. Stig's APC jerked forward, not a moment too soon. A round from one of the recoilless rifles trailing smoke sizzled past the APC and smashed into a building behind it with a devastating roar that collapsed the whitewashed tropical structure.

For a week the seesaw battle continued outside of the Katangan capital. Ethiopian troops arrived and were deployed at various points that were under fire. However, they kicked off a series of attacks that left a bitter taste in the mouhs of Belgian civilians who, at the time, were not averse to sniping at *les Onusiens* from their homes and apartments.

The Ethiopians, members of some mutinous units shipped out of their country for disciplinary reasons after the ill-fated revolt smashed by their emperor, arrived in Elisabethville and were immediately ordered into action by ONUC headquarters. Brigadier Raja desperately required as many troops in the field as he could obtain and, rather than easing the Ethiopians into the fray by perhaps deploying them around the airfield, he ordered them into Elisabethville. The blue-helmeted soldiers from East Africa immediately came under fire from snipers. In an effort to end the threat to their patrols, Ethiopian soldiers shot up a number of Belgians, killing some women in the process. The cry from a group of Belgian doctors, who called themselves "forty-six angry men," was one that smacked of the ugly word "atrocity."

The doctors later compiled a number of case histories charging numerous U.N.O. violations. However, the Ethiopians considered themselves at war. They reacted accordingly, shooting up homes and people without attempting to weigh the merits of each combat situation. The Red Cross announced that fifteen ambulances would be used to carry wounded to a hospital located near the airport. Within days the fifteen vehicles painted with red crosses on a white square numbered fifty as the additional so-called ambulances sped through the city carrying food, ammunition and reinforcements for the *gendarmerie.*

In the case of the Ethiopian troops, the language barrier prevented them from communicating with suspected enemies before opening fire. Some of these peacekeepers shot first and then tried to ask questions later. A number of ambulances were shot up, including some actually carrying casualties. International Red Cross chief in Elisabethville, Georges Olivet and two of his associates were killed when the ambulance they were traveling in was machine gunned during the fighting. They could have been killed by either side.

From Stig's vantage point as intelligence officer, he was able to keep abreast of most of the fighting. Five days after the shooting began Brigadier Raja requested his senior field commanders to return to ONUC headquarters at the airfield for a strategy conference. The only vehicle available to transport the battalion commanders was a Swedish armored car. Colonel Waern was ordered to send the APC to the various parts of the city where ONUC units were dug in and pick up the senior officers.

"Lieutenant, you will come with me," he told Stig. The APC the began the perilous journey from one sector to another, first picking up the Irish C.O. and his chief of staff, then to the Indian sector and finally to the Ethiopian sector. On the way to the airport the APC came under heavy Katangese fire. Stig kneeled at one of the gun ports firing his submachine gun at the *gendarmerie* dug in along the road. Overhead, a Swedish soldier in the gun turret fired off rapid bursts from the twin machine guns.

The senior UN field commanders quietly sat inside the APC as the vehicle ran through a gantlet of machine gun and mortar fire. One lucky hit against this vehicle and the Katangans could kill or capture the most important officers in the ONUC force.

Stig saw a flash off to the side and stiffened. He triggered off several short bursts from his Karl Gustaf. "Faster! Faster!" he shouted. Before he could tell the driver that the *gendarmerie* were firing a recoiless rifle the APC rocked from an explosion that slammed into the turret above. Shrapnel whizzed downward and a numbing blow struck Stig's arm while chunks of metal battered his helmet. The bloody body of the mortally wounded turret gunner slipped down and was grasped by the outstretched hands of the senior officers. Bullets thudded into the thick tires of the APC as the driver gunned it forward. The armored vehicle weaved from side to side nearly out of control. Colonel Waern climbed into the turret and began manning the twin machine guns as the vehicle roared through the noisy crossfire.

Stig's right arm hung limply at his side. He turned to one of the senior officers and asked him to reload the submachine gun with another clip.

"But you're wounded!" the officer shouted over the barking of the twin machine guns and the noise of war outside the APC. Stig shook his head.

"Reload for me!" he virtually ordered the senior officer who was several ranks above him. The officer slammed in another clip and handed the weapon back to Stig. Bracing the submachine gun's barrel on the gun port Stig continued adding his firepower to the defense of the swaying APC. They arrived at the airport headquarters just as a flight of huge U. S. Air Force C-124 Globemasters touched down. The transports disgorged reinforcements and a number of additional armored cars.

During the two-hour conference plans were made for the final series of assaults against *gendarmerie* positions. As intelligence officer, Stig briefed the battalion commanders with whatever information he had to offer. While he spoke, a medic bandaged his wounds. The battle plan that was formulated called for an attack by the Irish battalion against the underpass; a Swedish battalion attack to capture Camp Massart; Indian troops were to create diversionary attacks and the Ethiopians would secure the western part of Elisabethville.

Once the meeting was over the various battalion commanders split up and returned to their respective units in the newly arrived armored vehicles which had been unloaded from the Globemasters. The final attack to crush the *gendarmerie* kicked off at 0300 hours on December 16 during a miserable downpour. Stig had asked Colonel Waern for permission to accompany the attack in one of the APCs. His request was turned down. The colonel wanted Stig to monitor intercepted Katangese radio messages and keep him abreast of the enemy's movements.

The downpour turned some of the dirt roads into mud and gullies into small rivers which impeded the movement of the ONUC forces. However, despite Nature's own counteroffensive, the various units succeeded in winning their objectives after several days of heavy fighting. The Swedes took Camp Massart; later, on the same day they launched their attack and captured a large amount of military equipment. However, the plan to cut off all roads leading in and out of the city failed because the Ethiopians and the Indians were unable to secure their objectives according to the battle plan timetable. Most of the *gendarmerie* escaped to fight another day.

But Elisabethville was taken.

A cease-fire was scheduled to become effective at 1100 hours on December 19. Christmas was less than one week away. Peace! The word itself sounded wonderful to the European troops. The shooting died down with the exception of sporadic firing as diehard civilian snipers and *gendarmerie* held out at isolated points that had been cut off by the ONUC troops. It was clearly a UN victory. That is, if this term could be used to describe a military situation as confusing as the Congo itself where the word or solemn oath of national leaders was not worth the paper on which it was given.

There were prisoners to be exchanged and battle damage to be cleaned up. New plans had to be made for Katanga while at UN headquarters in New York and in world capitals ONUC was taken to task for becoming involved in "offensive" operations. However, the discussions taking place on the highest rarified levels of government meant little to the soldiers in the field. They were just happy to be alive. A total of twenty-one ONUC soldiers were killed and eighty-four wounded; 206 *gendarmerie* and six mercenaries also lost their lives along with fifty civilians who were killed and wounded.

If this was war, it was just as strange to the peacekeepers as the aftermath of the battle was to Stig. Two trucks from the Irish Battalion arrived at the Swedish unit's headquarters several hours after the cease-fire. An Irish officer accompanying the trucks sought out Stig. He needed the Swedish officer's assistance.

"I've got three thousand botttles of liquor and wine," he confided to Stig in a low voice. "There's some danger that if we left it where we found it, the bloody natives would have looted it."

"Why can't you keep it at your camp?" Stig asked. The ONUC officer's reply was amusingly Irish.

"We can't spare the men to guard it. The problem is that we'd have to assign guards to guard the guards."

Stig sagely nodded. He looked at the two trucks. Then he placed his arm around the Irish officer's shoulder and they slowly walked away from the trucks. Remarkably enough, the entire shipment was eventually turned over intact to the owner, who apparently had such great faith in the integrity of the soldiers that he did not even bother to say thanks for the safekeeping of his property.

22

The smugglers

THE "PEACE ON EARTH, goodwill toward men" that Christmas usually reflects was impossible to come by in the Congo. Chaos continued. The cohesive force that ONUC was supposed to represent was missing. There were problems in the Congo that just could not be solved by ONUC. This African nation, approaching its second birthday on June 30, 1962, was faced by imponderables that would require at least a generation to solve. The forces of civilization represented by the UN presence were hardpressed to maintain the decorum that was expected of ONUC. The peacekeepers were professional soldiers who disliked being shot at without shooting back; and some sniping continued from all directions.

In the Congo the undisciplined and mutinous ANC continued their sporadic attacks against the peacekeepers; tribesmen attacked the blue-helmets; Katangans repeatedly broke the cease-fire agreement reached just before Christmas of 1961. In the United Nations itself the Secretary General was faced with a financial problem of great significance: some of the big powers refused to pay their share of the cost of peacekeeping in the Congo.

In January, 1962, a band of ANC soldiers burst into a Catholic mission of the Order of the Holy Spirit near Kongolo in north Katanga and brutally murdered twenty-two Belgian priests. There were other missionaries in the area and ONUC dispatched Major Richard Lawson, a British officer serving with a Nigerian battalion at Luluabourg, to Kongolo to warn others of the Lord's calling of the danger they faced. A light plane touched down on a field near the mission and Lawson and the pilot hopped out. The pilot and the blonde, thirty-seven-year-old major were on their own.

They managed to cover a wide area on foot and visit several of the missions. At one point they were surrounded by a group of Balubakat *jeunesse* clad in tribal skins and feathers. They still did not know why they were not killed and chalked up the experience to the erratic psychology of the Congolese. One of the warriors jabbed Lawson in the back with a spear. The English officer turned in anger and threw a well-aimed fist that smashed into the warrior's face, knocking him to the ground.

Here was a lion, a *simba,* the warriors thought and for some unknown reason let both men go in peace.

As the year unraveled, the Tshombe government began importing more mercenaries and rebuilding the Katangese *gendarmerie* into a stronger force. Clearly, another round of shooting was in the making.

Meanwhile, Stig continued in his intelligence and troubleshooting assignment until it was decided by ONUC that perhaps it was time to incorporate one or two ANC battalions into the UN peacekeeping force. Both the ONUC civilian political advisers and the UN Secretariat had been so engrossed in their attempts to pacify the troubled nation that any disarming or retraining of the mutinous ANC had virtually been overlooked. Critics of UN policies in the Congo contend that by ignoring the ANC the infant nation's problems were increased tenfold.

After returning from home leave in Sweden Stig was assigned as liaison officer with the Second ANC Battalion and ordered to report to Congolese military headquarters in Leopoldville. The modern eleven-story military headquarters building belied the uniformed rabble it represented. Staff officers in smartly tailored uniforms were busily engaged in paperwork and military red tape. However, the central government's army was strictly a paper organization. The ANC numbered thousands on official rosters. At many military posts, however, the troops were no more than bandit gangs held together by a fraction of military discipline and their knowledge that they could effectively use their weapons to good advantage if they stuck together.

It was a frustrating assignment for Stig. The Congolese troops were an undisciplined lot who Stig personally believed were unfit to wear the ONUC shoulder patch and blue berets and helmets they were issued. Stig's assignment was to observe training of these troops who he knew were the cause of most of the Congo's problems. His suggestions to Congolese officers went unheeded. An uneducated lot, they believed that as officers in the Army they knew everything there was to know about soldiering—an unsound opinion that was to prove disastrous during the troublesome period after the last ONUC troops departed the Congo.

Enlisted men considered Stig an outsider. They never accepted orders from officers other than their own, they repeatedly barked at the Swedish captain. They cried "discrimination" when he issued orders and would brook none of the endless discussion and arguments they had with their own officers. As Stig observed with a shudder, none of the orders of the Congolese officers were ever carried out without a shouting bout between the enlisted men and their superiors.

It was one helluva way to run an army. But Stig was a professional soldier and he was determined to do whatever possible to weld the recalcitrant Congolese into a first-rate battalion.

ONUC military strength rose to more than eighteen thousand men during the year, but seventy per cent were deployed in Katanga in an effort to keep the rapidly diminishing peace from exploding into another round of shooting. Stig tried to spend as much time as possible with the men of his ANC battalion at Kamina base. The task of training the Congolese seemed next to impossible.

After a few months with the ANC, Stig and the Second Battalion were ordered to Kamina Base in West Central Katanga which ONUC had set up as a major base in the province. The situation in Katanga had deteriorated to the point where Kamina base was entirely surrounded by heavily armed *gendarmerie* forces and vehicle convoys were permitted to enter or leave only by permission of the Tshombe government in Elisabethville, and all supplies to the base were airlifted. The presence of ANC troops in Kamina base angered Tshombe. In October an Ethiopian F-86 Sabrejet failed to return after a patrol flight in the Kamina area. Stig was ordered to lead a small search party to a town sixty miles east of Kamina where the jet fighter might have gone down.

It was one of Stig's most memorable missions and he nearly ended his peacekeeping career before a firing squad. Armed with his submachine gun and a pistol he had shoved in his pocket almost as an afterthought, Stig escorted an Ethiopian officer to an H-19 helicopter piloted by a Swedish officer, warrant officer Olsson, copiloted by a Danish sergeant. The helicopter easily covered the distance and set down near *gendarmerie* headquarters. Stig stepped out to be greeted by a squad of Katangese troops dressed in mottled green and brown camouflaged uniforms.

The greeting was pleasant. The soldiers were relaxed as Stig told the sergeant in charge of the detachment that he had permission to search for the missing jet. Stig called to the Ethiopian officer to step out of the helicopter. The East African officer complied. But his appearance set off a near riot. Before Stig could introduce the Ethiopian one of the *gendarmerie* soldiers shouted: "Spy!"

"Kill the pigs!" another voice shrieked. "Let's show them how we treat spies."

The sound of the commotion brought a number of other Katangese soldiers on the run and within a few minutes a hundred of them were caught up in the frenzy. The pilots, who had clambered out of their cockpit to escape the hot sun beating on the helicopter, were shoved beside Stig and the Ethiopian and their weapons were taken with the exception of Stig's hidden pistol. Stig tried to reason with the soldiers. After several months of service with the ANC, he was aware of the volatile spirit of the Congolese, no matter what tribe they belonged to or to which political leader they owed a tenuous fealty.

The shouts continued. "Shoot them! Burn the helicopter! Kill the spies!"

Stig was the only person among the four who understood what the *gendarmerie* were shouting about. He held up his hand to quiet the mob and vainly attempted to explain that the government in Elisabethville had granted permission for the search.

Once again, Stig tried to speak his piece. The blow from a rifle butt slammed against the small of his back. He almost fell to his knees. Rifle butts struck the other three ONUC peacekeepers. The noncom ordered the four men taken to the small headquarters building about fifty feet away. Protesting without success, Stig and the others were painfully prodded with the muzzles of loaded guns. If one shot was fired, it would be curtains for the four men. The first shot would trigger off others and every bullet would strike down the four prisoners.

As they were prodded on their way, Stig glanced behind. Some of the *gendarmerie* were still trying to light a small fire under the Sikorsky. When they reached the buildiing the noncom ordered the ONUC officers to stand against the bullet-pocked wall of the building.

"*Forbannat!*" Stigg exclaimed in Swedish. "Dammit all!" he muttered under his breath. They were going to shoot the ONUC officers. The wall of the building obviously had seen similar duty.

The noncom ordered twelve men to form up for a firing squad. The rest of the *gendarmerie* loudly voiced approval. These were central government spies. Obviously, the tall Ethiopian was from a tribe allied to the central government and was sent to Katanga as a spy.

The noncom called his execution squad to attention. Stig demanded that a *gendarmerie* officer be contacted adding: "You are making a great mistake."

"Ready!" the noncom ordered. The rifles were lifted to port arms and the smooth clicking of bolts shoving bullets into firing chambers cut through the noisy chatter of the onlooking Katangese soldiers.

"Aim!"

"You are making a serious mistake," Stig called out again. "We have permission from Tshombe, your chief. This will mean big trouble for you."

Stig shoved his hand in his pocket and gripped the pistol. There was only one thing left to do; he would have to time it just right—fall to the ground and begin shooting. They'd kill him. But at least he would get some of them, and he was determined to shoot first at the noncommissioned officer.

The roar of an engine and the screeching of brakes cut into the scene pregnant with death; a jeep driven by a *gendarmerie* driver with an officer at his side pulled to a halt.

"What's going on here?" the officer asked the noncom. He was told about the spies. Despite his presence, the soldiers kept clamoring for the lives of *les Onusiens*. The captain, a Katangan, began arguing with his men. It was obvious to Stig and his comrades that even the vaunted *gendarmerie* were about as ill-disciplined a lot as the ANC. Their superior told them that he would have to telephone Elisabethville for permission to shoot the prisoners. The shouting lowered to a grumble. Meanwhile, flames began rising beneath the helicopter. The Katangese officer ordered the fire extinguished and then instructed the execution squad to escort the four peacekeepers to his own quarters. While the prisoners nervously waited, the captain tried to get through to Elisabethville. Two hours later he made contact with one of Tshombe's military advisers who ordered the prisoners released.

The latent temper of the *gendarmerie*, paralleled by the explosive character of the ANC, boded no good for the Congo's future. During the return flight to Kamina—the search for the jet was all but forgotten after this close brush with death—Stig mentally examined the situation. He shook his head. There was no solution for the Congo. ONUC was in for serious trouble. He was never more right.

On Christmas eve ONUC launched Operation Grandslam against the *gendarmerie* and whatever mercenaries were in Katanga. Tshombe, as Stig had reasoned and predicted after his narrow escape the previous October, had lost all control over his military force. He fled the country when Grandslam opened ONUC's offensive. Unfortunately, a breakdown in communications occurred outside of Jadotville. A column of Indian troops crossed the Lufira River after orders had been issued by UN headquarters in New York to halt just west of the natural barrier. Both the highway bridge and railroad trestle had been demolished by retreating *gendarmerie*. The orders from the Secretary General failed to reach the ONUC field commander until some of his troops were actually on the Jadotville side.

It appeared to be a question of either obeying New York and withdrawing or pressing what was distinctly a military advantage. The Secretary General's orders were disregarded; he just was not aware of the situation of the moment. The Indian units crossed the Lufira using the debris from the demolished bridges to build a temporary structure.

At this particular point the blue-helmeted troops became involved in a serious military and diplomatic *faux pas*. An advance patrol spotted a small Volkswagen driving away. They shouted for the driver to halt. There was a language barrier. The Indians did not speak French. The Belgian driver did not understand Hindi. As the vehicle picked up speed, the Indians opened fire. The auto dizzily careened and ground to a halt. The driver, covered with blood, staggered out dazed with his hands outstretched as if pleading for mercy. Inside the vehicle were the bodies of two women. They had been killed by the shots fired at the fleeing car.

Throughout the entire peacekeeping operation the ONUC command had no public information organization or psychological warfare operation to counteract the well-directed and heavily financed propaganda machine that Union Minière had launched on behalf of Tshombe and Katanga. Moreover, during this particular phase of Operation Grandslam news correspondents from a number of nations had been given permission to follow this particular Indian column. They were on the scene when this unfortunate incident occurred. Photos graced the front pages of newspapers throughout the world within 12 hours after the incident. It was a black eye that the United Nations would be forced to wear for quite some time.

Indeed, peacekeeping became a duty compounded of trials and tribulations.

"Mon capitaine, we can use your services . . . and pay well for them."

Stig nodded to the Congolese provincial official; he turned to Vladimir Jerkovic, the ONUC senior political officer stationed in Kasai Province, and winked ever so imperceptibly.

"Yes, yes, go on. I am listening," Stig replied to the Congolese.

The official, clad in a Western business suit, white shirt, and necktie affected by the professional politicians and civilian leaders in the Congo, blatantly offered to bribe Stig and his civilian counterpart with a bottle of diamonds if they would cooperate.

"What do you want me to do?" Stig asked.

"The President of Unitée Kasaienne wants you to send a unit of *les Onusiens* to Tshikapa and arrest his opponents."

"For this you want to pay only one bottle?" the Swedish officer sneered. "And what about my colleague, Monsieur Jerkovic? Surely you must want to pay him too!"

For several minutes Stig and the political leader haggled over the payment of one or two bottles of valuable diamonds from the diamond-rich Kasai Province. He was playing out his role as ONUC liaison and intelligence officer in the summer of 1963. A semblance of peace had finally come to the Congo although beneath the surface the Swedish officer, now a captain, felt that trouble was brewing despite the surface calm.

Tshombe had been forced to end the secession of Katanga and the rebellious province was brought back into the Leopoldville government's fold. The mercenaries had either fled or were rounded up by ONUC and deported. Three men including a twenty-seven-year-old passport-less Hungarian, Bela Szabados, who claimed to have served in the U. S. Army Special Forces, and two Belgians had escaped from ONUC custody at Kamina base in early January and disappeared into the bush —never to be heard from again. By mid-March, ONUC forces in the Congo numbered 19,872 and the decision had been made at UN headquarters in New York to decrease the number of blue-helmeted peacekeepers now that some semblance of law and order prevailed.

As the ONUC units withdrew and left the country, the various military outposts they had established were handed over to these still untrained and poorly disciplined ANC troops. The end of the "military phase" of the peacekeeping operation was announced by the Secretary General. Civilian assistance was the order of the day and various additional government, public health and financial experts began arriving to assist the officials of the government and train them in the art of governing.

The Soviets reopened their embassy but were still not welcomed by the Leopoldville government. A pair of Soviet diplomatic officials succeeded in antagonizing the Congolese and were severely beaten up. The Kremlin protested; but for once Soviet protests fell on deaf ears.

Stig covered a lot of territory, visiting out-of-the way villages with his ONUC civilian counterparts. Peace. It was wonderful. Only, remember always to carry a weapon.

The corruption among the Congo's civilian officials in the provinces—and even in the capital—ran rampant. ONUC personnel were approached time and again for various favors that would be repaid in diamonds or gold. Take your pick. And there were a few who took their share of bribes.

But on this warm summer day that Stig bargained over the size of his bribe, he was only doing his duty. That was to report the flagrancies of Congolese like the man who was offering him diamonds in return for the services of the blue-helmets. Stig finally "accepted" two bottles of diamonds. He returned to his headquarters with Jerkovic and they reported the bribery attempt. From the civilian point of view Kasai was diamond-rich and money-rich. However, it was economically poor. The control of diamond buying and selling was difficult. The Congolese tribesmen in Kasai Province refused to work for wages. They preferred to mine for diamonds, which called for very little labor, and then sell them to the many diamond smugglers who infested the province. Stig reported that at least 80 per cent of the diamonds coming out of Kasai were illicitly purchased and then smuggled out of the country.

The tribes of Kasai were close to starvation. They had more than enough money. But the province's economy had broken down. There was nothing they could purchase with their franc notes, especially food.

The diamond scandal first came to Stig's attention when a Congolese interpreter working for ONUC complained to him that the Ghanaian soldiers owed him money for 265 diamonds that he had sold to members of this battalion.

"I would like to get my money as soon as possible," he told the Swedish officer. He had heard that the Ghanaians were going to return to their own country. Stig said he'd take the interpreter's request under consideration. After investigating the diamond situation, Stig came to the conclusion that this was a touchy problem. He had not asked the interpreter for the names of the Ghanaians involved. Later, after delving into the subject of diamonds, he came to the conclusion that an official ONUC investigation might prove embarrassing. There was the possibility that too many important people in the African battalion were involved. He told the interpreter that diamond smuggling was a civil police matter and that's where he should report it. Of course, Stig knew that if the interpreter did file a complaint with the police the Congolese would face arrest himself for breaking the law.

As for the law, it was being broken daily by members of the Congolese Government. During his tours through Kasai with Jerkovic, Stig would point out various officials and political leaders.

"That one there has a Swiss bank account," he'd advise the ONUC political officer. "Now, that one owns a villa in Europe and a hotel in Leopoldville."

Jerkovic quickly caught on to what was really going on behind the scenes; in fact, he was given an opportunity personally to see the Congolese type of bribery at work. An airplane from Leopoldville landed at Luluabourg airport one day and five Senegalese clad in robes and burnooses stepped down from the DC-3. Everybody who arrives in Kasai must undergo a rigid customs inspection and the two ONUC officials watched the passengers disembark from the aircraft. The five men carrying suitcases approached the customs counter which was in what had once been a modern building in good condition but was now dirty and in poor maintenance.

The first of the five Arabs opened his suitcase. It was filled with neat bundles of franc notes. He handed his Senegalese passport to the Congolese customs inspector.

"What will you buy with this money?" the customs inspector asked the Arab.

"Why, clothing and other local things here," the Senegalese replied in fluent French.

"But you know there is nothing to buy in this province, except one thing."

"Ah, now we understand each other," the Senegalese answered with a nod of his head. He lowered his eyes toward his packed wealth and reached for a packet of money. "Take it and we won't discuss this any more."

"Thank you," the customs officer said. He excused himself. The spokesman for the Senegalese turned to his companions. Everything was taken care of. The fix was on. The customs officer returned. He still had a sheaf of money in his hand, but Stig noticed that it wasn't as thick and wondered aloud to Jerkovic if other customs people had to be paid off, too.

The drama continued to unfold. A Belgian pilot came out of the terminal building and told the Arabs to follow him. They proceeded to a small Cessna twin-engine aircraft and the men clambered aboard. The engines turned over and the propeller began spinning and flashing in the sunlight as the aircraft slowly pulled away and gently bounced along the runway toward the end of the runway bordered by heavy green foliage.

Stig and Jerkovic saw the cabin door open; a suitcase fell to the ground. Then a white robed figure tumbled out, rolled and got to his feet. The customs officers also were watching. The officer who had taken the bribe shouted for his colleagues to apprehend the Senegalese. His robes flowing behind him, the smuggler headed for the bush and the customs police took off after him, shouting and firing their pistols. Stig and Jerkovic watched wide-eyed. As he ran, the Senegalese opened a side pocket of his suitcase, reached in and pulled out a sheaf of francs which he flung into the air. The money was caught by the slip stream of the plane which was still warming up and blown in the direction of the pursuing customs police.

They suddenly stopped and began bending down picking up and chasing the francs. With a roar the pilot gunned his engine and the airplane took off; he had no idea of what was going on behind him. The scene was so ludicrous that Stig and Jerkovic bent over in laughter. It was slapstick at its very best.

After composing themselves, Stig and Jerkovic approached the customs officer who had taken the bribe. The ONUC officer wanted to know what had transpired between the customs officer and the pilot. He told them:

"It's against the law to smuggle diamonds. It's also against the law to aid smugglers. Gentlemen, I did not aid these smugglers. They wanted to fly into the bush and transact business with the diamond sellers. I just helped them believe I would be of service. I rented the airplane in their name, paid the pilot seventy-five thousand francs which is the official price and ordered him to fly them back to Leopoldville."

The Congolese official smiled innocently. "It seems that they found out they were going to Leopoldville and one of them jumped out. He won't get far."

"But what of the money you kept?" Stig asked.

"Oh," the customs officer replied, "that's my commission, *mon capitaine.*"

The Senegalese smuggler did manage to escape and the illegal trade in diamonds continued. There was no way to halt it. Stig learned through his intelligence work that the black market in diamonds was even encouraged by a Soviet mission in the neighboring capital of Brazzaville, Congo—a next-door country bearing the same name as the nation ruled from Leopoldville. The Russian industrial machine, badly in need of diamonds for tooling, obtained many of the valuable gems from Kasai Province. But this was not a UN matter.

However, the extent of diamond smuggling can be measured by a 1964 economic report from the "other Congo," as the former French colony across the river from Leopoldville is called. In 1961 the Brazzaville government was staggering under a deficit of 58.7 million dollars. By mid-1964 the deficit had been pared to 5.6 million dollars. The key to this fiscal success: diamond smuggling from Kasai Province to the amount of nearly 25 million dollars in 1964 alone.

As Stig and his civilian colleague returned to their headquarters in Luluabourg, they continued to chuckle over the bribery incident. But it was not a UN matter and both men silently asked themselves if many of the peacekeepers of diverse nationalities had possibly succumbed to the "easy money" that could be illegally earned in the Congo.

23

Jadex One

IT HAS BEEN SAID that money is the root of all evil. Money has also been the root of the major problem that has befallen the United Nations. Specifically, the refusal of big powers like France and the Soviet Union to pay their share of the peacekeeping costs in the Congo which by June 30, 1964, saw the last ONUC troops depart this central African country. The bill after nearly four years of the peacekeeping effort reached a massive 402 million dollars of which at least 42 per cent came from the United States.

The Congo in reality had become pawn in the Cold War as first the Soviet Union and then Communist China attempted to gain a foothold on the dark continent. As early as 1961 the Soviets began criticizing the UN's role in the Congo. But then the U.S.S.R. was wont to criticize any situation that ran counter to the Kremlin's plans or wishes. First, the Soviets appeared to have a champion in the Congo's first prime minister, Patrice Lumumba. The aid that Russia sent to Lumumba was offered outside of the channels set up by the UN. Later, the Soviets were literally "booted" out of the Congo. During the central government's efforts to entice Tshombe and Katanga to return to the fold, the Soviets sided with Leopoldville. Katanga was ripe for a Soviet propaganda campaign directed against the rebellious province supported by the "capitalists" and "colonialists."

Despite the opposition from the Communist bloc, the peacekeeping force in the Congo ultimately was backed by thirty-five nations all of which provided military forces or personnel, including non-member Switzerland and the troubled Congo itself. Meanwhile, other UN peacekeeping operations continued in Kashmir, along Israel's frontiers edging along the borders of neighboring Arab states, and in the Gaza strip. In Korea the UN flag still flew outside U. S. Eighth Army headquarters and the United Nations Command continued to discuss armistice violations with Communist North Korea in a conference hall where a tiny village called Panmunjom once stood.

Strife in the Congo had been a serious issue at the UN for eighteen months when, in December, 1961, fighting suddenly broke out in the West New Guinea area between Indonesian and Netherlands forces. On December 19, 1961, the day that a ceasefire was to become effective in the Congo, Secretary General U Thant sent identical cables to the prime minister of the Netherlands and the president of Indonesia, expressing his deep concern over the possibility of a serious situation arising between both countries. He expressed his sincere hope that both parties to the dispute might come together to seek a peaceful solution to the problem. The following month small naval craft of both countries clashed off the coast of West New Guinea. Military prisoners were captured by the Netherlands and for a number of months Indonesian Army commandos continued their raids, inflicting casualties and destruction on Dutch forces and territory.

It was a vest-pocket war that had been continuing sporadically since 1954. It was no more than a pimple on the face of the globe; and it was a minor infection that could spread. Despite the more serious problem in the Congo, the hard-pressed then Acting Secretary General U Thant found the time to establish a settlement between the Netherlands and its former colony. A peacekeeping force designated the United Nations Temporary Executive Authority (UNTEA) was established with the help of 1,661 military personnel from 10 nations, including a force of nearly 1,500 troops from Pakistan. Their mission: to keep the peace and maintain law and order.

Meanwhile, in the tiny mountain kingdom of Yemen near the southwest tip of the Saudi Arabian peninsula fighting broke out in late 1962 between United Arab Republic forces supporting the republican government and Saudi Arabian military units supporting the royalist forces of the *imam,* or king. The royalists requested the United Nations to investigate their charges that the United Arab Republic was an aggressor. By late 1962, however, the composition of the UN had changed. The new nations, all of which had smarted for generations under colonial rule, sided with the republicans who had toppled a thousand years of despotism. The General Assembly voted seventy-four to three to seat Yemen's new government.

On the other hand, the situation in the isolated country called for positive measures. In early 1963, at a time when the boiling situation in the Congo apparently was cooling off, Secretary General U Thant began consultations with what the diplomats refer to as "parties to the dispute." The three nations involved in the dispute agreed to permit military observers to supervise a ceasefire. Eleven nations provided 247 men to UNYOM—the United Nations Observation Mission to Yemen—and the value of a uniformed peacekeeping force even for observer purposes was proved once again.

The UN peacekeeping efforts in West Irian and Yemen were of a temporary nature; neither lasted longer than a year. Nor did these smaller-scale peacekeeping operations go unnoticed. The officers and men in ONUC from several of the more advanced nations began openly discussing the pros and cons of a permanent military peacekeeping force of professional soldiers who would serve under the UN flag—anywhere, anytime, and against any threat to world peace.

A UN peacekeeping force wearing UN uniforms and serving

under the familiar flag emblazoned with the blue and white olive branch and globe symbol was something to think about. The idea appealed to Captain Stig von Bayer.

The message directed to ONUC headquarters in Leopoldville was stamped SECRET and signed by the team of von Bayer and Jerkovic based in Luluabourg. The date was October 15, 1963, and the message concerned a revolt by ANC troops. The Congolese troops had, according to the message, arrested their officers after word was received that the National Assembly had voted a raise for the military but that General Mobutu had vetoed the pay boost. The soldiers of the ANC were furious and it was, as Stig recalled, for a similar reason why the new Armée Nationale Congolaise in 1960 had mutinied a few days after independence. It was obvious that the ANC was in no position to keep the peace in the Congo once the forces of ONUC left. The termination of the UN peacekeeping effort was changed from the end of June, 1963, to the end of December. By the time December rolled around, another six months would be added to the ONUC peacekeeping operation.

Perhaps it was too late, but toward the end of 1963 it was becoming apparent to many observers, commentators, and participants in international affairs that the former Belgian colony was *not* a nation in the classical sense but a conglomeration of tribes; each with only a primitive understanding of the world known to these people of the bush. Few ONUC officers understood the Congo as well as Stig. In late 1963 the pattern of the troubled nation's first two years began to repeat itself. The tribes began to war on each other; the ancient hatreds could not and, indeed, would not be ignored by the warriors who believed only in vengeance.

Stig's secret messages to ONUC in Leopoldville followed one upon another. There was trouble brewing, but he couldn't quite put his finger on it. On October 30 he messaged ONUC:

SECRET FROM JERKOVIC VON BAYER POPULATION HAS STRONGLY PROTESTED ARRIVAL OF ONE PLATOON FROM KABINDA, STATING

THAT THESE ARE LOMAMI SOLDIERS AND THAT THEIR OBJECTIVE IS TO START WAR AGAINST LUNTU POPULATION. CIVILIANS ARRIVING FROM LOMAMI PROVINCE REPORTED KILLED BY LUNTU IN AREA. REASON APPARENTLY THEY BELONG TO BASONGE TRIBE WITH LOMAMI.

Intelligence reports like this were routine and somewhat insignificant with one exception: a pattern was beginning to take form and it boded ill for the Congo. The tribes were in a state of unrest in newly formed Kwilu Province, carved out of Leopoldville Province. Prime Minister Adoula during the year had reorganized the provinces along tribal lines, breaking six large areas into twenty small ones. In Kwilu only two of the five major tribes were involved in a fast-spreading rebellion against the Leopoldville Government. The Bapende and the Babunde numbering half a million began a series of vicious attacks against the Bambala, Bayanzi and Baboma numbering nearly one million. The reports arriving at ONUC headquarters and passed out to field intelligence and liaison officers like Stig described countless incidents. In Kwilu marauding Babunde warriors were captured, killed and eaten by the normally peaceful Baboma, and then the Babunde launched a series of retaliatory attacks killing three hundred Baboma cannibals.

"Here we go again," Stig remarked to ONUC colleagues. The peacekeeping officers looked at one another. Would the chaos in the Congo never end?

In Leopoldville Prime Minister Adoula and General Mobutu, commander of the ANC, publicly demanded that ONUC withdraw its forces. The central government was no longer willing to use ONUC troops for any purpose. The sooner the blue-helmeted troops departed the Congo, the sooner the troubled nation's leaders could, they claimed, get down to pacifying their country with the ANC. And to make matters worse, as 1963 faded Ghana's president Nkrumah wrote to U Thant calling for an all-African UN force to replace ONUC in order to forestall a military coup by Mobutu or Tshombe. Adoula vigorously protested this blatant "interference" in the Congo's internal affairs.

If the central government's leaders were at odds with ONUC, Nkrumah, and what appeared to be the world at large, they were slow to recognize that the Kwilu uprising had firmly pulled the Congo into the East-West conflict.

What Stig first determined to be a slowly forming pattern quickly took on a new dimension. His reports in October and November described attacks by *jeunesse*. It was all reminiscent of the Balubakat *jeunesse* violence in Katanga in 1960 and 1961. In December his secret reports to ONUC described the *jeunesse* as "partisans." The clues to a new outbreak of violence finally pointed to the establishment of a well-led rebel movement that was anti-Central Government and anti-ONUC.

It was against everything and anything that stood for law and order. It was also pro-communist! Once again the troubled Congo was a cold war cockpit. Only this time the leftist elements were led by well-trained revolutionaries headed by Pierre Mulele, former minister of education in Patrice Lumumba's government.

"Who is Mulele?" ONUC headquarters asked its intelligence officers when the final form of the revolt took shape and size. Mulele, a Communist since 1959, had fled Leopoldville after Lumumba was toppled from power. He joined the leftwing government of Antoine Gizenga in Orientale Province as the Stanleyville leader's envoy in Cairo where the Egyptians presumably were holding a five million dollar gold cache and tons of arms in safekeeping. Once Gizenga's government fell Mulele went on to Peking where he spent eighteen months studying guerrilla warfare under the tutelage of the men who helped Mao Tse-tung write his widely discussed "wars of liberation" theories. Africa was ripe for guerrilla warfare and Red China was quick to grasp any opportunity to get a foothold on the dark continent.

Mulele returned to the Congo during the summer of 1963 and for nearly six months was left alone as he recruited and trained his *jeunesse* partisans into a formidable force of nearly ten thousand warriors who were not exhorted to violence by the tenets of Marx, Lenin, or Mao Tse-tung, but by witch doctors in the employ of the Reds.

In early 1964, the prospect of withdrawal of ONUC, scheduled for June 30, hung over the Congo like an oppressive cloud. An emergency was proclaimed by the Central Government which referred to the "Muleliste" rebellion. Stig reported that the ANC garrisons, which had replaced ONUC peacekeeping troops, could not be counted on to withstand attacks by the Muleliste *jeunesse*. And caught in the middle of this chaos which now was taking on a new dimension were the European and American missionaries and their Congolese converts and followers.

The stench of death hung everywhere over Kwilu Province and the columns of thick black smoke that lazily floated skyward from burning religious missions cast an appalling black shadow across the bush country. To add to the confusion, the Communist-oriented rebellion spread to Kivu Province where Anicet Kashamura, Lumumba's former minister of propaganda, challenged the authority of the Leopoldville Government by his attempt to establish a leftwing regime leaning toward Peking.

There were now slightly less than five thousand ONUC troops remaining in the Congo, not enough to maintain law and order in the light of a carefully planned guerrilla campaign. The orders issued by ONUC headquarters to Stig were now of a humanitarian nature. He was assigned to rescue operations and his first important mission was called Jadex One which brought together a team of hard-hitting, hard-shooting, fast-moving blue-helmets from six countries who rescued 106 missionaries of seven nations. The rescue team, commanded by Lt. Col. Paul Mayer, a Canadian Army officer, included Stig as second-in-command, two helicopters and an Otter light reconnaissance aircraft piloted by a huge black-bearded Viking named Thorwald Lars ("Larser") Glantz, often called the Mad Swede by those who had the nerve to fly with him a second time.

For ten perilous days the Jadex One rescue team covered most of Kwilu Province, tangling almost daily with the Mulele *jeunesse* who began to call themselves "partisans" at the suggestion of Mulele himself. The partisans, mainly teen-agers recruited from the bush country and fed with a combination of Marx, Mao, and jungle magic, burned their way through the province, killing and destroying the Catholic and Protestant missions that had taken years to build.

Once reports began arriving in Leopoldville that the partisans were running amuck, the U.S., Canadian, Italian, Belgian, Netherlands, and Swiss embassies requested ONUC to do something about it. The United States ambassador ordered two U. S. Army officers who were pilots and a sergeant to assist ONUC with the embassy's smallest aircraft, a single engine L-20. The first rescue of three fathers from a Catholic mission came off without a hitch. But three days later another rescue operation kicked off a small battle between the partisans on the ground and the ONUC force in the air.

The Catholic mission at Kandale was located about six miles from an American Protestant mission that the two ONUC helicopters had evacuated. Lt. Col. Mayer, flying in the same helicopter with Stig, ordered the pilot to pass over the Catholic mission for one final reconnaissance. The Sikorsky made one pass and then lowered to nearly ground level beside one of the mission buildings. Stig pointed to Mayer to look through the window of the building. Two nuns were struggling and it was obvious they were being prevented from running out. The pilot was ordered to land and the copilot, a submachine gun in his hand, ran out just as a mob of painted partisans burst from their hiding places in the brush and from the far side of one of the mission buildings.

Overhead, Lt. Glantz pushed forward on the stick and aimed the Otter at the charging mob, coming down man-high along the field in an effort to frighten or scatter the partisans. They neither scared nor scattered. Arrows whooshed at the Otter and spears and war clubs were hurled into the air at the oncoming high-winged aircraft, some of them bouncing off the plane's metal skin. The Nigerian soldier in Stig's helicopter fired out the open compartment door at the attacking Mulelists and the copilot on the ground triggered off short bursts. The nuns broke away from their captors and ran from the building toward the helicopter loaded with people from the American mission.

"Hold your fire!" Stig shouted to the copilot and the Nigerian soldier. "You're likely to hit the nuns!" He jumped to the ground. Aided by the many outstretched hands from the men standing braced in the copter's wide open door assisted the sisters into the chopper. The copilot ducked beneath the slowly revolving rotor blades and ran to his side of the cockpit, clambering inside just as Lt. Peter Karlsen, a Norwegian, hit the throttle hard and lifted the now overloaded helicopter into the air. As the helicopter slowly beat its way back to the town the rescuers were using as a headquarters, Stig spotted two men in white cassocks. The sisters told him they were two priests who surely would be killed if they were not rescued.

"Please, please, rescue them," they pleaded with Stig who tried to calm the women. There was no sense trying to talk with them in their hysteria, with the engine of the Sikorsky erasing any possibility of talk. When they landed at their temporary base at Tchikapa, Stig assured the nuns that he would indeed return to the mission to rescue the fathers. With Colonel Mayer's permission he ordered the two helicopters refueled, and he huddled with the pilots, the Nigerian soldier and Sgt. Leonce Lessard, the Canadian noncom who served as Mayer's assistant.

Stig told the men they would probably have to fight their way into the mission to rescue the two priests. "If they are still alive," he added softly. "Let's take plenty of ammunition and grenades. We may need all of this firepower." The Sikorskys took off again and headed back to the mission. When they sighted the mission cathedral's spire, Lt. Karlsen dropped to treetop level in an effort to come in low with as little warning as possible and surprise the partisans if any were still there. They were there, indeed, and what Stig observed was a page out of Mao Tse-tung's handbook on the kind of guerrilla warfare then practiced in South Vietnam.

Partisans were scattered all across the soccer field, frantically digging holes to prevent any aircraft from landing and also sticking sharpened stakes into the ground high enough to puncture the low slung fuel tanks of any helicopter that dared to land.

Lt. Karlsen made a pass over the field in an effort to spot any clearing where he might be able to set down. Stig waved to the partisans in a gesture of friendship. After all, it was better to land without being shot at. He was encouraged when some of them waved back, but as the Sikorsky lowered to a small clearing spotted by the pilot a cloud of arrows were unstrung from bows and clattered against the settling helicopter. The Sikorsky touched down and rolled a few feet bouncing slightly until it suddenly tipped where a wheel had dropped into one of the freshly dug holes that had escaped the sharp eyes of both Karlsen and Warrant Officer Bo Lehman, his Swedish co-pilot.

The Norwegian pilot gunned the engine and succeeded in gaining enough lift to pull the Sikorsky up and away while Stig, the Nigerian soldier and Sgt. Lessard opened fire. It was close, too close, Stig thought. He had two ammo magazines for his submachine gun—seventy-two bullets—and a holstered pistol to fight it out on the ground and still save one final pistol shot for himself. He shuddered when he thought of what might happen to him if he were taken alive.

In the center of the field were the two fathers, guarded like two staked-out animals waiting for a lion whom the hunters wished to kill. They still had to be rescued. Colonel Mayer's helicopter which had been circling overhead dipped toward the ground and Karlsen followed. Submachine guns opened up against the Mulelists while Stig, Sgt. Lessard and the Nigerian quickly pulled the pins from grenades and dropped them on the partisans chasing on the ground below. The grenades exploded with dull crumps, killing and wounding the excited Congolese on the field.

However, it was like throwing rotten eggs. Nothing happened. Men fell to the ground and others appeared out of nowhere to take their places. Stig snapped the safety off his Karl Gustaf and squeezed the trigger in short bursts as the helicopter headed toward where the two fathers were standing under guard. An arrow glanced off Stig's submachine gun. Another fell in the cabin and struck Stig's shoe where, spent in flight, it lodged itself in the toe. A third arrow struck the Nigerian soldier in the arm and he painfully yelped once but continued shooting.

Karlsen set his Sikorsky down and Stig jumped out followed by Sgt. Lessard. Dodging arrows and spears, they crouched low as they ran triggering off short bursts of fire until they reached the priests, shoved them in the direction of the helicopters and then roughly pushed them aboard while Colonel Mayer's helicopter remained overhead with the rescue mission's commander and his Nigerian soldier pouring out a curtain of covering fire. It was no time for the niceties or respect for the cloth—only a matter of saving lives—the fathers' and those of the helicopter's rescue crew.

The days blended together and Jadex One rushed toward its conclusion while the exhausted rescue team continued to court death at the hands of the marauding partisans. They were, indeed, receptive students of Mao Tse-tung's guerrilla principles of warfare as taught by his Congolese disciple, Pierre Mulele.

24

Rescue and recognition

JADEX ONE still had three days to go as February 1, 1964, rolled around. Nearly every mission in Kwilu Province had been evacuated. The ONUC rescuers continued to be exposed to the dangerous Communist-led partisans and they learned more about Pierre Mulele. The wily Congolese, a member of the Bapende tribe, relied on his Red Chinese guerrilla training and jungle hocus-pocus to inflame his *jeunesse* partisans.

"You are invincible," he screamed to his warriors. "The bullets of *les Onusiens* or your other enemies cannot kill you. They will turn to water. See!"

One of his henchmen would suddenly aim a rifle at Mulele and squeeze the trigger. The explosion would shock the young rebels watching the show and they would gasp in amazement when Mulele continued standing, smiling in self-satisfaction. Of course, he had planned well. A blank round was enough to convince his impressive followers that here stood a god in league with the most powerful of witch doctors and all of the spirits that infested the jungle and savanna.

"If you believe in Mulele," the witch doctors in the Communist leader's entourage chanted, "no danger will befall you. If you don't believe, you will die!"

Mulele and his witch doctors, in the pay of their present highest bidder for primitive services rendered, easily explained away the deaths and wounds of rebel warriors who fell before the guns and grenades of the ONUC rescue teams.

Simply stated, the casualties were "unbelievers." This was about as simple an explanation of death in this jungle war as any ever devised by guerrilla experts in Peking.

The Belgian mission at Kisandji finally remained to be evacuated. Eight Italian nuns, their priest, and an undetermined number of Congolese nuns reportedly were held prisoner by a band of six hundred partisans. Five helicopters were assigned to the mission by Colonel Mayer. The ANC's small air force manned by anti-Castro Cubans and American civilian pilots in the pay of the U. S. Central Intelligence Agency furnished two low-winged, propeller-driven T-28 fighter bombers. The U. S. military attaché, Major Harold D. Asbury, piloted the U. S. embassy plane reconnaissance flights during the rescue operation. The heavily armed T-28's were to be used for fire support.

Each of the helicopters carried two or three heavily armed Nigerians. Stig and Sgt. Lessard each rode in the two lead copters; they would touch down first. Hovering over the mission, the ONUC rescuers couldn't help but spot heavily armed bands of partisans.

"Dammit," Stig muttered to himself. He spotted rifles among the milling warriors. Stig's helicopter settled to the ground and he jumped out shooting at the same time that arrows and spears were loosed in his direction. A Cuban pilot, who had been circling overhead, leaned against the stick and his T-28 thundered in a steep dive as he directed the fighter-bomber at one of the massed groups of rebels. Flame blinked from his machine guns and tracer sizzled toward the partisans who scattered when the massive outpouring of hot lead struck among them, toppling warriors like ten pins.

Lessard's helicopter touched down beside Stig's. Seven of

the eight sisters and their priest, who had been standing in the clearing as bait, were hustled to the helicopters. The eighth sister was lying ill on a stretcher. Lessard ran to her and singlehandedly lifted the stretcher and its burden and stumbled back to his helicopter while the two Nigerian soldiers aboard covered him with rifle fire. The partisans noisily surged forward. They were determined to capture at least one helicopter filled with the hated *les Onusiens.* It was apparent to the ONUC officers flying this particular rescue operation that the rebels were out to capture the rescuers and their weapons.

From out of nowhere four painted, skin-clad rebels hurled themselves on the brawny French Canadian sergeant without realizing until too late that they were tangling with a wildcat. The Nigerians couldn't shoot without fear of hitting the nun and when Lessard finally reached the open helicopter they pulled the sister aboard. Lessard's iron fists hammered at the warriors who were in too close to use their deadly *panga* knives or spears.

"Take off!" he cried out and with a last desperate flurry of blows he grabbed for the helicopter just as the pilot gunned the engine jerking the Sikorsky upward with Lessard pulling himself into the cabin. The rescue was completed.

Jadex One had ended and in an official letter of commendation to the ONUC Force Commander, Colonel Mayer commended Stig for heroism and reported how Captain von Bayer "on his own initiative . . . displayed extreme bravery in rescuing people under both arrow and rifle fire . . . without regard for flying arrows, spears and bullets, led them to safety."

Operation Strawberry, another in the series of rescue missions, quickly followed on the heels of Jadex One. The Mulelist revolt began to spread to Kivu Province and it appeared to Stig that as time ran out for ONUC's peacekeeping mission in the Congo, the final months would be spent in a new type of military operation combining rescues and a serious guerrilla war that would make the events that occurred in Katanga during ONUC's first two and a half years look like child's play.

The rescued missionaries were grateful to Stig and his comrades, but there were moments when he wondered what kind of people were these men and women who lived and worked in the bush in an effort to bring Christianity to the tribesmen. Stig never considered himself a religious person and never equated his humanitarian duties for ONUC with any religious belief. He simply considered himself a peacekeeper fighting beneath a banner which represented a world unity desired by nations and men of good will.

During his rescue flights he had been shot at and nearly killed time and again. The constant danger and fighting was beginning to wear on his nerves. The Mulelist partisans began to launch probing attacks against Kikwit which Stig and his chief pilot, Peter Karlsen, were using as a base of operations. They were headquartered at an American mission and its director finally took exception to the presence of both ONUC officers. Stig and Karlsen were astonished at this treatment. The Swedish officer and his Danish pilot quickly composed an undiplomatically indignant telegram and sent it off to ONUC headquarters in Leopoldville. It read in part:

> FROM VON BAYER KARLSEN. WE ARE MOST ASTONISHED TO LEARN THAT AMERICAN BAPTIST MISSION ARE CHARGING US FOR OUR STAYING AT THE MISSION. SUGGEST WE SHOULD CHARGE THE MISSION FOR RECCE [RECONNAISSANCE], RESCUE FLIGHTS AND OTHER ASSISTANCE MADE UNTIL NOW.

A few days later Stig received his reply. A message that had been received by Secretary General U Thant on March 15, 1964—two days after the two ONUC officers complained about the mission's treatment—and forwarded to UN headquarters in Leopoldville. It read in part:

> . . . MY CONCERN WAS ESPECIALLY GREAT BECAUSE THE LIVES OF A NUMBER OF MY COUNTRYMEN WERE ENDANGERED. NOW, WE CAN TAKE SATISFACTION THAT SO MANY OF THE FOREIGN RESIDENTS HAVE BEEN BROUGHT TO SAFETY.
>
> . . . I AM TOLD THAT THE PERSONNEL OF THE UNITED NATIONS MILITARY FORCES IN THE CONGO WHO EFFECTED THE RESCUE WORKED UNDER EXCEPTIONALLY DIFFICULT AND DANGEROUS CIR-

CUMSTANCES. THIS WELL EXECUTED AIR EVACUATION OPERATION MERITS THE WORLD'S ATTENTION AND PRAISE.

WOULD YOU CONVEY MY WARM PERSONAL GRATITUDE, AS WELL AS THE HIGHEST APPRECIATION OF MY GOVERNMENT, TO ALL THOSE RESPONSIBLE FOR THIS OPERATION. IN PARTICULAR, I WOULD LIKE TO COMMEND THE EXTRAORDINARY COURAGE, PERSEVERANCE AND DEVOTION TO DUTY. . . .

Among the thirteen names listed in the message were those of Stig and Peter Karlsen. The message was signed by President Lyndon B. Johnson. The two-man ONUC rescue team knew that there were some Americans who appreciated their efforts and the UN military presence.

25

From Congo to Cyprus

THE UNITED NATIONS presence in the Congo came to an end exactly four years to the day that Dr. Ralph Bunche, representing Secretary General Dag Hammarskjold, heartily applauded the establishment of what was on June 30, 1960, the world's newest nation and fledgling member of the United Nations. On June 30, 1964, the last small detachments of ONUC boarded aircraft for the return flight to their homelands. Among the last Swedish soldiers who had served in the international peacekeeping force was Captain Stig Erik Otto von Bayer.

With mixed emotions, Stig boarded the aircraft that would take him back to his country. He would return to Sweden with the unique distinction of having been the only one, of more than ninety-three thousand men from thirty-five foreign nations, who while fighting to maintain peace in the Congo had served the longest duty tour in that troubled country.

When he said his final farewells to Congolese friends and ONUC staff officers from other nations, he had packed away in his bags personal papers that included any number of citations for his bravery and heroism, and devotion and outstanding service as a United Nations peacekeeper.

He had received Sweden's Vasa Medal in gold, one of his country's highest military decorations, for gallantry in action. He had been awarded Belgium's Medaille de la Reconnaissance and he had been cited by the President of the United States.

If any one of *les Onusiens* stood out as a shining example of the perfect international peacekeeper, Stig was probably that man as ONUC closed its four-year-old headquarters for the last time. His military service in the Congo had not gone unnoticed at United Nations headquarters in New York. His name, signed to many important military reports that circulated in the rarified atmosphere of the Secretary General's office, had caught the attention of the men who served on the UN's small military advisory staff as well as their civilian superiors. Stig von Bayer was personally known to all of the Secretariat headquarters staff who had visited or served in the Congo at one time or another.

When the UN's Congo operation finally folded Stig had carved out a niche. He was a professional officer in the Swedish army; he had seen combat service; he was a hero and, above all, he was young and clearly an officer on the way up. All he had to do was attend the staff schools, serve with the troops in the field and the promotions would naturally follow. It was the same in all armies.

However, the Congo had been a soul-searching experience for Stig. He had left for duty in the land of his youth more out of a quest for adventure than out of any deep-rooted idealism. During his four years in the Congo he had matured. Nor was he alone. Many other professional soldiers of Stig's generation from among the peacekeeping force had also undergone a similar change.

They had seen 126 of their comrades killed in action, 75 in accidents and 34 die from "natural" causes induced by the harsh and primitive living conditions in the Congo. They had seen death and disorder at its ugliest. Like Stig, they asked themselves if it all was worth the candle.

Many of them openly and often idealistically—and unrealistically—debated the merits of a permanent peacekeeping military force in which they could serve in other Congos. Of course, they agreed, no duty could be as rough as military service in the Congo. These people were savages, they declared, and what could ONUC troops expect other than savage violence and vituperation from the people they had tried to protect and help.

From the beginning of 1964, when ONUC began closing up shop, on the one hand, and rescuing missionaries while fighting a new force of evil, on the other hand, another trouble spot on the globe demanded United Nations action. Trouble was flaring up in the historic island of Cyprus located in the heart of the ancient world in the eastern Mediterranean. Throughout the millennia of recorded history this strategically located island stepping stone had attracted a succession of foreigners—colonists, merchants, and invaders. Greeks and Phoenicians settled there long before the Christian era, and waves of conquerors—Egyptian, Assyrian, Persian, and Roman—came and went. In 1191 King Richard Coeur de Lion (The Lion Hearted) of England led his knights to the Holy Land during the Third Crusade and stopped off at Cyprus on his journey, setting up a Frankish dynasty that lasted until the Venetian navy finally conquered the island. A century later, in 1571, the Ottoman Empire, wrested control from the Kingdom of Venice and subdued the predominantly Greek islanders. Not until 1878 did Britain re-enter Cypriote history. By then the enmity of Greeks and Turks on the island had been forged in the crucible of terror, turmoil, and time.

The Sultan of Turkey in exchange for help in averting Russian aggression agreed to let Britain occupy and administer Cyprus. This mutually satisfactory arrangement lasted until World War I when Turkey sided with Germany against the Allies and Britain promptly annexed the island which, in 1925, became a crown colony—a status that lasted until the independence of Cyprus in 1960.

Cyprus, an island touched by the Western world's earliest civilization, was—and still is—torn in bloody hatred between Greek and Turk. In the late 1950's Britain fought a losing battle as nationalistic Greek terrorists fought to wrest the island from the United Kingdom. At the core of this problem was the Cypriote desire for one of two things—*enosis* (annexation of Cyprus by Greece) or complete independence with the 77 per cent Greek majority of half a million people prevailing over the 23 per cent Turkish population.

Independence for Cyprus resulted in an unworkable constitution patched together by Britain, Greece, and Turkey as the guarantor powers. Each sought advantages; each received them. Britain retained its military bases in exchange for giving up its most troublesome colony. Greece gave up *enosis* and therefore dampened its serious friction with neighboring Turkey. Turkey dropped its demand for *taksim* (partition of the island) with the constitution's assurance for the safety of the minority population.

But generations of bloodletting and the historic hatred between Greeks and Turks that spans centuries is almost as impossible a problem to solve as are the tribal hatreds in the Congo. Nevertheless, a United Nations peacekeeping force was requested by Cyprus President Archbishop Makarios III.

At the very time that Stig was rescuing missionaries in the Congo, the vanguard of seven thousand blue-helmeted troops from ten nations began landing in Cyprus on March 13, 1964, and a new acronym found its place in the United Nations glossary of peacekeeping terms—UNFICYP, for United Nations Forces in Cyprus. Stig didn't know it at the time, but Cyprus was to become his next peacekeeping mission.

Stig's departure for Sweden on June 27, 1964, was followed by a month-long holiday. In late July he reported to his headquarters at Stragnas and was asked if he wanted to join a battalion from his regiment that had been sent to Cyprus to join the UN peacekeeping force.

"There's a little shooting now going on there, captain," the regimental adjutant advised with a wink. "However, I'm sure that it won't be as rough as the Congo. The people on Cyprus are *civilized.*"

He was, of course, referring to the European background of the Greeks and the civilized traditions that he assumed the Greek Cypriotes followed. "Remember, captain," he chuckled, "the travel agents call this the island of love."

Stig had heard all about this so-called island of love. He knew of the legends about Aphrodite, goddess of love, who was born in the foam of the sea where the blue Mediterranean touches the island's sandy beaches. During the few days he had left before flying off to the troubled island, he naturally did what any good intelligence officer would do: he did some reading and studied both classified official and unofficial documents.

Cyprus, Greek by history and tradition, is the third largest island in the Mediterranean and forty miles from the southwestern shore of Turkey. However, peace has been elusive because of the ingrained dislike of the Greeks and the Turks for one another. It was a combination of two things, two cultures and two religions that successfully kept the majority and minority populations apart for hundreds of years.

Stig knew that when fighting broke out again in late 1963 between the Greek and Turkish Cypriotes, the British had moved troops from their base at Limassol in an effort to keep the peace. In high diplomatic circles the suggestion was made that forces from North Atlantic Treaty countries should be sent in to maintain law and order and keep the warring factions apart. However, Archbishop Makarios, the island's bearded president, a man of the Greek majority's Orthodox Christian faith, took the position that Cyprus was not a NATO country and therefore should not be policed by NATO troops. He would have nothing less than a United Nations peacekeeping force with an option to keep the blue-helmeted troops present for periods of three months before picking up the next option for a brief period.

At first the British were all alone trying to act as a peacekeeping force with twenty-seven hundred troops from its base on the island. Then the UN passed a resolution during the first week of March, 1964, for a seven thousand-man UNFICYP peacekeeping force. There was one final decision lacking, however. No agreement could be reached on which countries would furnish troops, and there the matter stalled until warfare in mid-March broke out in the town of Ktima on the southwest coast which brought the smouldering hatred of six thousand Greeks and three thousand Turks to a fresh and bloody explosion.

On a morning when the market place was crowded the Turks allegedly opened fire on Greeks. Armed Turks came pouring from their houses shooting indiscriminately as they ran through the streets. An armored bulldozer driven by a Turk came out of hiding and clanked through the streets followed by heavily armed Turkish Cypriotes who began rounding up their enemies. Six Greeks were killed in the first outburst of shooting. The British hurried to the scene just in time to release three hundred Greek prisoners, before mayhem was committed, and then arrange for a temporary cease-fire. But the following morning the Greeks struck back in an all-out offensive. Small arms and mortar fire poured into the Turkish section of the city and the Turks fought back from streets filled with rubble as burning buildings collapsed.

The Cypriote Army blocked off all roads leading into the small town and refused to permit British peacekeeping troops to enter. After a bloody twelve-hour battle the Turks surrendered to the Greeks. Both sides had lost a total of eighty-six killed and wounded. The savagery and scale of fighting forced the UN to make a speedy decision for providing a peacekeeping force. Canada and Sweden immediately sent advance detachments, until a total of seven thousand men representing the armed forces of Austria, Denmark, Finland, Ireland, New Zealand, Australia, and India had joined Britain, Sweden, and Canada.

U.S. Army Photograph

U.N. ceremonies at Pusan, Korea.

U.S. Army Photograph

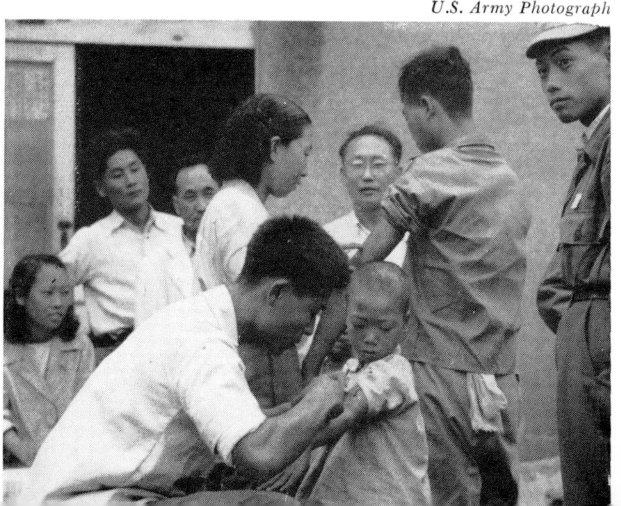

U.N. personnel vaccinating civilians at Pusan.

U.S. Army Photograph

Gen. MacArthur at the Capitol Building, Seoul.

U.S. Army Photograph

The Mayor of Pusan on the 8th Anniversary of the U.N.

Photo from European

U.N. military police patrolling Panmunjom peace negotiations site.

U.N. peace negotiator, Arthur H. Dean, leaving negotiating session.

Wide World Photos

P.I.P.

Indian paratroopers serving under U.N. flag in Port Said.

P.I.P.

U.N. soldier on the one yard deep border between the Gaza Strip and Israel.

Danish troops boarding plane for U.N. service in Cyprus.

U.S. Air Force Photo

Danish vehicle arrives in Cyprus for U.N. service.

U.S. Air Force Photo

P.I.P.

Off-duty.

U.S. Air Force Photo

Taps for Finnish peace-keeping soldier.

U.S. Air Force Photo

U.N. Ghanian troops in the Congo.

P.I.P.

Maintaining peace in Cyprus.

U.N. soldier on guard duty.

P.I.P.

P.I.P. (next page)

Photo from European

Ghana troops in U.N. blue helmets keeping the peace in the Congo.

Photo from European

U.N. Madras Indian troops in the Congo.

Photo from European

Capturing white mercenaries.

Indian soldiers removing explosives.

Photo from European

U.S. Air Force Photo

Mission to rescue hostages in Stanleyville.

U.N. troops at Leopoldville holding back agents provocateurs.

Photo from European

On the day that Stig returned the background report on the Cyprus situation to his regimental adjutant and picked up his travel orders, the administrative officer asked the young captain what he now thought of the new peacekeeping assignment.

"It's not much different from the Congo," Stig laughed. "In Africa we had two hundred tribes to contend with; in Cyprus there are only two—Greeks and Turks." He bade the adjutant farewell. The cause of peace awaited the arrival of Capt. Stig von Bayer.

The transport in which Stig flew to Cyprus circled Nicosia Airport once, as if the pilot had to make sure that fighting was not taking place on the runways, and then landed to disgorge its passengers. It was old home week for Stig, when he reported to UNFICYP headquarters near the airport. He felt good at seeing so many familiar faces. Colonel Waern, his commander in the Congo was present along with officers from Ireland, Denmark, and Canada, whom he had known in the Congo. They warmly greeted the young Swede.

"How come you're here?" they asked each other.

"Well, somebody had to keep the peace," was the stock reply. Each man knew that the other had volunteered for UNFICYP as soon as his respective country offered to provide military personnel. For Stig it was a warm feeling, not so much a reunion with former comrades but a sudden awareness that he was, indeed, serving a just cause in the company of giants.

Shortly after his arrival shooting broke out on the northwest coast of the island. Greek Cypriotes reported that Turks were preparing a beachhead to receive troops from Turkey. They attacked and in the ensuing violence more deaths were added to the already frightening toll. The UNFICYP command dispatched a battalion of troops into the area to halt the fighting. Meanwhile, as assistant intelligence officer for the Swedish Battalion, Stig learned that if a beachhead really was being set up by the Turks, the Greeks already had established theirs and secretly unloaded an unusually large amount of weapons and ammunition—including artillery—from small boats that had come from Greece and Egypt. The arms shipments were transported to hiding places in the mountains.

Cyprus was unlike Africa in one respect: the United Nations military force specifically was not involved in the fighting between both sides but wherever and whenever appropriate was to inject itself between combatants and attempt to talk them into a cease-fire. From his headquarters in Xeros one day Stig watched Turkish jet fighters bomb Greek Cypriote positions along the coastal area and sink a Cypriote gunboat. The situation was indeed explosive and Stig joined several UNFICYP patrols in an effort to learn more about the situation from a field trip rather than try to cope with it from behind a desk.

Cyprus, so it appeared to Stig and his comrades in arms, was a country that ran straight up and down despite its relatively small area of thirty-five hundred square mile. The top of every hill and mountain, large or small, was a potential Greek or Turkish outpost. The peaks manned by armed men of each side either had a Greek or Turkish national flag fluttering from a pole; rarely did the Cypriote national flag make an appearance although the island nation's bearded leader, whom the British referred to as "Black Mac," made several half-hearted attempts to bring the fighting to a halt.

It was obvious to Stig what had to be done by UNFICYP troops. They had to claim the empty peaks, deploy throughout the valleys, and set up fortified observation outposts. It was a dangerous approach. Rarely were the empty mountain and hilltops higher than those nearby on which Greeks or Turks were dug in. More often than not they were located squarely between the combatants of both sides. It was a ticklish position for the UN peacekeepers to be in, but the most effective. Soon a third banner joined the Greek and Turkish national flags. The blue and white United Nations flag, its insignia of two olive branches of peace embracing the globe, took its rightful place on the island of love that in reality was one of deep, dark, and violent hatred.

On one mission Stig had led a patrol deep inside the Greek

lines. He began marking his map and radioing information to his battalion headquarters about the location of armed and fortified strongpoints, when his detachment was spotted by the Greeks and a group of angry heavily armed men quickly surrounded the Swedes. One of the Greek Cypriotes, obviously an officer, was fuming behind his heavy jet black mustache. Fire literally flashed from angry eyes. As far as he and his men were concerned, the United Nations soldiers were not welcome visitors. In fact, they were "spies and should be shot," he angrily growled. He ordered the Swedish soldiers to write their names on a pad of paper that he proferred. "None of your damned business," they scribbled in Swedish and with poker-stiff features solemnly handed the paper pad back to the captain.

Stig, who had been a short distance away observing the area through binoculars, returned to where the swarthy Greek officer was berating the Swedish soldiers.

"What the hell do you think you are doing!" the Cypriote exclaimed to Stig in English, the common *lingua franca* of the island. "We shoot spies!"

Stig sized up the man. Obviously, if he could get him to cool off they could discuss the UN's peacekeeping mission in civilized terms. "If there's any civilization on this island at all," he remarked to himself.

The Swedish intelligence officer had just returned from a rough climb. He wasn't used to traveling up and down the island's steep heights. Stig sat down on a rock, fanning himself with the folded map he was holding in one hand.

"Please, don't talk for a few minutes," the UNFICYP intelligence officer replied. "I have to relax. These mountains are killing me. I can't speak when I'm so tired."

"The Cypriote officer quieted down for a moment or two and then once again began to berate Stig.

"Please, please, I'd like to have a cigarette," the Swedish officer said. "Then we can discuss this more calmly if we are relaxed. Have one?"

Stig pulled a pack of Pall Malls from his breast pocket. He gained time by slowly and deliberately making a production out of his normal smoking habit. The long, slender hand-carved ivory cigarette holder was methodically pulled from a pocket. The cigarette was tapped and inserted in the holder. Stig pulled out the Zippo emblazoned with his regimental crest and leaned toward the Greek, thumbing a flame and offering a light. Then Stig lit his own cigarette, inhaled and exhaled slowly, so very slowly, before he looked directly at the Greek Cypriote officer.

"Now that I feel better, we can talk," Stig finally broke the silence. It was a one-sided conversation. If the Greek officer wondered how much Stig had learned about the sector under his command, he quickly found out as the Swedish intelligence officer diplomatically and unexpectedly praised his opposite number. He told the Greek that he had done an excellent job of camouflaging his positions.

"In fact, I have never seen anything better, even in the Congo," Stig grudgingly admitted. The Greek's hard, swarthy features began to soften. Then the Swedish officer pointed to other positions that he said could stand a bit more camouflage. It was obvious to the Greek captain that the slim Swedish officer was an unusual person. By the time they had spent half an hour together, with Stig doing most of the talking, the Greek's violent temper had cooled off. In fact, they became friends. Stig learned that the Cypriote spoke French. The Greek, happy to have found somebody with whom he could converse in the language of the diplomats, invited his Swedish opposite number to have dinner at his camp. It was an extremely unusual invitation because the United Nations peacekeepers were considered interlopers by both the Greek and Turk hotheads on the island.

As Stig moved about the island on his inspection tours and peace patrols, he soon discovered that somehow or other the Greek forces had been able to smuggle in tanks and ground-to-air anti-aircraft missiles along with other heavy weapons and vehicles all bearing a made-in-Russia trademark. It soon wasn't that much of a military secret.

"Black Mac is playing with fire," the peacekeeping troops

remarked among themselves. Whether or not the bearded, black-garbed cleric who was Cyprus's chief of state realized the implications of this dangerous association with the Kremlin, his willingness to accept Red Army military equipment was not lost on the seven thousand soldiers in the UNIFCYP force. Nor did his flirtation go unnoticed among the Turkish population. Incidents occurred and although they resulted in the loss of very few lives after a flurry of shooting, the presence of the peacekeepers prevented the serious large-scale outbreaks that had occurred before the arrival of UNFICYP.

Stig mingled with Greeks and Turks and finally came to the conclusion that Cyprus was as impossible a situation as the Congo because of the deep hatred of each ethnic group for the other. The radio transcripts that passed across his desk told him how the enmity of the Cypriotes runs deep. "Will you avenge your father's death?" the commercial on Radio Nicosia booms. "Yes," the voice of young Christos replies, "when I grow up I will bring you the heads of six Turks."

Stig finally departed from Cyprus in April 1965 for a new military assignment in Sweden, convinced from personal experience a permanent United Nations peacekeeping force is a must. He couldn't help but notice as he boarded the aircraft that would fly him back to his own country the United Nations banner that fluttered from the staff in front of UNFICYP headquarters. He paused at the transport plane's door and his eyes rested for a few moments on the flag that had been his for nearly five years.

"Perhaps it will be mine to serve again," he thought to himself. His hand came up in a quick salute. A feeling of pride surged within him.

He had served and he had fought—for peace.

26

Beginnings without end

"WHY DOESN'T THE United Nations do something about this?"

This universal question has been asked time and again since World War II ended in 1945. In times of international crisis, when shooting has broken out or when the threat of war stirs the world, thinking people of many nations have posed this question. After all, they reason, the purpose or *raison d'etre* of the United Nations is the prevention of war and the maintenance of peace.

The UN itself is a creature born of conflict and created by those very nations that have suffered the agonies of World War II and by statesmen who lived through two world wars and were determined that the world never again would experience a global conflict. In an effort to prevent war itself they gave teeth to the United Nations by providing in the international organization's Charter a number of articles dedicated to preventing hostilities by the raising of armed forces to keep the peace and oppose aggression.

Since the final ratification on October 24, 1945 of the UN Charter by the original fifty-one nations who became the first members of this family of nations, an extremely large number of men have served beneath the blue and white international banner. Specifically, an impressive total of some 3,859,000 have fought or served—and are now serving—under the United Nations flag.

The armed forces of fifty-three nations have provided men in eleven different situations to either keep the peace or prevent aggression since 1948 when a small detachment of ten observers from ten countries—seven of them wearing the uniforms of their respective military services—were dispatched to Greece during the fighting between Communist guerrillas and the lawful government.

These peacekeepers have carried from nothing more than UN armbands and maps to the very latest in weapons and weapons systems short of nuclear bombs. They have served on peacekeeping missions as small as seven military officers in Greece to as many as 2,323,000 men from twenty-two nations who fought or served beneath the UN flag during the three years of the Korean War.

Since the first observer mission in Greece men in uniform have served the United Nations in disputed Kashmir, Indonesia, Israel, Korea, Gaza Strip, Lebanon, Congo, West Irian, Yemen, and Cyprus. During the seventeen years since 1948, and the twenty years since the founding of the United Nations, a grand total of 3,859,000 have fought and served and are presently serving beneath the United Nations flag flying in Kashmir, Korea, Gaza Strip and Cyprus.

Tens of thousands of men have given their lives fighting beneath the United Nations banner, battling aggression in Korea and serving as peacekeepers in remote places like the Gaza Strip, the Congo, and Cyprus.

If the United Nations has fielded nearly four million soldiers it certainly has set the precedent for establishing and maintaining a permanent peacekeeping force in which idealistic peacekeepers like Captain Stig von Bayer would volunteer to serve. Unfortunately, the realities of international politics do not serve the cause of a permanent UN military force. When member nations refuse to pay for peacekeeping forces that were voted into existence by the majority, the UN's military power is hamstrung and virtually useless. The peacekeeping forces, usually drawn from the smaller nations which have no axe to grind nor a grand design affecting the status quo, have kept the peace during the first twenty years of the UN's hectic life.

Compared to the League of Nations, which died before it even reached the age of twenty, the record shows that the United Nations has become a standing diplomatic conference and town hall of international politics in this modern, complex world. Many of the UN's member nations would be fighting today if there was no forum to air disagreements. The record shows, time and again, that UN military forces or observers have helped preserve the peace, after it was broken, eleven times in the past score of years. Men called to the UN's blue and white colors have assisted nations unable to act alone. As a result, the United Nations has not died and will undoubtedly survive during this era of changing national alignments.

Today's United Nations undoubtedly is in a crisis and, therefore, has been made virtually useless as a peacekeeping organization because France and the Soviet Union refuse to support past peacekeeping missions; paying their share of the battles that were "avoided" by troops in blue helmets and blue berets.

The United Nations is not a world government but an organization of governments participating by consent. A good number of nations believe in the UN and what it stands for. In the twentieth century the UN stands for peace; it has to. "We have the power," stated the late President John F. Kennedy a few months before he was assassinated, "to make this the best generation in the history of mankind—or to make it the last."

Unfortunately, member nations are not yet willing to unquestionably hand over to UN authority the power required to organize the permanent peacekeeping force that many idealists have discussed time and again. On the other hand, a nation under attack by another country or threatened either by an attack or from violently disrupted forces from within acting on instructions from without usually will seek military aid from the United Nations. Again, unfortunately, the UN's peacekeeping machinery can only function as fast as the member states wish. Within days after chaos broke out in the Congo and UN military assistance was requested, the first detachments of peacekeeping troops had been landed in this troubled Central African nation. Early peacekeeping operations required more time. Later ones have gotten underway within twenty-four hours. Future ones can be organized within hours if the UN's member states vote for a United Nations peacekeeping force to be deployed immediately by air to a particular nation at the troubled country's request.

When violence threatened in Cyprus and two NATO allies, Greece and Turkey, were faced with a confrontation over the fighting between Cypriotes of Greek or Turkish extraction, the lawful government of the eastern Mediterranean island requested and received UN military aid to keep the protagonists apart. On the other hand, the question is being asked why the UN hasn't done anything in South Vietnam. The lawful government of South Vietnam, although not a member of the United Nations, had not requested an international peacekeeping force because of the military aid being received from the United States. Moreover, if South Vietnam were to ask for UN military aid, the very fact that this request was made would imply that U. S. policy in South Vietnam has failed. The United States, then, is not about to permit South Vietnam to request an international peacekeeping force to take over where Washington has failed.

Meanwhile, an assessment of the Congo peacekeeping operation is still undergoing study at the UN. The military errors made in the Congo by the United Nations peacekeeping force are being studied at great length in an effort to avoid making similar mistakes in the future. The Secretary General's small military advisory staff has presented a number of so-called contingency plans for future peacekeeping operations in some of the more prominent of the world's troublespots. These plans can only encompass particular situations for which less than six thousand peacekeeping troops are initially available.

On the other hand, the more recent UN peacekeeping experiences have given the Secretary General's military staff an insight into the need for adequate and standardized weapons, ammunition, communications, vehicles, operational aircraft, medical facilities, quartermaster supplies, and the use of English as the common language of the next peacekeeping force.

When all is said and done, the United Nations has not yet died. If there is a definite and obvious requirement for another peacekeeping force, there are enough nations who will vote to establish a UN military operation.

The Dominican crisis in the spring of 1965 proved that a United Nations peacekeeping force, if requested and approved, could have landed on the troubled Caribbean island faster than the Latin American regional force representing the Organization of American States. The hasty unilateral United States committment of troops, in what Washington considers its own traditional sphere of influence, was defended on the floor of the United Nations General Assembly against charges of aggression hurled by Communist Cuba and the Soviet Union.

If a request for a United Nations peacekeeping presence on the island had been made, it would first have gone to the Security Council where an all but certain Soviet veto would have passed the problem to the General Assembly under the Uniting for Peace resolution of November 3, 1950. This resolution prevents a Security Council veto from hamstringing collective action that the majority of member nations may deem necessary during an international crisis.

Once a decision had been reached in the General Assembly to send a peacekeeping force to the Dominican Republic (and the delegates to the UN now have a reputation for not deliberating *ad nauseam* during a crisis), a well armed and well trained army of some seventy-five hundred men would have been flown to Santo Domingo. Unknown to the general public, and virtually unreported in any detail, there is a standing composite military force representing twelve members of the

United Nations who have earmarked troops, supplies, equipment and transportation facilities whenever required by the Secretary General upon the approval of either the Security Council or General Assembly.

In the summer of 1963, after five years of quiet discussion and deliberation, the four Scandinavian countries—Denmark, Finland, Norway and Sweden—earmarked five thousand specially trained officers and troops evenly divided into four reinforced battalions. The mission: keeping the peace anywhere and anytime the United Nations needed a peacekeeping force. By mid-1965 eight other nations had gone on record as offering to the Secretary General the military wherewithal to provide a peace force to serve under the United Nations flag.

Canada offered Army, Navy and Air Force support when and if requested. Iran offered a small army detachment for UN peacekeeping service. Italy set up a United Nations contingency group of officers for observer and headquarters staff duties.

Malta has earmarked a small army unit.

Netherlands has a force of three hundred Royal Marines immediately available on twenty-four hours notice with other troops to follow at a later date.

New Zealand is putting together a plan for using its troops for peacekeeping purposes.

United Kingdom has offered support and transport troops for as many as six infantry battalions. If requested, the UK commitment will provide short-range aircraft, engineering and signal troops, ambulance and medical detachments, and ordnance and transport units.

United States long-range transport aircraft and weapons, ammunition, supplies and equipment, and military vehicles have been earmarked for immediate availability.

Undoubtedly, other nations will join this paper army which members of the United Nations fervently hope will never have to be activated. There are those on this rapidly shrinking planet who reject any thought of a permanent United Nations peacekeeping force. There are those who question its need.

There are men of goodwill who are critical of even this paper military force and fervently hope that someday a larger army of peacekeepers will be on standby. "There is, after all," pondered Adlai Stevenson, U. S. ambassador to the UN, in an address in New York to American newspaper publishers on April 22, 1965, "something grotesque, unreal, and nightmarish about a world with 20 million men under arms and a military budget of 120 billion dollars when we can't seem to find 20 thousand men and 120 million dollars for international peacekeeping by the United Nations."

There are nations which have offered thanks to the United Nations for providing a peacekeeping force. Despite the internal strife that actually turned the Congolese against *les Onusiens,* the Democratic Republic of the Congo on September 19, 1964, expressed on behalf of itself and people, "its sincere and profound gratitude for the remarkable efforts made by the United Nations forces to preserve the unity and integrity of the Congo.

"Being unable to meet the danger . . . and placing its trust in the United Nations, the Congolese people appealed to that lofty international body. . . .

"The Congo's appeal did not go unheeded. No sooner was the alarm sounded than troops from both African and European countries poured into the Congo. Animated solely by a desire to defend the Congo's territorial integrity, the United Nations troops moved in wherever their intervention was needed, without a thought for their personal safety. After three years of untiring efforts . . . unremitting struggle and continuous combat, the United Nations forces are withdrawing . . . with the moral satisfaction of a job well done.

"May the Ministry (of Foreign Affairs) be permitted to salute the memory of His Excellency Secretary General Dag Hammarskjold and all the officers and men of the United Nations who gave their lives for the Congolese cause. . . ."

Finally, there are men like Captain Stig Otto Erik von Bayer who take a strictly military view of the practical rather than a so-called realistic political view of the impractical. They believe in the United Nations. They consider it a privilege and honor to have served under a flag other than their own.

They know that twenty thousand men would volunteer immediately to serve in an international peacekeeping force. They are well aware of the huge stocks of arms, equipment and aircraft that are available for such a force. They have discussed and debated and dreamed of a UN task force either based on land or aboard a task force of transports and aircraft carriers at sea, roaming the hemispheres like knights of old, battling the evil war dragons rearing up wherever peaceful men live.

Theirs is a dream; not of battles to be won or lost, but of the peace that must be maintained in order to preserve this planet and all those who live on it. In the words of humorist Ogden Nash, whose verse is seldom bitter:

> When geniuses of every nation
> Hasten us towards obliteration,
> Perhaps it will take the dolts
> and geese
> To drag us backward into peace.*

Appendixes

A: United Nations charter articles pertinent to military peace-keeping measures and forces.

B: Selected United Nations Security Council and General Assembly resolutions covering four different types of peace-keeping and military forces.

B-1: Korea—The United Nations Command (UNC)

B-2: Gaza-Sinai—The United Nations Emergency Force (UNEF)

B-3: Congo—Opération des Nations Unies au Congo (ONUC)

B-4: Cyprus—The United Nations Peace-Keeping Force in Cyprus (UNFICYP)

C: Selected statements and addresses on peace-keeping military forces and problems.

C-1: "Keeping the Peace," an address by Prime Minister Lester B. Pearson delivered as the Dag Hammarskjold Lecture at Carleton University, Ottawa, on May 7, 1964.

C-2: "United Nations Peace Force," an address by United Nations Secretary-General U Thant delivered to the Harvard Alumni Association in Cambridge, Massachusetts on June 13, 1963.

C-3: "United Nations Emergency Force," a summary study of the experience derived from the establishment of UNEF including the "Concluding Observations and Principles" made by United Nations Secretary-General Dag Hammarskjold in UN Document A/3943, October 9, 1958.

D: List of 11 United Nations peace-keeping operations requiring the use of military personnel and armed forces, and the armed forces and/or military personnel involved from the nations listed.

D-1: List of all nations whose troops or military personnel have served under the United Nations flag 1945-1965.

D-2: Cyprus (UNFICYP) 1964-

D-3: Congo (ONUC) 1960-1964

D-4: Yemen (UNYOM) 1962-1963

D-5: Lebanon (UNOGIL) 1958

D-6: Gaza-Sinai (UNEF) 1956-

D-7: West Irian (UNTEA) 1962-1963

D-8: Korea (UNC) 1950-

D-9: Palestine-Israel (UNTSO) 1949-

D-10. Indonesia (UNCI) 1948-1949

D-11: Kashmir (UNMOGIP) 1948-

D-12: Greece (UNSCOB) 1948-1950

Appendix A

United Nations Charter articles pertinent to military peace-keeping measures and forces

ARTICLE 2

4. All Members shall refrain in their international relations from the threat or use of force against the territorial integrity or political independence of any state, or in any other manner inconsistent with the Purposes of the United Nations.

5. All Members shall give the United Nations every assistance in any action it takes in accordance with the present Charter, and shall refrain from giving assistance to any state against which the United Nations is taking preventive or enforcement action.

7. Nothing contained in the present Charter shall authorize the United Nations to intervene in matters which are essentially within the domestic jurisdiction of any state or shall require the Members to submit such matters to settlement under the present Charter; but this principle shall not prejudice the application of enforcement measures under Chapter VII.

ARTICLE 22

The General Assembly may establish such subsidiary organs as it deems necessary for the performance of its functions.

ARTICLE 25

The Members of the United Nations agree to accept and carry out the decisions of the Security Council in accordance with the present Charter.

ARTICLE 27

1. Each member of the Security Council shall have one vote.

2. Decisions of the Security Council on procedural matters shall be made by an affirmative vote of seven members.

3. Decisions of the Security Council on all other matters shall be made by an affirmative vote of seven members including the concurring votes of the permanent members; provided that, in decisions under Chapter VI, and under paragraph 3 of Article 52, a party to a dispute shall abstain from voting.

ARTICLE 29

The Security Council may establish such subsidiary organs as it deems necessary for the performance of its functions.

CHAPTER VII: ACTION WITH RESPECT TO THREATS TO THE PEACE, BREACHES OF THE PEACE, AND ACTS OF AGGRESSION

ARTICLE 39

The Security Council shall determine the existence of any threat to the peace, breach of the peace, or act of aggression and shall make recommendations, or decide what measures shall be taken in accordance with Articles 41 and 42, to maintain or restore international peace and security.

ARTICLE 40

In order to prevent an aggravation of the situation, the Security Council may, before making the recommendations or deciding upon the measures provided for in Article 39, call upon the parties concerned to comply with such provisional measures as it deems necessary or desirable. Such provisional measures shall be without prejudice to the rights, claims, or position of the parties concerned. The Security Council shall duly take account of failure to comply with such provisional measures.

ARTICLE 41

The Security Council may decide what measures not involving the use of armed force are to be employed to give effect to its decisions, and it may call upon the Members of the United Nations to apply such measures. These may include complete or partial interruption of economic relations and of rail, sea, air, postal, telegraphic, radio, and other means of communication, and the severance of diplomatic relations.

ARTICLE 42

Should the Security Council consider that measures provided for in Article 41 would be inadequate or have proved to be inadequate, it may take such action by air, sea, or land forces as may be necessary to maintain or restore international peace and security. Such action may include demonstrations, blockade, and other operations by air, sea, or land forces of Members of the United Nations.

ARTICLE 43

1. All Members of the United Nations, in order to contribute to the maintenance of international peace and security, undertake to make available to the Security Council, on its call and in accordance with a special agreement or agreements, armed forces, assistance, and facilities, including rights of passage, necessary for the purpose of maintaining international peace and security.

2. Such agreement or agreements shall govern the numbers and types of forces, their degree of readiness and general location, and the nature of the facilities and assistance to be provided.

3. The agreement or agreements shall be negotiated as soon as possible on the initiative of the Security Council. They shall be concluded between the Security Council and Members or between the Security Council and groups of Members and shall be subject to ratification by the signatory states in accordance with their respective constitutional processes.

ARTICLE 44

When the Security Council has decided to use force it shall, before calling upon a Member not represented on it to provide armed forces in fulfillment of the obligations assumed under Article 43, invite that Member, if the Member so desires, to participate in the decisions of the Security Council concerning the employment of contingents of that Member's armed forces.

ARTICLE 45

In order to enable the United Nations to take urgent military measures, Members shall hold immediately available national air-force contingents for combined international enforcement action. The strength and degree of readiness of these contingents and plans for their combined action shall be determined, within the limits laid down in the special agreement or agreements referred to in Article 43, by the Security Council with the assistance of the Military Staff Committee.

ARTICLE 46

Plans for the application of armed force shall be made by the Security Council with the assistance of the Military Staff Committee.

ARTICLE 47

1. There shall be established a Military Staff Committee to advise and assist the Security Council on all questions relating to the Security Council's military requirements for the maintenance of international peace and security, the employment and command of forces placed at its disposal, the regulation or armaments, and possible disarmament.

2. The Military Staff Committee shall consist of the Chiefs of Staff of the permanent members of the Security Council or their representatives. Any Member of the United Nations not permanently represented on the Committee shall be invited by the Committee to be associated with it when the efficient discharge of the Committee's responsibilities requires the participation of that Member in its work.

3. The Military Staff Committee shall be responsible under the Security Council for the strategic direction of any armed forces placed at the disposal of the Security Council. Questions relating to the command of such forces shall be worked out subsequently.

4. The Military Staff Committee, with the authorization of the Security Council and after consultation with appropriate regional agencies, may establish regional subcommittees.

ARTICLE 48

1. The action required to carry out the decisions of the Security Council for the maintenance of international peace and security shall be taken by all the Members of the United Nations or by some of them, as the Security Council may determine.

2. Such decisions shall be carried out by the Members of the United Nations directly and through their action in the appropriate international agencies of which they are members.

ARTICLE 49

The Members of the United Nations shall join in affording mutual assistance in carrying out the measures decided upon by the Security Council.

ARTICLE 50

If preventive or enforcement measures against any state are taken by the Security Council, any other state, whether a Member of the United Nations or not, which finds itself confronted with special economic problems arising from the carrying out of those measures shall have the right to consult the Security Council with regard to a solution of those problems.

ARTICLE 51

Nothing in the present Charter shall impair the inherent right of individual or collective self-defense if an armed attack occurs against a Member of the United Nations, until the Security Council has taken measures necessary to maintain international peace and security. Measures taken by Members in the exercise of this right of self-defense shall be immediately reported to the Security Council and shall not in any way affect the authority and responsibility of the Security Council under the present Charter to take at any time such action as it deems necessary in order to maintain or restore international peace and security.

. . . . . .

ARTICLE 99

The Secretary-General may bring to the attention of the Security Council any matter which in his opinion may threaten the maintenance of international peace and security.

Appendix B

Selected United Nations Security Council and General Assembly resolutions covering four different types of peace-keeping and military forces

Appendix B-1

Korea

SECURITY COUNCIL RESOLUTION OF JUNE 25, 1950.

The Security Council,

Recalling the finding of the General Assembly in its resolution of 21 October 1949 that the Government of the Republic of Korea is a lawfully established government "having effective control and jurisdiction over that part of Korea where the United Nations Temporary Commission on Korea was able to observe and consult and in which the great majority of the people of Korea reside; and that this Government is based on elections which were a valid expression of the free will of the electorate of that part of Korea and which were observed by the Temporary Commission; and that this is the only such Government in Korea";

Mindful of the concern expressed by the General Assembly in its resolutions of 12 December 1948 and 21 October 1949 of the consequences which might follow unless Member States refrained from acts derogatory to the results sought to be achieved by the United Nations in bringing about the complete independence and unity of Korea; and the concern expressed that the situation described by the United Nations Commission on Korea in its report menaces the safety and well being of the Republic of Korea and of the people of Korea and might lead to open military conflict there;

Noting with grave concern the armed attack upon the Republic of Korea by forces from North Korea,

Determines that this action constitutes a breach of the peace,

I. *Calls for* the immediate cessation of hostilities; and

Calls upon the authorities of North Korea to withdraw forthwith their armed forces to the thirty-eighth parallel;

II. *Requests* the United Nations Commission on Korea

(a) To communicate its fully considered recommendations on the situation with the least possible delay;

(b) To observe the withdrawal of the North Korean forces to the thirty-eighth parallel; and

(c) To keep the Security Council informed on the execution of this resolution;

III. *Calls upon* all Members to render every assistance to the United Nations in the execution of this resolution and to refrain from giving assistance to the North Korean authorities.

SECURITY COUNCIL RESOLUTION OF JUNE 27, 1950.

The Security Council,

Having determined that the armed attack upon the Republic of Korea by forces from North Korea constitutes a breach of the peace,

Having called for an immediate cessation of hostilities, and

Having called upon the authorities of North Korea to withdraw forthwith their armed forces to the 38th parallel, and

Having noted from the report of the United Nations Commission for Korea that the authorities in North Korea have neither ceased hostilities nor withdrawn their armed forces to the 38th parallel and that urgent military measures are required to restore international peace and security, and

Recommends that the Members of the United Nations furnish such assistance to the Republic of Korea as may be necessary to repel the armed attack and to restore international peace and security in the area.

SECURITY COUNCIL RESOLUTION OF JULY 7, 1950.

The Security Council, having determined that the armed attack upon the Republic of Korea by forces from North Korea constitutes a breach of the peace, having recommended that members of the United Nations furnish such assistance to the Republic of Korea as may be necessary to repel the armed attack and to restore international peace and security in the area,

(1) *Welcomes* the prompt and vigorous support which governments and peoples of the United Nations have given to its resolutions of 25 and 27 June 1950 to assist the Republic of Korea in defending itself against armed attack and thus to restore international peace and security in the area,

(2) *Notes* that members of the United Nations have transmitted to the United Nations offers of assistance for the Republic of Korea;

(3) *Recommends* that all Members providing military forces and other assistance pursuant to the aforesaid Security Council resolutions make such forces and other assistance available to a unified command under the United States;

(4) *Requests* the United States to designate the commander of such forces;

(5) *Authorizes* the unified command at its discretion to use the United Nations flag in the course of operations against North Korean forces concurrently with the flags of the various nations participating;

(6) *Requests* the United States to provide the Security Council with reports, as appropriate, on the course of action taken under the unified command.

THE PROBLEM OF THE INDEPENDENCE OF KOREA. RESOLUTION 376 (V) OF THE UNITED GENERAL ASSEMBLY, OCTOBER 7, 1950.

The General Assembly,

Having regard to its resolutions of 14 November 1947 (112 (II)), of 12 December 1948 (195 (III)) and of 21 October 1949 (293 (IV)),

Having received and considered the report of the United Nations Commission on Korea,

Mindful of the fact that the objectives set forth in the resolutions referred to above have not been fully accomplished and, in particular, that the unification of Korea has not yet been achieved, and that an attempt has been made by an armed attack from North Korea to extinguish by force the Government of the Republic of Korea,

Recalling the General Assembly declaration of 12 December 1948 that there has been established a lawful government (the Government of the Republic of Korea) having effective control and jurisdiction over that part of Korea where the United Nations Temporary Commission on Korea was able to observe and consult and in which the great majority of the people of Korea reside; that this government is based on elections which were a valid expression of the free will of the electorate of that part of Korea and which were observed by the Temporary Commission; and that this is the only such government in Korea,

Having in mind that United Nations armed forces are at present operating in Korea in accordance with the recommendations of the Security Council of 27 June 1950, subsequent to its resolution of 25 June 1950, that Members of the United Nations furnish such assistance to the Republic of Korea as may be necessary to repel the armed attack and to restore international peace and security in the area,

Recalling that the essential objective of the resolution of the General Assembly referred to above was the establishment of a unified, independent and democratic Government of Korea,

1. *Recommends that*

(a) All appropriate steps be taken to ensure conditions of stability throughout Korea;

(b) All constituent acts be taken, including the holding of elections, under the auspices of the United Nations, for the establishment of a unified, independent and democratic government in the sovereign State of Korea;

(c) All sections and representative bodies of the population of Korea, South and North, be invited to cooperate with the organs of the United Nations in the restoration of peace, in the holding of elections and in the establishment of a unified government;

(d) United Nations forces should not remain in any part of Korea otherwise than so far as necessary for achieving the objectives specified in sub-paragraphs (a) and (b) above;

(e) All necessary measures be taken to accomplish the economic rehabilitation of Korea;

2. *Resolves* that

(a) A Commission consisting of Australia, Chile, Netherlands, Pakistan, Philippines, Thailand and Turkey, to be known as the United Nations Commission for the Unification and Rehabilitation of Korea, be established to (i) assume the functions hitherto exercised by the present United Nations Commission on Korea; (ii) represent the United Nations in bringing about the establishment of a unified, independent and democratic government of all Korea; (iii) exercise such responsibilities in connexion with relief and rehabilitation in Korea as may be determined by the General Assembly after receiving the recommendations of the Economic and Social Council. The United Nations Commission for the Unification and Rehabilitation of Korea should proceed to Korea and begin to carry out its functions as soon as possible;

(b) Pending the arrival in Korea of the United Nations Commission for the Unification and Rehabilitation of Korea, the governments of the States represented on the Commission should form an Interim Committee composed of representatives meeting at the seat of the United Nations to consult with and advise the United Nations Unified Command in the light of the above recommendations; the Interim Committee should begin to function immediately upon the approval of the present resolution by the General Assembly;

(c) The Commission shall render a report to the next regular session of the General Assembly and to any prior special session which might be called to consider the subject-matter of the present resolution, and shall render such interim reports as it may deem appropriate to the Secretary-General for transmission to Members;

The General Assembly furthermore,

Mindful of the fact that at the end of the present hostilities the task of rehabilitating the Korean economy will be of great magnitude,

3. *Requests* the Economic and Social Council, in consultation with the specialized agencies, to develop plans for relief and rehabilitation on the termination of hostilities and to report to the General Assembly within three weeks of the adoption of the present resolution by the General Assembly;

4. *Also recommends* the Economic and Social Council to expedite the study of long-term measures to promote the economic development and social progress of Korea, and meanwhile to draw the attention of the authorities which decide requests for technical assistance to the urgent and special necessity of affording such assistance to Korea;

5. *Expresses* its appreciation of the services rendered by the members of the United Nations Commission on Korea in the performance of their important and difficult task;

6. *Requests* the Secretary-General to provide the United Nations Commission for the Unification and Rehabilitation of Korea with adequate staff and facilities, including technical advisers as re-

quired; and authorizes the Secretary-General to pay the expenses and *per diem* of a representative and alternate from each of the States members of the Commission.

CHINESE COMMUNIST INTERVENTION IN KOREA. RESOLUTION OF THE UNITED NATIONS GENERAL ASSEMBLY, DECEMBER 14, 1950

The General Assembly,

Viewing with grave concern the situation in the Far East,

Anxious that immediate steps should be taken to prevent the conflict in Korea spreading to other areas and to put an end to the fighting in Korea itself and that further steps should then be taken for a peaceful settlement of existing issues in accordance with the Purposes and Principles of the United Nations,

Requests the President of the General Assembly to constitute a group of three persons including himself to determine the basis on which a satisfactory cease-fire in Korea can be arranged and to make recommendations to the General Assembly as soon as possible.

CHINESE COMMUNIST INTERVENTION IN KOREA. RESOLUTION OF THE UNITED NATIONS GENERAL ASSEMBLY, FEBRUARY 1, 1951.

The General Assembly,

Noting that the Security Council because of lack of unanimity of the permanent members, has failed to exercise its primary responsibility for the maintenance of international peace and security in regard to Chinese communist intervention in Korea,

Noting that the Central People's Government of the People's, Republic of China has not accepted United Nations proposals to bring about a cessation of hostilities in Korea with a view to peaceful settlement, and that its armed forces continue their invasion of Korea and their large-scale attacks upon United Nations forces there,

1. *Finds* that the Central People's Government of the People's Republic of China, by giving direct aid and assistance to those who were already committing aggression in Korea and by engaging in hostilities against United Nations forces there, has itself engaged in aggression in Korea;

2. *Calls upon* the Central People's Government of the People's Republic of China to cause its forces and nationals in Korea to cease hostilities against the United Nations forces and to withdraw from Korea;

3. *Affirms* the determination of the United Nations to continue its action in Korea to meet the aggression;

4. *Calls upon* all states and authorities to continue to lend every assistance to the United Nations action in Korea;

5. *Calls upon* all states and authorities to refrain from giving any assistance to the aggressors in Korea;

6. *Requests* a committee composed of the members of the Collective Measures Committee as a matter of urgency to consider additional measures to be employed to meet this aggression and to report thereon to the General Assembly, it being understood that the committee is authorized to defer its report if the Good Offices Committee referred to in the following paragraph reports satisfactory progress in its efforts;

7. *Affirms* that it continues to be the policy of the United Nations to bring about a cessation of hostilities in Korea and the achievement of United Nations objectives in Korea by peaceful means, and requests the President of the General Assembly to designate forthwith two persons who would meet with him at any suitable opportunity to use their good offices to this end.

CHINESE COMMUNIST INTERVENTION IN KOREA. RESOLUTION OF THE UNITED NATIONS GENERAL ASSEMBLY, MAY 18, 1951.

The General Assembly,

Noting the report of the Additional Measures Committee dated May 14, 1951,

Recalling its resolution 498 (V) of February 1, 1951,

Noting that:

(a) The Additional Measures Committee established by that resolution has considered additional measures to be employed to meet the aggression in Korea,

(b) The Additional Measures Committee has reported that a number of states have already taken measures designed to deny contributions to the military strength of the forces opposing the United Nations in Korea,

(c) The Additional Measures Committee has also reported that certain economic measures designed further to deny such contributions would support and supplement the military action of the United Nations in Korea and would assist in putting an end to the aggression,

1. *Recommends* that every state:

(a) Apply an embargo on the shipment to areas under the control of the Central People's Government of the People's Republic of

China and of the North Korean authorities of arms, ammunition and implements of war, atomic energy materials, petroleum, transportation materials of strategic value, and items useful in the production of arms, ammunition and implements of war;

(b) Determine which commodities exported from its territory fall within the embargo, and apply controls to give effect to the embargo;

(c) Prevent by all means within its jurisdiction the circumvention of controls on shipments applied by other states pursuant to the present resolution;

(d) Co-operate with other states in carrying out the purposes of this embargo;

(e) Report to the Additional Measures Committee, within 30 days and thereafter at the request of the Committee, on the measures taken in accordance with the present resolution;

2. *Requests* the Additional Measures Committee:

(a) To report to the General Assembly, with recommendations as appropriate, on the general effectiveness of the embargo and the desirability of continuing, extending, or relaxing it;

(b) To continue its consideration of additional measures to be employed to meet the aggression in Korea, and to report thereon further to the General Assembly, it being understood that the Committee is authorized to defer its report if the Good Offices Committee reports satisfactory progress in its efforts;

3. *Reaffirms* that it continues to be the policy of the United Nations to bring about a cessation of hostilities in Korea, and the achievement of United Nations objectives in Korea by peaceful means, and requests the Good Offices Committee to continue its good offices.

KOREA. RESOLUTION 610 (VII) OF THE UNITED NATIONS GENERAL ASSEMBLY, DECEMBER 3, 1952.

The General Assembly,

Having received the special report of the United Nations Command of 18 October 1952 on "the present status of the military action and the armistice negotiations in Korea" and other relevant reports relating to Korea,

Noting with approval the considerable progress towards an armistice made by negotiation at Panmunjom and the tentative agreements to end the fighting in Korea and to reach a settlement of the Korean question,

Noting further that disagreement between the parties on one remaining issue, alone, prevents the conclusion of an armistice and that a considerable measure of agreement already exists on the principles on which this remaining issue can be resolved,

Mindful of the continuing and vast loss of life, devastation and suffering resulting from and accompanying the continuance of the fighting,

Deeply conscious of the need to bring hostilities to a speedy end and of the need for a peaceful settlement of the Korean question,

Anxious to expedite and facilitate the convening of the political conference as provided in article 60 of the draft armistice agreement,

1. *Affirms* that the release and repatriation of prisoners of war shall be effected in accordance with the Geneva Convention relative to the Treatment of Prisoners of War, dated 12 August 1949, the well-established principles and practice of international law and the relevant provisions of the draft armistice agreement;

2. *Affirms* that force shall not be used against prisoners of war to prevent or effect their return to their homelands, and that they shall at all time be treated humanely in accordance with the specific provisions of the Geneva Convention and with the general spirit of the Convention;

3. *Accordingly requests* the President of the General Assembly to communicate the following proposals to the Central People's Government of the People's Republic of China and to the North Korean authorities as forming a just and reasonable basis for an agreement so that an immediate cease-fire would result and be effected; to invite their acceptance of these proposals and to make a report to the General Assembly during its present session and as soon as appropriate:

Proposals

I. In order to facilitate the return to their homelands of all prisoners of war, there shall be established a Repatriation Commission consisting of representatives of Czechoslovakia, Poland, Sweden and Switzerland, that is, the four States agreed to for the constitution of the Neutral Nations Supervisory Commission and referred to in paragraph 37 of the draft armistice agreement, or constituted, alternatively, of representatives of four States not participating in hostilities, two nominated by each side, but excluding representatives of States that are permanent members of the Security Council.

II. The release and repatriation of prisoners of war shall be effected in accordance with the Geneva Convention relative to the Treatment of Prisoners of War, dated 12 August 1949, the well-established principles and practice of International Law and the relevant provisions of the draft armistice agreement.

III. Force shall not be used against the prisoners of war to prevent or effect their return to their homelands and no violence to their persons or affront to their dignity or self-respect shall be permitted in any manner or for any purpose whatsoever. This duty is enjoined on and entrusted to the Repatriation Commission and each of its members. Prisoners of war shall at all times be treated humanely in accordance with the specific provisions of the Geneva Convention and with the general spirit of that Convention.

IV. All prisoners of war shall be released to the Repatriation Commission from military control and from the custody of the detaining side in agreed numbers and at agreed exchange points in agreed demilitarized zones.

V. Classification of prisoners of war according to nationality and domicile as proposed in the letter of 16 October 1952 from General Kim Il Sung, Supreme Commander of the Korean People's Army, and General Peng Teh-huai, Commander of the Chinese People's Volunteers, to General Mark W. Clark, Commander-in-Chief, United Nations Command, shall then be carried out immediately.

VI. After classification, prisoners of war shall be free to return to their homelands forthwith, and their speedy return shall be facilitated by all parties concerned.

VII. In accordance with arrangements prescribed for the purpose by the Repatriation Commission, each party to the conflict shall have freedom and facilities to explain to the prisoners of war "depending upon them" their rights and to inform the prisoners of war on any matter relating to their return to their homelands and particularly their full freedom to return.

VIII. Red Cross teams on both sides shall assist the Repatriation Commission in its work and shall have access, in accordance with the terms of the draft armistice agreement, to prisoners of war while they are under the temporary jurisdiction of the Repatriation Commission.

IX. Prisoners of war shall have freedom and facilities to make representations and communications to the Repatriation Commission and to bodies and agencies working under the Repatriation Commission, and to inform any or all such bodies of their desires on any matter concerning themselves, in accordance with arrangements made for the purpose by the Commission.

X. Notwithstanding the provisions of paragraph III above, nothing in this Repatriation Agreement shall be construed as derogating from the authority of the Repatriation Commission (or its authorized representatives) to exercise its legitimate functions and responsibilities for the control of the prisoners under its temporary jurisdiction.

XI. The terms of this Repatriation Agreement and the arrangements arising therefrom shall be made known to all prisoners of war.

XII. The Repatriation Commission is entitled to call upon parties to the conflict, its own member governments, or the Member States of the United Nations for such legitimate assistance as it may require in the carrying out of its duties and tasks and in accordance with the decisions of the Commission in this respect.

XIII. When the two sides have made an agreement for repatriation based on these proposals, the interpretation of that agreement shall rest with the Repatriation Commission. In the event of disagreement in the Commission, majority decisions shall prevail. When no majority decision is possible, an umpire agreed upon in accordance with the succeeding paragraph and with article 132 of the Geneva Convention of 1949 shall have the deciding vote.

XIV. The Repatriation Commission shall at its first meeting and prior to an armistice proceed to agree upon and appoint the umpire who shall at all times be available to the Commission and shall act as its Chairman unless otherwise agreed. If agreement on the appointment of the umpire cannot be reached by the Commission within the period of three weeks after the date of the first meeting this matter should be referred to the General Assembly.

XV. The Repatriation Commission shall also arrange after the armistice for officials to function as umpires with inspecting teams or other bodies to which functions are delegated or assigned by the Commission or under the provisions of the draft armistice agreement, so that the completion of the return of prisoners of war to their homelands shall be expedited.

XVI. When the Repatriation Agreement is acceded to by the parties concerned and when an umpire has been appointed under paragraph 14 above, the draft armistice agreement, unless otherwise altered by agreement between the parties, shall be deemed to have been accepted by them. The provisions of the draft armistice agreement shall apply except in so far as they are modified by the Repatriation Agreement. Arrangements for repatriation under this agreement will begin when the armistice agreement is thus concluded.

XVII. At the end of ninety days, after the Armistice Agreement has been signed, the disposition of any prisoners of war whose return to their homelands may not have been effected in accordance with the procedure set out in these proposals or as otherwise agreed, shall be referred with recommendations for their disposition, including a target date for the termination of their detention to the political conference to be called as provided under article 60 of the draft armistice agreement. If at the end of a further thirty days there are any prisoners of war whose return to their homelands has not been effected under the above procedures or whose future has not been provided for by the political conference, the responsibility for their care and maintenance and for their subsequent disposition shall be transferred to the United Nations, which in all matters relating to them shall act strictly in accordance with international law.

Appendix B-2

Gaza-Sinai

UN GENERAL ASSEMBLY RESOLUTIONS ESTABLISHING UNEF, NOVEMBER, 1956.

RESOLUTION 997 (ES-I)

The General Assembly,

Noting the disregard on many occasions by parties to the Israel-Arab armistice agreements of 1949 of the terms of such agreements, and that the armed forces of Israel have penetrated deeply into Egyptian territory in violation of the General Armistice Agreement between Egypt and Israel of 24 February 1964,

Noting that armed forces of France and the United Kingdom of Great Britain and Northern Ireland are conducting military operations against Egyptian territory,

Noting that traffic through the Suez Canal is now interrupted to the serious prejudice of many nations,

Expressing its grave concern over these developments,

1. *Urges* as a matter of priority that all parties now involved in hostilities in the area agree to an immediate cease-fire and, as part thereof, halt the movement of military forces and arms into the area;

2. *Urges* the parties to the armistice agreements promptly to withdraw all forces behind the armistice lines, to desist from raids across the armistice lines into neighboring territory, and to observe scrupulously the provisions of the armistice agreements;

3. *Recommends* that all Member States refrain from introducing military goods in the area of hostilities and in general refrain from any acts which would delay or prevent the implementation of the present resolution;

4. *Urges* that, upon the cease-fire being effective, steps be taken to reopen the Suez Canal and restore secure freedom of navigation;

5. *Requests* the Secretary-General to observe and report promptly on the compliance with the present resolution to the Security Council and to the General Assembly, for such further action as they may deem appropriate in accordance with the Charter;

6. *Decides* to remain in emergency session pending compliance with the present resolution.

562nd plenary meeting,
2 November 1956.

RESOLUTION 998 (ES-I)

The General Assembly,

Bearing in mind the urgent necessity of facilitating compliance with its resolution 997 (ES-I) of 2 November 1956,

Requests, as a matter of priority, the Secretary-General to submit to it within forty-eight hours a plan for the setting up, with the consent of the nations concerned, of an emergency international United Nations Force to secure and supervise the cessation of hostilities in accordance with all the terms of the aforementioned resolution.

563rd plenary meeting,
4 November 1956.

RESOLUTION 999 (ES-I)

The General Assembly,

Noting with regret that not all the parties concerned have yet agreed to comply with the provisions of its resolution 997 (ES-I) of 2 November 1956,

Noting the special priority given in that resolution to an immediate cease-fire and, as part thereof, to the halting of the movement of military forces and arms into the area,

Noting further that the resolution urged the parties to the armistice agreements promptly to withdraw all forces behind the armistice lines, to desist from raids across the armistice lines into neighboring territory, and to observe scrupulously the provisions of the armistice ageements,

1. *Reaffirms* its resolution 997 (ES-I), and once again calls upon the parties immediately to comply with the provisions of the said resolution;

2. *Authorizes* the Secretary-General immediately to arrange with the parties concerned for the implementation of the cease-fire and the halting of the movement of military forces and arms into the area, and requests him to report compliance forthwith and, in any case, not later than twelve hours from the time of adoption of the present resolution;

3. *Requests* the Secretary-General, with the assistance of the Chief of Staff and the members of the United Nations Truce Supervision Organization, to obtain compliance of the withdrawal of all forces behind the armistice lines;

4. *Decides* to meet again immediately on receipt of the Secretary-General's report referred to in paragraph 2 of the present resolution.

563rd plenary meeting,
4 November 1956.

RESOLUTION 1000 (ES-I)

The General Assembly,

Having requested the Secretary-General, in its resolution 998 (ES-I) of 4 November 1956, to submit to it a plan for an emergency international United Nations Force, for the purposes stated,

Noting with satisfaction the first report of the Secretary-General on the plan, and having in mind particularly paragraph 4 of that report,

1. *Establishes* a United Nations Command for an emergency international Force to secure and supervise the cessation of hostilities in accordance with all the terms of General Assembly resolution 997 (ES-I) of 2 November 1956;

2. *Appoints*, on an emergency basis, the Chief of Staff of the United Nations Truce Supervision Organization, Major-General E. L. M. Burns, as Chief of the Command;

3. *Authorizes* the Chief of the Command immediately to recruit, from the observer corps of the United Nations Truce Supervision Organization, a limited number of officers who shall be nationals of countries other than those having permanent membership in the Security Council, and further authorizes him, in consultation with the Secretary-General, to undertake the recruitment directly, from various Member States other than the permanent members of the Security Council, of the additional number of officers needed;

4. *Invites* the Secretary-General to take such administrative measures as may be necessary for the prompt execution of the actions envisaged in the present resolution.

565th plenary meeting,
5 November 1956.

RESOLUTION 1001 (ES-I)

The General Assembly,

Recalling its resolution 997 (ES-I) of 2 November 1956 concerning the cease-fire, withdrawal of troops and other matters related to the military operations in Egyptian territory, as well as its resolution 998 (ES-I) of 4 November 1956 concerning the request to the Secretary-General to submit a plan for an emergency international United Nations Force,

Having established by its resolution 1000 (ES-I) of 5 November 1956 a United Nations Command for an emergency international Force, having appointed the Chief of Staff of the United Nations Truce Supervision Organization as Chief of the Command with authorization to him to begin the recruitment of officers for the Command, and having invited the Secretary-General to take the administrative measures necessary for the prompt execution of that resolution,

Noting with appreciation the second and final report of the Secretary-General on the plan for an emergency international United Nations Force as requested in General Assembly resolution 998 (ES-I), and having examined that plan,

1. *Expresses its approval* of the guiding principles for the organi-

zation and functioning of the emergency international United Nations Force as expounded in paragraphs 6 to 9 of the Secretary-General's report;

2. *Concurs* in the definition of the functions of the Force as stated in paragraph 12 of the Secretary-General's report;

3. *Invites* the Secretary-General to continue discussions with Governments of Member States concerning offers of participation in the Force, toward the objective of its balanced compositions;

4. *Requests* the Chief of the Command, in consultation with the Secretary-General as regards size and composition, to proceed forthwith with the full organization of the Force;

5. *Approves provisionally* the basic rule concerning the financing of the Force laid down in paragraph 15 of the Secretary-General's report;

6. *Establishes* an Advisory Committee composed of one representative from each of the following countries: Brazil, Canada, Ceylon, Colombia, India, Norway and Pakistan, and requests this Committee, whose Chairman shall be the Secretary-General, to undertake the development of those aspects of the planning for the Force and its operation not already dealt with by the General Assembly and which do not fall within the area of the direct responsibility of the Chief of the Command;

7. *Authorizes* the Secretary-General to issue all regulations and instructions which may be essential to the effective functioning of the Force, following consultation with the Committee aforementioned, and to take all other necessary administrative and executive action;

8. *Determines* that, following the fulfilment of the immediate responsibilities defined for it in operative paragraphs 6 and 7 above, the Advisory Committee shall continue to assist the Secretary-General in the responsibilities falling to him under the present and other relevant resolutions;

9. *Decides* that the Advisory Committee, in the performance of its duties, shall be empowered to request, through the usual procedures, the convening of the General Assembly and to report to the Assembly whenever matters arise which, in its opinion, are of such urgency and importance as to require consideration by the General Assembly itself;

10. *Requests* all Member States to afford assistance as necessary to the United Nations Command in the performance of its functions,

including arrangements for passage to and from the area involved.

567th plenary meeting,
7 November 1956.

RESOLUTION 1002 (ES-I)

The General Assembly,

Recalling its resolutions 997 (ES-I) of 2 November 1956, 998 (ES-I) and 999 (ES-I) of 4 November 1956 and 1000 (ES-I) of 5 November 1956, adopted by overwhelming majorities,

Noting in particular that the General Assembly, by its resolution 1000 (ES-I), established a United Nations Command for an emergency international Force to secure and supervise the cessation of hostilities in accordance with all the terms of its resolution 997 (ES-I),

1. *Reaffirms* the above-mentioned resolutions;
2. *Calls once again upon* Israel immediately to withdraw all its forces behind the armistice lines established by the General Armistice Agreement between Egypt and Israel of 24 February 1949;
3. *Calls once again upon* the United Kingdom and France immediately to withdraw all their forces from Egyptian territory, consistently with the above-mentioned resolutions;
4. *Urges* the Secretary-General to communicate the present resolution to the parties concerned, and requests him promptly to report to the General Assembly on the compliance with this resolution.

567th plenary meeting,
7 November 1956.

Appendix B-3

Congo

SECURITY COUNCIL, JULY 14, 1960

Considering the report of the Secretary-General on a request for United Nations action in relation to the Republic of the Congo,

Considering the request for military assistance addressed to the Secretary-General by the President and the Prime Minister of the Republic of the Congo (document S/4382),

1. *Calls upon* the Government of Belgium to withdraw their troops from the territory of the Republic of the Congo;

2. *Decides* to authorize the Secretary-General to take the necessary steps, in consultation with the Government of the Republic of the Congo, to provide the Government with such military assistance as may be necessary, until, through the efforts of the Congolese Government with the technical assistance of the United Nations, the national security forces may be able, in the opinion of the Government, to meet fully their tasks;

3. *Requests* the Secretary-General to report to the Security Council as appropriate.

SECURITY COUNCIL, JULY 22, 1960

Having considered the first report by the Secretary-General on the implementation of Security Council resolution S/4387 of 14 July 1960 (document S/4389),

Appreciating the work of the Secretary-General and the support so readily and so speedily given to him by all Member States invited by him to give assistance,

Noting that as stated by the Secretary-General the arrival of the troops of the United Nations force in Leopoldville has already had a salutary effect,

Recognizing that an urgent need still exists to continue and to increase such efforts,

Considering that the complete restoration of law and order in the Republic of the Congo would effectively contribute to the maintenance of international peace and security,

Recognizing that the Security Council recommended the admission of the Republic of the Congo to membership in the United Nations as a unit,

1. *Calls upon* the Government of Belgium to implement speedily the Security Council resolution of 14 July 1960, on the withdrawal of their troops, and *authorizes* the Secretary-General to take all necessary action to this effect;

2. *Requests* all States to refrain from any action which might tend to impede the restoration of law and order and the exercise by the Government of the Congo of its authority and also to refrain from any action which might undermine the territorial integrity and the political independence of the Republic of the Congo;

3. *Commends* the Secretary-General for the prompt action he has taken to carry out resolution S/4387 of the Security Council and his first report;

4. *Invites* the specialized agencies of the United Nations to render to the Secretary-General such assistance as he may require;

5. *Requests* the Secretary-General to report further to the Security Council as appropriate.

UN SECURITY COUNCIL RESOLUTION OF AUGUST 9, 1960, ON THE CONGO

The Security Council,

Recalling its resolution of July 22, 1960 (S/4405), *inter alia*, calling upon the Government of Belgium to implement speedily the Security Council resolution of July 14 (S/4387) on the withdrawal of their troops and authorizing the Secretary-General to take all necessary action to this effect,

Having noted the second report by the Secretary-General on the implementation of the aforesaid two resolutions and his statement before the Council,

Having considered the statements made by the representatives of Belgium and the Republic of the Congo to this Council at this meeting,

Noting with satisfaction the progress made by the United Nations in carrying out the Security Council resolutions in respect of the territory of the Republic of the Congo other than the Province of Katanga,

Noting however that the United Nations had been prevented from implementing the aforesaid resolutions in the Province of Katanga although it was ready, and in fact attempted, to do so,

Recognizing that the withdrawal of Belgian troops from the Province of Katanga will be a positive contribution to and essential for the proper implementation of the Security Council resolutions,

1. *Confirms* the authority given to the Secretary-General by the Security Council resolutions of July 14 and July 22, 1960, and requests him to continue to carry out the responsibility placed on him thereby;

2. *Calls upon* the Government of Belgium to withdraw immediately its troops from the Province of Katanga under speedy modalities determined by the Secretary-General and to assist in every possible way the implementation of the Council's resolutions;

3. *Declares* that the entry of the United Nations force into the Province of Katanga is necessary for the full implementation of this resolution;

4. *Reaffirms* that the United Nations force in the Congo will not be a party to or in any way intervene in or be used to influence the outcome of any internal conflict, constitutional or otherwise;

5. *Calls upon* all member states, in accordance with Articles 25 and 49 of the Charter, to accept and carry out the decisions of the Security Council and to afford mutual assistance in carrying out measures decided upon by the Security Council;

6. *Requests* the Secretary-General to implement this resolution and to report further to the Security Council as appropriate.

GENERAL ASSEMBLY, SEPTEMBER 20, 1960

[*Resolution A/4510 was adopted by 70 votes to 0. There were 11 abstentions—Albania, Bulgaria, Byelorussia, Czechoslovakia, France, Hungary, Poland, Romania, the Ukraine, Union of South Africa and the Soviet Union. Bolivia was absent.*]

Having considered the situation in the Republic of the Congo,

Taking note of the resolutions of 14 and 22 July and of 9 August 1960 of the Security Council,

Taking into account the unsatisfactory economic and political conditions that continue in the Republic of the Congo,

Considering that, with a view to preserving the unity, territorial integrity and political independence of the Congo, to protecting and advancing the welfare of its people, and to safeguarding international peace, it is essential for the United Nations to continue to assist the Central Government of the Congo,

1. *Fully supports* the resolutions of 14 and 22 July and of 9 August of the Security Council;

2. *Requests* the Secretary-General to continue to take vigorous action in accordance with the terms of the aforesaid resolutions and to assist the Central Government of the Congo in the restoration and maintenance of law and order throughout the territory of the Republic of the Congo and to safeguard its unity, territorial integrity and political independence in the interests of international peace and security;

3. *Appeals* to all Congolese within the Republic of the Congo to seek a speedy solution by peaceful means of all their internal conflicts for the unity and integrity of the Congo, with the assistance,

as appropriate, of Asian and African representatives appointed by the Advisory Committee on the Congo, in consultation with the Secretary-General, for the purpose of conciliation;

4. *Appeals* to all Member Governments for urgent voluntary contributions to a United Nations Fund for the Congo to be used under United Nations control and in consultation with the Central Government for the purpose of rendering the fullest possible assistance to achieve the objective mentioned in the preamble;

5. *Requests*

(a) All States to refrain from any action which might tend to impede the restoration of law and order and the exercise by the Government of the Congo of its authority and also to refrain from any action which might undermine the unity, territorial integrity and political independence of the Republic of the Congo;

(b) All Member States, in accordance with Articles 25 and 49 of the Charter, to accept and carry out the decisions of the Security Council and to afford mutual assistance in carrying out measures decided upon by the Security Council;

6. Without prejudice to the sovereign rights of the Republic of the Congo, *calls upon* all States to refrain from the direct and indirect provision of arms or other material of war and military personnel and other assistance for military purposes in the Congo during the temporary period of military assistance through the United Nations, except upon the request of the United Nations through the Secretary-General for carrying out the purposes of this resolution and of the resolutions of 14 and 22 July and of 9 August 1960 of the Security Council.

SECURITY COUNCIL, FEBRUARY 21, 1961

A

Having considered the situation in the Congo,

Having learned with deep regret the announcement of the killing of the Congolese leaders, Mr. Patrice Lumumba, Mr. Maurice Mpolo and Mr. Joseph Okito,

Deeply concerned at the grave repercussions of these crimes and the danger of wide-spread civil war and bloodshed in the Congo and the threat to international peace and security,

Noting the Report of the Secretary-General's Special Representative (S/4691) dated 12 February 1961 bringing to light the development of a serious civil war situation and preparations therefor,

1. *Urges* that the United Nations take immediately all appropriate measures to prevent the occurrence of civil war in the Congo, including arrangements for cease-fires, the halting of all military operations, the prevention of clashes, and the use of force, if necessary, in the last resort;

2. *Urges* that measures be taken for the immediate withdrawal and evacuation from the Congo of all Belgian and other foreign military and para-military personnel and political advisers not under the United Nations Command, and mercenaries;

3. *Calls* upon all States to take immediate and energetic measures to prevent the departure of such personnel for the Congo from their territories, and for the denial of transit and other facilities to them;

4. *Decides* that an immediate and impartial investigation be held in order to ascertain the circumstances of the death of Mr. Lumumba and his colleagues and that the perpetrators of these crimes be punished;

5. *Reaffirms* the Security Council resolutions of 14 July, 22 July, and 9 August 1960 and the General Assembly resolution 1474 (ES-IV) of 20 September 1960 and reminds all States of their obligation under these resolutions.

B

The Security Council,

Gravely concerned at the continuing deterioration in the Congo, and the prevalence of conditions which seriously imperil peace and order, and the unity and territorial integrity of the Congo, and threaten international peace and security,

Noting with deep regret and concern the systematic violations of human rights and fundamental freedoms and the general absence of rule of law in the Congo,

Recognizing the imperative necessity of the restoration of parliamentary institutions in the Congo in accordance with the fundamental law of the country, so that the will of the people should be reflected through the freely elected Parliament,

Convinced that the solution of the problem of the Congo lies in the hands of the Congolese people themselves without any interference from outside and that there can be no solution without conciliation,

Convinced further that the imposition of any solution, including the formation of any government not based on genuine conciliation would, far from settling any issues, greatly enhance the dangers of conflict within the Congo and threat to international peace and security,

1. *Urges* the convening of the Parliament and the taking of necessary protective measures in that connection;

2. *Urges* that Congolese armed units and personnel should be reorganized and brought under discipline and control, and arrangements be made on impartial and equitable bases to that end and with a view to the elimination of any possibility of interference by such units and personnel in the political life of the Congo;

3. *Calls upon* all States to extend their full co-operation and assistance and take such measures as may be necessary on their part, for the implementation of this resolution.

SECURITY COUNCIL, NOVEMBER 24, 1961

Recalling its resolutions S/4387, S/4405, S/4426 and S/4741,

Recalling further General Assembly resolutions 1474 (ES-IV), 1592 (XV), 1599 (XV), 1600 (XV) and 1601 (XV),

Reaffirming the policies and purposes of the United Nations with respect to the Congo (Leopoldville) as set out in the aforesaid resolutions, namely:

(a) To maintain the territorial integrity and the political independence of the Republic of the Congo;

(b) To assist the Central Government of the Congo in the restoration and maintenance of law and order;

(c) To prevent the occurrence of civil war in the Congo;

(d) To secure the immediate withdrawal and evacuation from the Congo of all foreign military, para-military and advisory personnel not under the United Nations Command, and all mercenaries; and

(e) To render technical assistance;

Welcoming the restoration of the national Parliament of the Congo in accordance with the *Loi fondamentale* and the consequent formation of a Central Government on 2 August 1961,

Deploring all armed action in opposition to the authority of the Government of the Republic of the Congo, specifically secessionist activities and armed action now being carried on by the Provincial Administration of Katanga with the aid of external resources and foreign mercenaries, and *completely rejecting* the claim that Katanga is a "sovereign independent nation,"

Noting with deep regret the recent and past actions of violence against United Nations personnel,

Recognizing the Government of the Republic of the Congo as exclusively responsible for the conduct of the external affairs of the Congo,

Bearing in mind the imperative necessity of speedy and effective action to implement fully the policies and purposes of the United Nations in the Congo to end the unfortunate plight of the Congolese people, necessary both in the interests of world peace and international cooperation, and stability and progress of Africa as a whole,

1. *Strongly deprecates* the secessionist activities illegally carried out by the provincial administration of Katanga, with the aid of external resources and manned by foreign mercenaries;

2. *Further deprecates* the armed action against United Nations forces and personnel in the pursuit of such activities;

3. *Insists* that such activities shall cease forthwith, and *calls upon* all concerned to desist therefrom;

4. *Authorizes* the Secretary-General to take vigorous action, including the use of a requisite measure of force, if necessary, for the immediate apprehension, detention pending legal action and/or deportation of all foreign military and para-military personnel and political advisers not under the United Nations Command, and mercenaries as laid down in paragraph A-2 of the Security Council resolution of 21 February 1961;

5. *Further requests* the Secretary-General to take all necessary measures to prevent the entry or return of such elements under whatever guise and also of arms, equipment or other material in support of such activities;

6. *Requests* all States to refrain from the supply of arms, equipment or other material which could be used for warlike purposes, and to take the necessary measures to prevent their nationals from doing the same, and also to deny transportation and transit facilities for such supplies across their territories, except in accordance with the decisions, policies and purposes of the United Nations;

7. *Calls upon* all Member States to refrain from promoting, condoning, or giving support by acts of omission or commission, directly or indirectly, to activities against the United Nations often resulting in armed hostilities against the United Nations forces and personnel;

8. *Declares* that all secessionist activities against the Republic of the Congo are contrary to the *Loi fondamentale* and Security Coun-

cil decisions and specifically *demands* that such activities which are now taking place in Katanga shall cease forthwith;

9. *Declares* full and firm support for the Central Government of the Congo, and the determination to assist that Government in accordance with the decision of the United Nations to maintain law and order and national integrity, to provide technical assistance and to implement those decisions;

10. *Urges* all Member States to lend their support, according to their national procedures, to the Central Government of the Republic of the Congo, in conformity with the Charter and the decisions of the United Nations;

11. *Requests* all Member States to refrain from any action which may directly or indirectly impede the policies and purposes of the United Nations in the Congo and is contrary to its decisions and the general purpose of the Charter.

AGREEMENT BETWEEN THE UNITED NATIONS AND THE CONGOLESE GOVERNMENT

Note: This "basic agreement" between Mr. Hammarskjold and the Congo was initialled on July 29, 1960.

1. The Government of the Republic of the Congo states that, in the exercise of its sovereign rights with respect to any question concerning the presence and functioning of the United Nations Force in the Congo, it will be guided, in good faith, by the fact that it has requested military assistance from the United Nations and by its acceptance of the resolutions of the Security Council of 14 and 22 July 1960; it likewise states that it will ensure the freedom of movement of the Force in the interior of the country and will accord the requisite privileges and immunities to all personnel associated with the activities of the Force.

2. The United Nations takes note of this statement of the Government of the Republic of the Congo and states that, with regard to the activities of the United Nations Force in the Congo, it will be guided, in good faith, by the task assigned to the Force in the aforementioned resolutions; in particular the United Nations reaffirms, considering it to be in accordance with the wishes of the Government of the Republic of the Congo, that it is prepared to maintain the United Nations Force in the Congo until such time as it deems the latter's task to have been fully accomplished.

3. The Government of the Republic of the Congo and the Secre-

tary-General state their intention to proceed immediately, in the light of paragraphs 1 and 2 above, to explore jointly specific aspects of the functioning of the United Nations Force in the Congo, notably with respect to its deployment, the question of its lines of communication and supply, its lodging and its provisioning; the Government of the Republic of the Congo, confirming its intention to facilitate the functioning of the United Nations Force in the Congo, and the United Nations have agreed to work together to hasten the implementation of the guiding principles laid down in consequence of the work of joint exploration on the basis of the resolutions of the Security Council.

4. The foregoing provisions shall likewise be applicable, as appropriate, to the non-military aspects of the United Nations operation in the Congo.

Appendix B-4

Cyprus

RESOLUTION ADOPTED BY THE SECURITY COUNCIL AT ITS 1102ND MEETING ON 4 MARCH 1964

The Security Council,

Noting that the present situation with regard to Cyprus is likely to threaten international peace and security and may further deteriorate unless additional measures are promptly taken to maintain peace and to seek out a durable solution,

Considering the positions taken by the parties in relation to the Treaties signed at Nicosia on 16 August 1960,

Having in mind the relevant provisions of the Charter of the United Nations and its Article 2, paragraph 4, which reads: "All Members shall refrain in their international relations from the threat or use of force against the territorial integrity or political independence of any State, or in any other manner inconsistent with the Purposes of the United Nations",

1. *Calls upon* all Member States, in conformity with their obligations under the Charter of the United Nations, to refrain from any action or threat of action likely to worsen the situation in the

sovereign Republic of Cyprus, or to endanger international peace;

2. *Asks* the Government of Cyprus, which has the responsibility for the maintenance and restoration of law and order, to take all additional measures necessary to stop violence and bloodshed in Cyprus;

3. *Calls upon* the communities in Cyprus and their leaders to act with the utmost restraint;

4. *Recommends* the creation, with the consent of the Government of Cyprus, of a United Nations peace-keeping force in Cyprus. The composition and size of the force shall be established by the Secretary-General, in consultation with the Governments of Cyprus, Greece, Turkey and the United Kingdom. The commander of the force shall be appointed by the Secretary-General and report to him. The Secretary-General, who shall keep the Governments providing the force fully informed, shall report periodically to the Security Council on its operation;

5. *Recommends* that the function of the force should be, in the interest of preserving international peace and security, to use its best efforts to prevent a recurrence of fighting and, as necessary, to contribute to the maintenance and restoration of law and order and a return to normal conditions;

6. *Recommends* that the stationing of the force shall be for a period of three months, all costs pertaining to it being met, in a manner to be agreed upon by them, by the Governments providing the contingents and by the Government of Cyprus. The Secretary-General may also accept voluntary contributions foı that purpose;

7. *Recommends further* that the Secretary-General designate, in agreement with the Government of Cyprus and the Governments of Greece, Turkey and the United Kingdom, a mediator, who shall use his best endeavours with the representatives of the communities and also with the aforesaid four Governments, for the purpose of promoting a peaceful solution and an agreed settlement of the problem confronting Cyprus, in accordance with the Charter of the United Nations, having in mind the well-being of the people of Cyprus as a whole and the preservation of international peace and security. The mediator shall report periodically to the Secretary-General on his efforts;

8. *Requests* the Secretary-General to provide, from funds of the United Nations, as appropriate, for the remuneration and expenses of the mediator and his staff.

RESOLUTION ADOPTED BY THE SECURITY COUNCIL AT ITS 1103RD MEETING ON 13 MARCH 1964

The Security Council,

Having heard the statements of the representatives of the Republic of Cyprus, Greece and Turkey,

Reaffirming its resolution of 4 March 1964 (S/5575),

Being deeply concerned over developments in the area,

Noting the progress reported by the Secretary-General in regard to the establishment of a United Nations peace-keeping force in Cyprus,

Noting the assurance from the Secretary-General that the United Nations Peace-Keeping Force in Cyprus envisaged in the Council's resolution of 4 March 1964 (S/5575) is about to be established, and that advance elements of that Force are already en route to Cyprus;

1. *Reaffirms* its call upon all Member States, in conformity with their obligations under the Charter of the United Nations, to refrain from any action or threat of action likely to worsen the situation in the sovereign Republic of Cyprus, or to endanger international peace;

2. *Requests* the Secretary-General to press on with his efforts to implement the Security Council resolution of 4 March 1964 and requests Member States to co-operate with the Secretary-General to that end.

REPORT BY THE SECRETARY-GENERAL ON THE ORGANIZATION AND OPERATION OF THE UNITED NATIONS PEACE-KEEPING FORCE IN CYPRUS

1. By an exchange of letters dated 31 March 1964 between the Secretary-General and the Foreign Minister of the Republic of Cyprus (Annexes I and II), an agreement was concluded concerning the status of the United Nations Peace-Keeping Force in Cyprus.

2. The Government of the Republic of Cyprus has further undertaken to give provisional application to the arrangements described in the letter of the Secretary-General and to use its best efforts to secure the earliest possible ratification of the agreement.

EXCHANGE OF LETTERS CONSTITUTING AN AGREEMENT BETWEEN THE UNITED NATIONS AND THE GOVERNMENT OF THE REPUBLIC OF CYPRUS CONCERNING THE STATUS OF THE UNITED NATIONS PEACE-KEEPING FORCE IN CYPRUS

ANNEX I

LETTER FROM THE SECRETARY-GENERAL OF THE UNITED NATIONS TO THE MINISTER FOR FOREIGN AFFAIRS OF CYPRUS

31 March 1964

Sir,

I have the honour to refer to the resolution adopted by the Security Council of the United Nations on 4 March 1964 (S/5575). In paragraph 4 of that resolution the Security Council recommended the creation, with the consent of the Government of the Republic of Cyprus, of a United Nations peace-keeping force in Cyprus. By letter of 4 March 1964, the Minister for Foreign Affairs of Cyprus informed the Secretary-General of the consent of the Government of the Republic of Cyprus to the creation of the Force. The Force was established on 27 March 1964. I have also the honour to refer to Article 105 of the Charter of the United Nations which provides that the Organization shall enjoy in the territory of its Members such privileges and immunities as are necessary for the fulfilment of its purposes, and to the Convention on the Privileges and Immunities of the United Nations to which Cyprus is a party. Having in view the provisions of the Convention on the Privileges and Immunities of the United Nations, I wish to propose that the United Nations and Cyprus should make the following *ad hoc* arrangements defining certain of the conditions necessary for the effective discharge of the functions of the United Nations Force while it remains in Cyprus. These arrangements are set out below under the following headings:

His Excellency
Mr. Spyros A. Kyprianou
Minister for Foreign Affairs
c/o Permanent Mission of Cyprus
to the United Nations
165 East 72nd Street
New York 21, New York

Definitions

1. The "United Nations Force in Cyprus" (hereinafter referred to as "the Force") consists of the United Nations Commander appointed by the Secretary-General in accordance with the Security

Council resolution of 4 March 1964 (S/5575) and all military personnel placed under his command. For the purpose of these arrangements the term "member of the Force" refers to any person, belonging to the military service of a State, who is serving under the Commander of the United Nations Force and to any civilian placed under the Commander by the State to which such civilian belongs.

2. "Cypriot authorities" means all State and local, civil and military authorities of the Government of the Republic of Cyprus called upon to perform functions relating to the Force under the provisions of these arrangements, without prejudice to the ultimate responsibility of the Government of the Republic of Cyprus (hereinafter referred to as "the Government").

3. "Participating State" means a Member of the United Nations that contributes military personnel to the Force.

4. "Area of operations" includes all areas throughout the territory of the Republic of Cyprus (which territory is hereinafter referred to as "Cyprus") where the Force is deployed in the performance of its functions as defined in operative paragraph 5 of the Security Council resolution of 4 March 1964 (S/5575); military installations or other premises referred to in paragraph 19 of these arrangements; and lines of communication and supply utilized by the Force pursuant to paragraphs 32 and 33 of these arrangements.

International status of the Force and its members

5. Members of the Force shall respect the laws and regulations of Cyprus and shall refrain from any activity of a political character in Cyprus and from any action incompatible with the international nature of their duties or inconsistent with the spirit of the present arrangements. The Commander shall take all appropriate measures to ensure the observance of these obligations.

6. The Government undertakes to respect the exclusively international character of the Force as established by the Secretary-General in accordance with the Security Council resolution of 4 March 1964 (S/5575) and the international nature of its command and function.

Entry and exit: Identification

7. Members of the Force shall be exempt from passport and visa regulations and immigration inspection and restrictions on entering or departing from Cyprus. They shall also be exempt from any regulations governing the residence of aliens in Cyprus, including registration, but shall not be considered as acquiring any right to perma-

nent residence or domicile in Cyprus. For the purpose of such entry or departure members of the Force will be required to have only (a) an individual or collective movement order issued by the Commander or an appropriate authority of the Participating State; and (b) a personal identity card issued by the Commander under the authority of the Secretary-General, except in the case of first entry, when the personal military identity card issued by the appropriate authorities of the Participating State will be accepted in lieu of the said Force identity card.

8. Members of the Force may be required to present, but not to surrender, their identity cards upon demand of such Cypriot authorities as may be mutually agreed between the Commander and the Government. Except as provided in paragraph 7 of these arrangements the identity card will be the only document required for a member of the Force. If, however, it does not show the full name, date of birth, rank and number (if any), service and photograph of a member of the Force, such member may be required to present likewise the personal military identity card or similar document issued by the appropriate authorities of the Participating State to which he belongs.

9. If a member of the Force leaves the service of the Participating State to which he belongs and is not repatriated, the Commander shall immediately inform the Government, giving such particulars as may be required. The Commander shall similarly inform the Government if any member of the Force has absented himself for more than twenty-one days. If an expulsion order against an ex-member of the Force has been made, the Commander shall be responsible for ensuring that the person concerned shall be received within the territory of the Participating State concerned.

Jurisdiction

10. The following arrangements respecting criminal and civil jurisdiction are made having regard to the special functions of the Force and to the interests of the United Nations, and not for the personal benefit of the members of the Force.

Criminal jurisdiction

11. Members of the Force shall be subject to the exclusive jurisdiction of their respective national States in respect of any criminal offences which may be committed by them in Cyprus.

Civil jurisdiction

12. (a) Members of the Force shall not be subject to the civil jurisdiction of the courts of Cyprus or to other legal process in any matter relating to their official duties. In a case arising from a matter relating to the official duties of a member of the Force and which involves a member of the Force and a Cypriot citizen, and in other disputes as agreed, the procedure provided in paragraph 38 (b) shall apply to the settlement.

(b) In these cases where civil jurisdiction is exercised by the courts of Cyprus with respect to members of the Force, the courts or other Cypriot authorities shall grant members of the Force sufficient opportunity to safeguard their rights. If the Commander certifies that a member of the Force is unable because of official duties or authorized absence to protect his interests in a civil proceeding in which he is a participant the aforesaid court or authority shall at his request suspend the proceeding until the elimination of the disability, but for not more than ninety days. Property of a member of the Force which is certified by the Commander to be needed by him for the fulfilment of his official duties shall be free from seizure for the satisfaction of a judgement, decision or order, together with other property not subject thereto under the law of Cyprus. The personal liberty of a member of the Force shall not be restricted by a court of other Cypriot authority in a civil proceeding, whether to enforce a judgement, decision or order, to compel an oath of disclosure, or for any other reason.

(c) In the cases provided for in sub-paragraph (b) above, the claimant may elect to have his claim dealt with in accordance with the procedure set out in paragraph 38 (b) of these arrangements. Where a claim adjudicated or an award made in favour of the claimant by a court of Cyprus or the Claims Commission under paragraph 38 (b) of these arrangements has not been made satisfied, the Government may, without prejudice to the claimant's rights, seek the good offices of the Secretary-General to obtain satisfaction.

Notification: certification

13. If any civil proceeding is instituted against a member of the Force before any court of Cyprus having jurisdiction, notification shall be given to the Commander. The Commander shall certify to the court whether or not the proceeding is related to the official duties of such member.

Military police: arrest: transfer of custody and mutual assistance

14. The Commander shall take all appropriate measures to ensure maintenance of discipline and good order among members of the Force. To this end military police designated by the Commander shall police the premises referred to in paragraph 19 of these arrangements, such areas where the Force is deployed in the performance of its functions, and such other areas as the Commander deems necessary to maintain discipline and order among members of the Force. For the purpose of this paragraph the military police of the Force shall have the power of arrest over members of the Force.

15. Military police of the Force may take into custody any Cypriot citizen committing an offence or causing a disturbance on the premises referred to in paragraph 19, without subjecting him to the ordinary routine of arrest, in order immediately to deliver him to the nearest appropriate Cypriot authorities for the purpose of dealing with such offence or disturbance.

16. The Cypriot authorities may take into custody a member of the Force, without subjecting him to the ordinary routine of arrest in order immediately to deliver him, together with any weapons or items seized, to the nearest appropriate authorities of the Force: (a) when so requested by the Commander, or (b) in cases in which the military police of the Force are unable to act with the necessary promptness when a member of the Force is apprehended in the commission or attempted commission of a criminal offence that results or might result in serious injury to persons or property, or serious impairment of other legally protected rights.

17. When a person is taken into custody under paragraph 15 and paragraph 16 (b), the Commander or the Cypriot authorities, as the case may be, may make a preliminary interrogation but may not delay the transfer of custody. Following the transfer of custody, the person concerned shall be made available upon request for further interrogation.

18. The Commander and the Cypriot authorities shall assist each other in the carrying out of all necessary investigations into offences in respect of which either or both have an interest, in the production of witnesses, and in the collection and production of evidence, including the seizure and, in proper cases, the handing over, of things connected with an offence. The handing over of any such things may be made subject to their return within the time specified by the

authority delivering them. Each shall notify the other of the disposition of any case in the outcome of which the other may have an interest or in which there has been a transfer of custody under the provisions of paragraphs 15 and 16 of these arrangements. The Government will ensure the prosecution of persons subject to its criminal jurisdiction who are accused of acts in relation to the Force or its members which, if committed in relation to the Cypriot army or its members, would have rendered them liable to prosecution. The Secretary-General will seek assurances from Governments of Participating States that they will be prepared to exercise jurisdiction with respect to crimes or offences which may be committed against Cypriot citizens by members of their national contingents serving with the Force.

Premises of the Force

19. The Government shall provide without cost to the Force and in agreement with the Commander such areas for headquarters, camps, or other premises as may be necessary for the accommodation and the fulfilment of the functions of the Force. Without prejudice to the fact that all such premises remain the territory of Cyprus, they shall be inviolable and subject to the exclusive control and authority of the Commander, who alone may consent to the entry of officials to perform duties on such premises.

United Nations flag

20. The Government recognizes the right of the Force to display within Cyprus the United Nations flag on its headquarters, camps, posts or other premises, vehicles, vessels and otherwise as decided by the Commander. Other flags or pennants may be displayed only in exceptional cases and in accordance with conditions prescribed by the Commander. Sympathetic consideration will be given to observations or requests of the Government concerning this last-mentioned matter.

Uniform: Vehicle, vessel and aircraft markings and registration: Operating permits

21. Members of the Force shall normally wear their national uniform with such identifying United Nations insignia as the Commander may prescribe. The conditions on which the wearing of civilian dress is authorized shall be notified by the Commander to the Government and sympathetic consideration will be given to

observations or requests of the Government concerning this matter. Service vehicles, vessels and aircraft shall carry a distinctive United Nations identification mark and licence which shall be notified by the Commander to the Government. Such vehicles, vessels and aircraft shall not be subject to registration and licensing under the laws and regulations of Cyprus. Cypriot authorities shall accept as valid, without a test or fee, a permit or licence for the operation of service vehicles, vessels and aircraft issued by the Commander.

Arms

22. Members of the Force may possess and carry arms in accordance with their orders.

Privileges and Immunities of the Force

23. The Force as a subsidiary organ of the United Nations, enjoys the status, privileges and immunities of the Organization in accordance with the Convention on the Privileges and Immunities of the United Nations. The provisions of article II of the Convention on the Privileges and Immunities of the United Nations shall also apply to the property, funds and assets of Participating States used in Cyprus in connexion with the national contingents serving in the Force. The Government recognizes that the right of the Force to import free of duty equipment for the Force and provisions, supplies and other goods for the exclusive use of members of the Force, members of the United Nations Secretariat detailed by the Secretary-General to serve with the Force, excluding locally recruited personnel, includes the right of the Force to establish, maintain and operate at headquarters, camps and posts, service institutes providing amenities for the persons aforesaid. The amenities that may be provided by service institutes shall be goods of a consumable nature (tobacco and tobacco products, beer, etc.), and other customary articles of small value. To the end that duty-free importation for the Force may be effected with the least possible delay, having regard to the interests of the Government, a mutually satisfactory procedure, including documentation, shall be arranged between the appropriate authorities of the Force and the Government. The Commander shall take all necessary measures to prevent any abuse of the exemption and to prevent the sale or resale of such goods to persons other than those aforesaid. Sympathetic consideration shall be given by the Commander to observations or requests of the Government concerning the operation of service institutes.

Privileges and immunities of officials and members of the Force

24. Members of the United Nations Secretariat detailed by the Secretary-General to serve with the Force remain officials of the United Nations entitled to the privileges and immunities of articles V and VII of the Convention on the Privileges and Immunities of the United Nations. With respect to the locally recruited personnel of the Force, however, who are not members of the Secretariat, the United Nations will assert its right only to the immunities concerning official acts, and exemption from taxation and national service obligations provided in sections 18 (a), (b) and (c) of the Convention on the Privileges and Immunities of the United Nations.

25. The Commander shall be entitled to the privileges, immunities and facilities of sections 19 and 27 of the Convention on the Privileges and Immunities of the United Nations. Officers serving on the Commander's Headquarters Staff and such other senior field officers as he may designate, are entitled to the privileges and immunities of article VI of the Convention on the Privileges and Immunities of the United Nations. Subject to the foregoing, the United Nations will claim with respect to members of the Force only those rights expressly provided in the present or supplemental arrangements.

Members of the Force: taxation, customs and fiscal regulations

26. Members of the Force shall be exempt from taxation on the pay and emoluments received from their national Governments or from the United Nations. They shall also be exempt from all other direct taxes except municipal rates for services enjoyed, and from all registration fees, and charges.

27. Members of the Force shall have the right to import free of duty their personal effects in connexion with their arrival in Cyprus. They shall be subject to the laws and regulations of Cyprus governing customs and foreign exchange with respect to personal property not required by them by reason of their presence in Cyprus with the Force. Special facilities for entry or exit shall be granted by the Cypriot immigration, customs and fiscal authorities to regularly constituted units of the Force provided that the authorities concerned have been duly notified sufficiently in advance. Members of the Force on departure from Cyprus may, notwithstanding the foreign exchange regulations, take with them such funds as the appropriate pay officer of the Force certifies were received in pay and emolu-

ments from their respective national Governments or from the United Nations and are a reasonable residue thereof. Special arrangements between the Commander and the Government shall be made for the implementation of the foregoing provisions in the mutual interests of the Government and members of the Force.

28. The Commander will co-operate with Cypriot customs and fiscal authorities in ensuring the observance of the customs and fiscal laws and regulations of Cyprus by the members of the Force in accordance with these or any relevant supplemental arrangements.

Communications and postal services

29. The Force enjoys the facilities in respect to communications provided in article III of the Convention on the Privileges and Immunities of the United Nations. The Commander shall have authority to install and operate a radio sending and receiving station or stations to connect at appropriate points and exchange traffic with the United Nations radio network, subject to the provisions of article 47 of the International Telecommunications Convention relating to harmful interference. The frequencies on which any such station may be operated will be duly communicated by the United Nations to the Government and to the International Frequency Registration Board. The right of the Commander is likewise recognized to enjoy the priorities of government telegrams and telephone calls as provided for the United Nations in article 39 and annex 3 of the latter Convention and in article 62 of the telegraph regulations annexed thereto.

30. The Force shall also enjoy, within its area of operations, the right of unrestricted communication by radio, telephone, telegraph or any other means, and of establishing the necessary facilities for maintaining such communications within and between premises of the Force, including the laying of cables and land lines and the establishment of fixed and mobile radio sending and receiving stations. It is understood that the telegraph and telephone cables and lines herein referred to will be situated within or directly between the premises of the Force and the area of operations, and that connexion with the Cypriot system of telegraphs and telephones will be made in accordance with arrangements with the appropriate Cypriot authorities.

31. The Government recognizes the right of the Force to make arrangements through its own facilities for the processing and trans-

port of private mail addressed to or emanating from members of the Force. The Government will be informed of the nature of such arrangements. No interference shall take place with, and no censorship shall be applied to, the mail of the Force by the Government. In the event that postal arrangements applying to private mail of members of the Force are extended to operations involving transfer of currency, or transport of packages or parcels from Cyprus, the conditions under which such operations shall be conducted in Cyprus will be agreed upon between the Government and the Commander.

Freedom of movement

32. The Force and its members together with its service vehicles, vessels, aircraft and equipment shall enjoy freedom of movement throughout Cyprus. Wherever possible the Commander will consult with the Government with respect to large movements of personnel, stores or vehicles on roads used for general traffic. The Government will supply the Force with maps and other information, including locations of dangers and impediments, which may be useful in facilitating its movements.

Use of roads, waterways, port facilities, and airfields

33. The Force shall have the right to the use of roads, bridges, canals and other waters, port facilities and airfields without the payment of dues, tolls or charges either by way of registration or otherwise, throughout Cyprus.

Water, electricity and other public utilities

34. The Force shall have the right to the use of water, electricity and other public utilities at rates not less favourable to the Force than those to comparable consumers. The Government will, upon the request of the Commander, assist the Force in obtaining water, electricity and other utilities required, and in the case of interruption or threatened interruption of service, will give the same priority to the needs of the Force as to essential Government services. The Force shall have the right where necessary to generate, within the premises of the Force either on land or water, electricity for the use of the Force, and to transmit and distribute such electricity as required by the Force.

Cypriot currency

35. The Government will, if requested by the Commander, make available to the Force, against reimbursement in such other mutually

acceptable currency, Cypriot currency required for the use of the Force, including the pay of the members of the national contingents, at the rate of exchange most favourable to the Force that is officially recognized by the Government.

Provisions, supplies and services

36. The Government will, upon the request of the Commander, assist the Force in obtaining equipment, provisions, supplies and other goods and services required from local sources for its subsistence and operation. Sympathetic consideration will be given by the Commander in purchases on the local market to requests or observations of the Government in order to avoid any adverse effect on the local economy. Members of the Force and United Nations officials may purchase locally goods necessary for their own consumption, and such services as they need, under conditions not less favourable than for Cypriot citizens. If members of the Force and United Nations officials should require medical or dental facilities beyond those available within the Force, arrangements shall be made with the Government under which such facilities may be made available. The Commander and the Government will co-operate with respect to sanitary services. The Commander and the Government shall extend to each other the fullest co-operation in matters concerning health, particularly with respect to the control of communicable diseases in accordance with international conventions; such co-operation shall extend to the exchange of relevant information and statistics.

Locally recruited personnel

37. The Force may recruit locally such personnel as required. The terms and conditions of employment for locally recruited personnel shall be prescribed by the Commander and shall generally, to the extent practicable, follow the practice prevailing in the locality.

Settlement of disputes or claims

38. Disputes or claims of a private law character shall be settled in accordance with the following provisions:

(a) The United Nations shall make provisions for the appropriate modes of settlement of disputes or claims arising out of contract or other disputes or claims of a private law character to which the United Nations is a party other than those covered in sub-paragraphs (b) and (c) following.

(b) Any claim made by

(i) a Cypriot citizen in respect of any damages alleged to result from an act or omission of a member of the Force relating to his official duties;

(ii) the Government against a member of the Force; or

(iii) the Force or the Government against one another, that is not covered by paragraphs 39 or 40 of these arrangements,

shall be settled by a Claims Commission established for that purpose. One member of the Commission shall be appointed by the Secretary-General, one member by the Government and a chairman jointly by the Secretary-General and the Government. If the Secretary-General and the Government fail to agree on the appointment of a chairman, the President of the International Court of Justice shall be asked by either to make the appointment. An award made by the Claims Commission against the Force or a member thereof or against the Government shall be notified to the Commander or the Government, as the case may be, to make satisfaction thereof.[1]

(c) Disputes concerning the terms of employment and conditions of service of locally recruited personnel shall be settled by administrative procedure to be established by the Commander.

39. All differences between the United Nations and the Government arising out of the interpretation or application of these arrangements which involve a question of principle concerning the Convention on the Privileges and Immunities of the United Nations shall be dealt with in accordance with the procedure of Section 30 of the Convention.

[1] In this respect attention must be drawn to operative paragraph 6 of the Security Council resolution of 4 March 1964 (S/5575) whereby the Council, *inter alia*, recommends that all costs pertaining to the Force be:

"met, in a manner to be agreed upon by them, by the Governments providing contingents and by the Government of Cyprus. The Secretary-General may also accept voluntary contributions for this purpose".

It is understood that the obligations of the Commander to make satisfaction as provided for in paragraph 38 (b) of the present arrangements are necessarily limited under the aforementioned paragraph of the Security Council resolution to the extent (a) that funds are available to him for this purpose and/or (b) alternative arrangements are arrived at with the Participating Governments and the Government of Cyprus.

40. All other disputes between the United Nations and the Government concerning the interpretation or application of these arrangements which are not settled by negotiation or other agreed mode of settlement shall be referred for final settlement to a tribunal of three arbitrators, one to be named by the Secretary-General of the United Nations, one by the Government and an umpire to be chosen jointly by the Secretary-General and the Government. If the two parties fail to agree on the appointment of the umpire within one month of the proposal of arbitration by one of the parties, the President of the International Court of Justice shall be asked by either party to appoint the umpire. Should a vacancy occur for any reason, the vacancy shall be filled within thirty days by the method laid down in this paragraph for the original appointment. The Tribunal shall come into existence upon the appointment of the umpire and at least one of the other members of the tribunal. Two members of the tribunal shall constitute a quorum for the performance of its functions, and for all deliberations and decisions of the tribunal a favourable vote of two members shall be sufficient.

Liaison

41. The Commander and the Government shall take appropriate measures to ensure close and reciprocal liaison in the implementation of the present agreement. Furthermore, arrangements will be made, *inter alia,* for liaison on a State and local level between the Force and the Government security forces to the extent the Commander deems this to be necessary and desirable for the performance of the functions of the Force in accordance with the Security Council resolution of 4 March 1964 (S/5575). In case of requests by the Government security forces for the assistance of the Force, the Commander, in view of the international status and function of the Force, will decide whether, within the framework of the aforesaid resolution, he may meet such requests. The Commander of the Force may make requests for assistance from the Government security forces, at the State or local level, as he may deem necessary in pursuance of the aforesaid resolution, and they will, as far as possible, meet such requests in a spirit of co-operation.

Deceased members: disposition of personal property

42. The Commander shall have the right to take charge of and dispose of the body of a member of the Force who dies in Cyprus

and may dispose of his personal property after the debts of the deceased person incurred in Cyprus and owing to Cypriot citizens have been settled.

Supplemental arrangements

43. Supplemental details for the carrying out of these arrangements shall be made as required between the Commander and appropriate Cypriot authorities designated by the Government.

Contacts in the performance of the function of the Force

44. It is understood that the Commander and members of the Force authorized by him may have such contacts as they deem necessary in order to secure the proper performance of the function of the Force, under the Security Council resolution of 4 March 1964 (S/5575).

Effective date and duration

45. Upon acceptance of this proposal by your Government, the present letter and your reply will be considered as constituting an agreement between the United Nations and Cyprus that shall be deemed to have taken effect as from the date of the arrival of the first element of the Force in Cyprus, and shall remain in force until the departure of the Force from Cyprus. The effective date that the departure has occurred shall be defined by the Secretary-General and the Government. The provisions of paragraphs 38, 39 and 40 of these arrangements, relating to the settlement of disputes, however, shall remain in force until all claims arising prior to the date of termination of these arrangements, and submitted prior to or within three months following the date of termination, have been settled.

In conclusion I wish to affirm that the activities of the Force will be guided in good faith by the task established for the Force by the Security Council. Within this context the Force, as established by the Secretary-General and acting on the basis of his directives under the exclusive operational direction of the Commander, will use its best endeavours, in the interest of preserving international peace and security, to prevent a recurrence of fighting and, as necessary, to contribute to the maintenance and restoration of law and order and a return to normal conditions.

Accept, Sir, the assurances of my highest consideration.

U THANT
Secretary-General

ANNEX II

REPLY FROM THE MINISTER FOR FOREIGN AFFAIRS OF THE REPUBLIC OF CYPRUS TO THE SECRETARY-GENERAL OF THE UNITED NATIONS

31 March 1964

Sir,

I have the honour to refer to your letter of 31 March 1964, in which you have proposed that the Republic of Cyprus and the United Nations should make the *ad hoc* arrangements contained therein which define certain of the conditions necessary for the effective discharge of the functions of the United Nations Force in Cyprus while it remains in Cyprus. Recalling that by letter of 4 March 1964, I informed you of the agreement of the Government of the Republic of Cyprus to the establishment of the Force, I now have the pleasure to inform you in the name of the Government of the Republic of Cyprus of its full agreement on, and its acceptance of, the terms of your letter.

The Government of the Republic of Cyprus agrees, furthermore, that subject to ratification by the Republic of Cyprus, your letter and this reply will be considered as constituting an agreement between Cyprus and the United Nations concerning the status of the United Nations Force in Cyprus. Pending such ratification the Government of the Republic of Cyprus undertakes to give provisional application to the arrangements contained in your letter and to use its best efforts to secure the earliest possible ratification of the agreement.

In conclusion, I wish to affirm that the Government of the Republic of Cyprus, recalling the Security Council resolution of 4 March 1964 (S/5575), and, in particular, paragraphs 2 and 5 thereof, will be guided in good faith, when exercising its sovereign rights on any matter concerning the presence and functioning of the Force, by its acceptance of the recommendation of the Security Council that a peace-keeping Force be established in Cyprus.

Accept, Sir, the assurances of my highest consideration.

Spyros A. Kyprianou
Minister for Foreign Affairs

RESOLUTION ADOPTED BY THE SECURITY COUNCIL AT ITS 1139TH MEETING HELD ON 20 JUNE 1964

The Security Council,

Noting that the report by the Secretary-General (S/5764) considers the maintenance in Cyprus of the United Nations Peace-Keeping Force created by the Security Council resolution of 4 March 1964 (S/5575) for an additional period of three months to be useful and advisable,

Expressing its deep appreciation to the Secretary-General for his efforts in the implementation of the Security Council resolutions of 4 March 1964 and 13 March 1964,

Expressing its deep appreciation to the States that have contributed troops, police, supplies and financial support for the implementation of the Security Council resolution of 4 March 1964,

1. *Reaffirms* its resolutions of 4 March 1964 and 13 March 1964;
2. *Calls upon* all Member States to comply with the above-mentioned resolutions;
3. *Takes note* of the Report by the Secretary-General (S/5764);
4. *Extends* the stationing in Cyprus of the United Nations Peace-Keeping Force established under the Security Council resolution of 4 March 1964 for an additional period of three months, ending 26 September 1964 (S/5575).

RESOLUTION ADOPTED BY THE SECURITY COUNCIL AT ITS 1159TH MEETING ON 25 SEPTEMBER 1964

The Security Council,

Noting the report of the Secretary-General and, in particular, that the Secretary-General considers necessary the extension of the stationing in Cyprus of the United Nations Peace-Keeping Force created by the Security Council resolution of 4 March 1964 (S/5575) beyond 26 September,

Noting that the Government of Cyprus has indicated its desire that the stationing of the United Nations Force in Cyprus should be continued beyond 26 September 1964,

Renewing the expression of its deep appreciation to the Secretary-General for his efforts in the implementation of the Security Council resolutions of 4 March 1964, 13 March 1964 and 20 June 1964,

Renewing the expression of its deep appreciation to the States that have contributed troops, police, supplies and financial support for the implementation of the Security Council resolution of 4 March 1964,

Paying tribute to the memory of Sakari Tuomioja for the outstanding services that he rendered to the cause of the United Nations,

Expressing satisfaction that a new Mediator has been appointed by the Secretary-General in conformity with the resolution of 4 March 1964,

1. *Reaffirms* its resolutions of 4 March 1964, 13 March 1964, 20 June 1964 and 9 August 1964 and the consensus expressed by the President at its 1143rd meeting on 11 August 1964;

2. *Calls upon* all Member States to comply with the above-mentioned resolutions;

3. *Extends* the period in which the United Nations Peace-Keeping Force (UNFICYP) shall be stationed in Cyprus for another three months ending 26 December 1964, in conformity with the terms of the resolution of 4 March 1964;

4. *Requests* the Secretary-General to keep the Security Council informed regarding the compliance of the parties concerned with the provisions of this resolution.

BOLIVIA, BRAZIL, IVORY COAST, MOROCCO AND NORWAY: JOINT DRAFT RESOLUTION

The Security Council,

Noting that the report by the Secretary-General (S/6102) recommends the maintenance in Cyprus of the United Nations Peace-Keeping Force created by the Security Council resolution of 4 March 1964 (S/5575) for an additional period of three months,

Noting that the Government of Cyprus has indicated its desire that the stationing of the United Nations Force in Cyprus should be continued beyond 26 December 1964,

Noting with satisfaction that the report of the Secretary-General (S/6102) indicates that the situation in Cyprus has improved and that significant progress has been made,

Renewing the expression of its deep appreciation to the Secretary-General for his efforts in the implementation of the Security Council resolutions of 4 March 1964, 13 March 1964, 20 June 1964 and 25 September 1964,

Renewing the expression of its deep appreciation to the States that have contributed troops, police, supplies and financial support for the implementation of the Security Council resolution of 4 March 1964,

1. *Reaffirms* its resolutions of 4 March 1964, 13 March 1964, 20 June 1964, 9 August 1964 and 25 September 1964, and the consensus expressed by the President at its 1143rd meeting on 11 August 1964;

2. *Calls upon* all Member States to comply with the above-mentioned resolutions;

3. *Takes note* of the Report by the Secretary-General (S/6102);

4. *Extends* the stationing in Cyprus of the United Nations Peace-Keeping Force established under the Security Council resolution of 4 March 1964 for an additional period of three months, ending 26 March 1965.

BOLIVIA, IVORY COAST, JORDAN, MALAYSIA, NETHERLANDS, URUGUAY: JOINT DRAFT RESOLUTION

The Security Council,

Noting that the report by the Secretary-General (S/6228 and Corr. 1 and Add. 1) recommends the maintenance in Cyprus of the United Nations Peace-Keeping Force created by the Security Council resolution of 4 March 1964 (S/5575) for an additional period of three months,

Noting that the Government of Cyprus has indicated its desire that the stationing of the United Nations Force in Cyprus should be continued beyond 26 March 1965,

Noting from the Report of the Secretary-General that while the military situation has on the whole remained quiet during the period under review and while the presence of the United Nations Force has contributed significantly to this effect, nevertheless the position remains one of uneasiness in several points, with the consequent danger of a renewal of fighting with all of is disastrous consequences,

Renewing the expression of its deep appreciation to the Secretary-General for his efforts in the implementation of the Security Council resolutions of 4 March 1964, 13 March 1964 (S/5603), 20 June 1964 (S/5778), 25 September 1964 (S/5987) and 18 December 1964 (S/6121),

Renewing the expression of its deep appreciation to the States that have contributed troops, police, supplies and financial support for the implementation of the Security Council resolution of 4 March 1964,

1. *Reaffirms* its resolutions of 4 March 1964, 13 March 1964, 20

June 1964, 9 August 1964 (S/5868), 25 September 1964 and 18 December 1964, and the consensus expressed by the President at its 1143rd meeting on 11 August 1964;

2. *Calls upon* all Member States to comply with the above-mentioned resolutions;

3. *Calls upon* the parties concerned to act with the utmost restraint and to co-operate fully with the United Nations Force;

4. *Takes note* of the Report by the Secretary-General (S/6228 and Corr. 1 and Add. 1);

5. *Extends* the stationing in Cyprus of the United Nations Peace-Keeping Force established under the Security Council resolution of 4 March 1964 for an additional period of three months, ending 26 June 1965.

Appendix C

Selected statements and addresses on peace-keeping military forces and problems

Appendix C-1

Lester B. Pearson

LECTURE BY THE RIGHT HONOURABLE LESTER B. PEARSON, PRIME MINISTER OF CANADA, IN THE DAG HAMMARSKJOLD MEMORIAL SERIES, AT CARLETON UNIVERSITY, MAY 7, 1964

Keeping the peace

When I received the invitation to speak in this Dag Hammarskjold Memorial Series of lectures, I considered it a privilege to be included among those close collaborators and friends of the late Secretary-General who would be paying tribute to his memory, and to his work, in this way. It is most fitting that in Canada this lecture should be given at Carleton University, from which Dag Hammarskjold received the first honorary degree given by this University and the first offered to him by any Canadian university.

I have chosen the subject "Keeping the Peace" because Mr. Hammarskjold gave so much of himself to the task of developing the peace-keeping work of the United Nations. Indeed he was on active service for peace when his life so tragically and so prematurely ended.

Dag Hammarskjold died, as he would have wished, in the service both of peace and the United Nations. I had the privilege of knowing him well and of working with him at the United Nations during some difficult years. I admired and respected the high character of the man and the great qualities of the statesman. He was tireless and selfless and wise. He was as sure and as resolute in carrying out instructions from the United Nations for international action in the cause of peace as he was skilful and objective in seeking to establish a basis for that action in the Charter.

His life was a triumph of service and achievement and his passing at the very height of his career was a tragic loss. His death must continue to inspire us all to do what we can to secure the triumph of the cause for which he died, peace and security in the world, through the United Nations.

At a press conference early in 1959, Dag Hammarskjold said this: "The basic policy line for this Organization is that the United Nations simply must respond to those demands which may be made of it. If we feel that those demands go beyond the present capacity, that in itself, from my point of view, is not a reason why the Organization should refuse to respond, because I do not know the exact capacity of this machine. It did take the very steep hill of Suez; it may take other and even steeper hills. I would not object beforehand unless I could say, and had to say in all sincerity, that I knew what was asked of the United Nations could not be done. So far, I am not aware of any question which has been raised which would cause me to give a negative or discouraging reply. For that reason, my policy attitude remains that the United Nations should respond and should have confidence in its strength and capacity to respond."

In this lecture, I am concerned with ways and means of increasing that "strength and capacity to respond."

To this end I wish to review developments in the field of United Nations peace-keeping in order to illustrate the various demands which have been made of the Organization and its response to them. I hope, as well, to suggest ways in which the capacity to respond can be strengthened, as it must be strengthened, if the United Nations is to fulfill its primary purpose of maintaining peace and security in future.

Intervention for War

As the nineteenth century came to an end, governments were beginning to think about international organization to prevent war.

But in the main they continued to rely for security on their own power, supplemented by military alliances which had replaced Mettennich's earlier Concert of Europe. Like the little old lady in Punch of 1914, they consoled themselves with the thought that, if threats to the peace occurred, such as the assassination of an Archduke in a Serbian town, "the powers are sure to intervene." After the shot at Sarejevo they did so—against each other and for national ends. The war to end war was on.

After World War I, experts on international affairs debated whether it could happen again. They hoped that it could be avoided by strengthening collective security. They looked to the new League of Nations for this. But most governments still showed a preference for arms and military pacts. When collective security and sanctions under the Covenant *were* advocated, it was primarily with a view to possible use against Germany. Later, in Italy's attacks on Ethiopia, the League rejected effective international action for peace. In consequence, we lost the race with re-armament, while Hitler and Mussolini scorned the treaties intended to maintain the balance of power. "Intervention," a dirty word in the case of Ethiopia, Spain and Czechoslovakia, became a necessity in Poland. Peace in our time dissolved in the global devastation of the Second World War.

Again there was a kind of peace, this time soon followed by cold war which had become so intense by the fifties that Great Power deadlock was in danger of destroying or rendering impotent the improved League which we now called the United Nations. Yet the world organization, in spite of limitations, and with varying success tried to keep the peace on the periphery of potential war —in Greece and Kashmir, in Palestine and Indonesia. Its method was one of persuasion and "watchdog" presence. It seemed a frail basis for collective security in the face of Soviet aggressiveness—and in the shadow of the Bomb.

Since the main Communist challenge at that time was in Europe, the North Atlantic states responded to the weakness of the United Nations by exercising their right of collective self-defence under the Charter. They formed NATO to ward off the threat of military attack in the Treaty area and, in essence, to safeguard peace by deterring aggression. NATO was not an alternative to the United Nations but a practical and regional means of cementing cracks which had appeared in the Charter security system.

In some ways, the situation in 1950 was unpleasantly like that of 1935. The international peace-keeping machinery was virtually stalled; the powers were once more turning to defence pacts. Tension in Europe remained explosive. A single incident from this tension could, and more than once almost did, result in general disaster.

But the flash of fighting actually occurred on a distant horizon—in Korea. This was no mere incident with possible alarming repercussions. This was an armed aggression, carefully calculated and prepared, and bolstered by the conventional military weapons of the Communist arsenal. It was a direct challenge which had to be met squarely by the Western powers if there was to be any hope of containing Communist military expansion. They were able to use the United Nations for this purpose because, luckily, the Russians stayed away from the Security Council when the Korean resolution was passed. It was an absence not likely to be repeated.

If the Great Powers had intervened in the manner of earlier times, Korea could have been the spark which ignited nuclear world war. Instead, the conflict was localized by improvising a collective response from the United Nations, by carefully defining the objectives of the United Nations military action and by making effective but limited use of United States military strength. In his thoughtful lecture in this series, Mr. Adlai Stevenson suggested that "*Perhaps* Korea was the end of the road for classical armed aggression against one's next door neighbour." It may also have signified the end of Communist gambling on *direct* aggression in areas of Great Power interest.

Intervention for Peace

In any event, Korea was the beginning of a new development in international affairs—the deployment of armed military force under the control and the flag of the United Nations. At San Francisco, this possibility had been provided for in Chapter VII of the Charter. But the international security force of that Chapter—intended to be the strong arm of an effectively functioning Security Council and to include all its permanent members—withered in the angry cold war debates of the late forties.

With the Security Council "frozen in futility," the General Assembly, under the stimulus of the Korean emergency, took its own action to give sinew to the United Nations peace-keeping arm.

It adopted certain recommendations under the heading "Uniting for Peace," including one to the effect that each member should maintain within its national armed forces elements so trained, organized and equipped that they could promptly be made available for service as a United Nations unit or units upon recommendation by the Security Council or the General Assembly. The same resolution provided for the General Assembly to act on short notice when there was a threat to the peace and the Security Council had failed to act because of the exercise of the veto.

Neither the procedure nor the collective measures proposed were pursued with any vigor in the next few years. The fighting in Korea died down. The wave of that crisis receded and with it the urge to be ready next time. The Soviet bloc was naturally opposed to the "Uniting for Peace" resolution and violently denounced it as a violation of the Charter. In any event, East-West tension had eased after the Summit meeting at Geneva and the West lost interest in the matter. In short, Great Power deadlock destroyed the hope of establishing the United Nations Security Council force envisaged in the Charter. Inertia and wishful thinking, among members generally, postponed any significant action on the 1950 resolution calling for the alternative of stand-by units. The world community was to wait for another crisis.

It came in 1956, mounting with increasing menace in the Middle East. In late October, Israeli armed forces raced to the Suez Canal. Britain and France delivered their ultimatum and moved in. The Soviet Union and later Communist China issued threats. War seemed imminent and the United Nations was called upon to intervene for peace.

The main demand was to end the fighting and bring about the withdrawal of the British and French forces. What was needed to accomplish this was an impartial military force to secure a ceasefire and withdrawal and to supervise a buffer zone, first near the Canal and later along the line dividing Israel and Egypt. Some security had to be restored after the shock of fighting, the humiliation of defeat, and the frustrations of withdrawal. But the United Nations force to be organized for this purpose would do no fighting except in self-defence and would rely mainly on its presence as representing the United Nations to accomplish its aims. "Intervention" by the United Nations was to acquire new meaning.

Problems of Ad Hoc Peace-keeping

The "Uniting for Peace" procedure had made it possible for the Assembly to meet in emergency special session to deal with the Suez crisis. It was able quickly to adopt broad directives governing the establishment and functioning of UNEF. But the Secretariat found little on their files concerning collective measures which might give a lead on how to proceed. It was a new course on new ground. Some experience could be drawn from the earlier activities of the military observer groups but no real precedent existed for a major, genuinely United Nations military operation which had to be carried out with speed, efficiency and even daring, if it were to succeed.

The Secretary-General and the participating governments had to start virtually from zero. There was no time for detailed planning, either in New York or in national capitals. An international command staff had to be gathered in the Canal Zone, and an *ad hoc* team of military advisers assembled overnight in United Nations Headquarters. Contingents, selected from the offers made, had to be moved to Palestine within a few days after the adoption of the Assembly resolution.

That UNEF did succeed in its initial tasks can largely be attributed to the ingenuity, skill and energy of Dag Hammarskjold; to the solid core of support which existed in the Assembly; and to the prompt response of the ten governments which provided the original contingents; finally, to the fact that the parties directly concerned with the Suez conflict consented to the stationing and functioning of the force in the area.

There were many anxious days in the long weeks from November 1956 to March 1957, when the withdrawal from Egyptian territory was completed and the United Nations force was fully deployed. There was noisy and acrimonious debate. There was also quiet and earnest consultation. At times it looked as though the UNEF experiment might fail, mainly because of political objections but also because of practical difficulties of establishing, organizing, and directing an international force which was the first of its kind in history.

A major question for Canada was the nature of its own participation. Our experience was revealing. To support our political initiative in the Assembly, the Government offered to provide a self-contained infantry battalion group. But after these troops had begun to move to the port of embarkation, it emerged that, of some two dozen offers of military assistance to the United Nations, most were infantry units and practically none included the supporting and technical services which the force would need—including an air component. Since the Great Powers were not participating in the force, Canada was one of a very few countries which was able, because of its military know-how and experience, to provide administrative and logistic specialists. In the end, the Canadian contingent included reconnaissance, transport, maintenance and supply units of the Canadian Army, and an observation and transport squadron of the RCAF. They were sneered at by some in the heat of partisan debate as a typewriter army, but they were indispensable to the success of UNEF. They played, and are still playing, a courageous and essential role.

This last-minute need to re-organize the Canadian contingent was not only a source of political embarrassment but a cause of delay in getting Canadian troops to Palestine. Both could have been avoided if there had been advance United Nations planning for such peace-keeping operations and co-ordinated preparations in the military establishments of the contributing countries.

Similar problems—the political problem of achieving balanced composition and the practical problem of finding qualified units and personnel for maintaining a mixed force—arose when the Congo crisis broke in 1960 and the United Nations was again asked to provide a peace-keeping force. There was no lack of infantry contingents and it was very desirable that the countries of Africa should provide most of them. Technical units and specialists were also needed, however, and national establishments had to be combed for suitable personnel.

The UNEF experience was available because the Secretary-General had produced a very useful study in 1958. But the United Nations faced a very different situation in the Congo and the demands on its military force were much more complicated. Quite apart from the political difficulties, which multiplied as the operation progressed, once again, as in the case of UNEF, there were technical delays and administrative and other difficulties.

Again our own experience can be cited. For both UNEF and ONUC, mainly because of the nature of our participation, it was necessary to organize new Canadian units to form the contingent. This caused some disruption in our armed services, for specialists had to be drawn from units and formations already committed to other tasks. While the personnel were well-trained in their technical duties, they had been taught, as part of their regular training, to think and act as fighting soldiers. In a peace-keeping role—largely passive and supervisory in nature—the troops were called upon to perform unaccustomed and difficult duties, often without clear directions.

I do not wish to leave the impression that the Canadian Armed Services in both the Suez and the Congo did not respond to United Nations needs with speed, efficiency, tact and inventiveness. The opposite is true. They were magnificent. What I do suggest is that the launching of these two vital peace-keeping operations—from the point of view both of the United Nations and of participating countries—would have been accomplished more easily and effectively if steps had been taken in advance to ensure technical and other forms of preparation for this kind of peace-keeping.

Now I am aware that earlier conditions are not likely to be duplicated when the United Nations embarks on a peace-keeping mission. The political circumstances vary; the composition of the force usually has to be adjusted to suit them; the climate and terrain in the area of operations may be quite different.

We also have to recognize that the kind of United Nations presence required may vary greatly from situation to situation. Mr. Hammarskjold spoke about the "uniqueness of the UNEF setting." He maintained that such a force could not have been deployed in Lebanon or in Jordan in 1958, although there was a need for other forms of United Nations presence on these occasions in which unarmed military observers were able to play a significant part in restoring stability. Similar operations—but with local variations—were carried out more recently in West New Guinea and in Yemen.

The method of operation has to be adapted to each situation. The truce supervision teams in Kashmir and Palestine investigate complaints about incidents; the observers in Lebanon, moving about in jeeps and helicopters, sought to check the illegal entry of arms and infiltrations. In Gaza, UNEF had been stationed at fixed posts. In the buffer zone and in Sinai it has engaged in mobile reconnaissance on the ground and in the air. In the Congo, the force has occupied key points in the main centres of the country. In some areas, the task has been one of patrolling demilitarized zones; in others, of calming and controlling local populations; and still others of persuading opposing factions to refrain from hostile acts.

The very fact that forces are composed of national contingents with their own military traditions and methods and disciplines adds to the complexity of the operation. Language can be a barrier; and problems of supply a difficulty. The many variations which occur require careful organization, through training and standardization of procedure.

But, in spite of all the difficulties and differences, the shocks and surprises, the United Nations has shown itself capable of brilliant improvisation and has succeeded in making its peace-keeping presence effective. Its record of achievement has been good; all the more so because it was never permitted to be prepared.

Cyprus Dilemma

How can we be complacent about this chronic state of unpreparedness; this necessity of improvising during a crisis when failure could mean war? Today in Cyprus, the United Nations is facing another severe test of its capacity to respond, without preparation, to a challenge to peace. On tomorrow's horizon, there may be other sudden and equally exacting demands. The halting response which the Organization made, after the Cyprus issue had been raised in the Security Council, reflected the deep-seated political dilemma which handicaps the United Nations peace-keeping role. It also served to remind us again that the protection of international peace should not be left to preparations made on the brink; to ad hoc arrangements and hasty organization.

Hesitations and difficulties over Cyprus were increased by division among the Great Powers. But this was a normal situation in the United Nations and outside it. More disturbing was the widespread disinterest or suspicion on the part of many middle and small powers. Some were too preoccupied with national and regional interests, which dulled their sense of danger at tensions smouldering in other parts of the world. Others had grown weary of the burden of international crises; and of finance, which, in recent years, has fallen heavily on the shoulders of a few states. All-pervading also was the suspicion that the Cyprus conflict was just too difficult and too domestic for United Nations treatment. It was too small a local tail to wag such a big international dog.

But, as in the Suez and the Congo, the United Nations while hesitant and unprepared, did not abandon its peace-keeping responsibilities thanks to the initiative taken by certain of its members.

So we can take comfort from the fact that in the Cyprus crisis, occurring even before the liquidation of the Congo problem, the Security Council decided to establish a force in that troubled Island; that five member governments agreed to provide contingents and ten to make contributions to the voluntary fund for financing the operation; that the force became quickly operational and that a mediator was chosen who took up his difficult assignment without delay.

While this result gives cause for satisfaction, it should not blind us to the need, demonstrated once more, to organize, plan and prepare in advance for prompt United Nations engagement in peace-keeping operations. It has become glaringly apparent that the Organization and its individual members must improve their capability to act quickly. I believe that there is a growing resolve to do this, reflecting a conviction that United Nations preparedness in the field of peace-keeping falls far short of the urgent demands being made on the Organization with increasing frequency.

The requirements of peace preservation in the future may not always be satisfied by skillful improvisation and by the willingness of a few to do their duty. The growing interest in improving peace-keeping methods must be broadly stimulated into advance planning and preparation. Canada, I know, is resolved to draw on its own experience in a way which will give leadership and encouragement in this effort.

Preparedness for Peace-keeping Operations

What can be done, then, to prepare the United Nations for the kind of peace-keeping operations which we have seen in the past and others which we can expect in future? Ideally the Organization should have its own permanent international force in being, under its orders, for peace-keeping duties. But this is not now feasible for political reasons.

As a next best, all member governments should have elements

in their armed services earmarked, trained and equipped for United Nations service; ready for call to such service. There should be a military planning staff in United Nations Headquarters to co-ordinate the national preparations and to improve the operating procedures of the Organization.

It has become apparent in the past ten years, however, that formal action by and in the United Nations to achieve even these limited ends is not immediately feasible because of political and practical difficulties. The most recent occasion when the United Nations showed some disposition to deal with the question of stand-by arrangements was in 1958. Dag Hammarskjold had made his report on the experience derived from the establishment and functioning of UNEF. A number of countries, including the United States, wished to take action in the General Assembly, based on that report. Political circumstances, however, were not favourable. United States support roused all the worst Soviet suspicions. So the matter was dropped. The report was not even discussed by the Assembly.

The Soviet bloc remained firmly opposed to any international security or peace-keeping force or any plan for such a force. The West was not willing to force the issue. The Arab world had been rocked by disturbances in Lebanon, Jordan and Iraq. Some non-aligned countries, suspicious of Western motives and not wishing to become involved in East-West argument, were unwilling to authorize the United Nations to put force behind international decisions and organize for the purpose. They failed to appreciate that by strengthening the United Nations capacity to meet threats to the peace, they would be strengthening as well their own security and creating conditions favourable to the economic and social development which they so badly needed.

Since that time, 1958, there has been some shift in the attitude of member states but not sufficient to ensure the kind of support needed if formal U.N. stand-by arrangements are to succeed. Nevertheless, the need continues and increases.

A few members have recognized this. Like Canada, they have earmarked units for United Nations service. Following an announcement last year, the Nordic countries—Denmark, Finland, Norway and Sweden—have introduced legislation setting up contingents which are designed for United Nations service and each of which may be used in conjunction with those established in the other Nordic countries.

This is an encouraging development. The Netherlands has followed suit by earmarking troops. There have been indications that other states, representing other geographical areas, have begun to think along those lines.

This is why I proposed recently that if the United Nations itself remains unable to agree on permanent arrangements for a stand-by peace force, members who believe that stand-by arrangements should be made could discharge their own responsibility, individually and collectively, by organizing such a force for use by the United Nations.

I do not wish to be misunderstood on this point. The stand-by arrangements made by the interested countries, because of existing circumstances in the United Nations, would have to be made outside its constitutional framework. But those arrangements would be squarely within the context of United Nations purposes; within the Charter.

The stand-by contingents which resulted from such an arrangement would not be used unless and until they had been requested by the United Nations to engage in one of its duly authorized peace-keeping operations.

In some situations this stand-by force might not necessarily serve as an entity; only some of its national contingents might be selected to serve. Parts might be used alone or be combined with contingents from other United Nations members not included in the stand-by arrangements. Political requirements would determine its role.

I emphasize this because there has been some disposition to interpret my proposal as an intention to turn away from the United Nations. The whole point of it was to strengthen the capability of the members concerned to serve and support the United Nations.

When I suggested that at first the stand-by arrangements might be confined to half a dozen or so middle powers, I had in mind, of course, the countries which have already earmarked contingents for United Nations service. They would be ready—and willing. Soon, I hope, others would be added until all the contingents would be represented.

Co-ordination would be a first requirement. This could be achieved in several ways. The governments concerned could consult closely about the kind of units and personnel which might be needed in future operations. They could perhaps agree to some allocation of responsibility for organizing and training their earmarked contingents. Exchanges of ideas, experience and key personnel could be arranged on a regular basis.

An international staff would be needed to co-ordinate the training and other activities of the earmarked contingents; to analyze and correlate with future needs the experience of past operations; to prepare contingency plans and operating procedures for a variety of situations. No stand-by arrangements would be complete without making provision for such a staff—at least in embryo.

It would be even better if a compact military planning staff could be set up in the office of the Secretary-General, one which could co-operate with the member states who have decided to work together in the United Nations peace-keeping field.

It is a matter of some satisfaction that the Secretariat now includes a Military Adviser. He should have a supporting staff to assist him in advising the Secretary-General on the establishment and conduct of military operations. The same staff could be planning ahead for possible peace-keeping missions.

I believe that, if a group of middle and small powers could be persuaded to work together along the lines indicated above, an effective stand-by arrangement could be brought into being.

I do not expect that even the most modest of such arrangements could be accomplished quickly. Nevertheless, the Canadian Government is determined to push ahead toward this goal. We have been considering plans for confidential discussions with certain other governments, primarily of military problems arising out of past and current peace-keeping operations. As a first stage, such discussions would be confined to countries which have taken steps to establish stand-by units for United Nations service. Later they might be extended.

Out of these discussions may come suggestions for improving the United Nations ability to conduct peace-keeping operations and for strengthening and co-ordinating arrangements for national participation in these operations. That is what I intended when I suggested at the eighteenth General Assembly that there should be a "pooling of available resources and the development in a co-ordinated way of trained and equipped collective forces for United Nations Service."

We shall be following up these exploratory talks with a more formal approach to the other governments concerned. We have reason to hope that they share Canadian views on the need to improve on the present improvised and haphazard approach to peace-keeping.

My concentration so far on the organization and employment of military force reflects my deep concern about the present operation in Cyprus, as well as a conviction which I have held for many years.

However, just as the United Nations is not the only instrument for keeping the peace in today's world, international military force is not the only peace-keeping United Nations machinery which should be readily available. There remains a growing need for unarmed supervisory teams, for experienced mediators and conciliators. This need should also be planned for.

Arising out of past operations, the United Nations has been able to compile an impressive list of individual soldiers and civilians who have demonstrated their qualification for serving as impartial international servants. Some member governments are aware of the need to keep this list up-to-date and up to strength. They have been proposing additional names to it. They know that there will be more situations requiring the prompt dispatch of observers and mediators ready and able to serve the Organization.

In many cases, the functions performed by an international force more closely resemble those of the police than the military. This is especially true in a country experiencing the breakdown of internal order or torn by civil disturbance.

Police training is not usually a part of military training but it should be, under any stand-by arrangement for an international peace force.

I would go further. If the United Nations, as such, cannot now organize its own peace-keeping force, it should at least recruit a small professional international police force specifically trained for such duties as traffic and crowd control, property protection, escort duty and crime investigation. Cyprus is showing the importance of having such a police force to supplement the soldiers.

Mr. Trygve Lie, the first Secretary-General, had this kind of force in mind when he put forth his proposal for a United Nations Guard in 1948. His proposal, like many others at that time, was a casualty of the cold war. But it had great merit then, as it has even greater merit today, in the light of recent experience of the United Nations in the field of peace-keeping.

Whatever may be the role of United Nations representatives in the field, it will always call for special qualities, in civilians and soldiers alike. They must make a quick transition from being a loyal citizen of one nationality to being a member of an international team with loyalty to the Organization and the Charter.

This means that training for UN service is of particular importance. Such training—military or para-military or civilian—should have a certain uniformity in all countries likely to participate in peace-keeping operations. It should take into account the training requirements of individual units. It should include a substantial content of United Nations philosophy. Personnel of all categories should be educated in the aims and purposes of the United Nations, in its political methods and administrative procedures, in the significance of the peace-keeping role.

This is particularly true for the soldiers of all ranks, who have been trained to be non-political and to owe one allegiance. It is a tribute to the character and discipline of United Nations troops that there have been very few instances in which they have broken the code of international service.

In the tasks of separating armies, supervising truce lines or calming hostile factions, the United Nations soldier will be frequently called upon to exert a mediatory rather than a military influence. He will be required to display unusual self-restraint often under severe provocation. In many cases, an explosive situation can be brought under control through coolness, good humour and common sense. And this applies not only to high-ranking officers but to NCO's and other ranks.

Behind this self-restraint and common sense there must, however, be force. The problem of the use of such force in United Nations peace-keeping operations can be a complicated and difficult business, especially for the commander on the spot. But the basic principles are clear enough and follow logically from the initial premise: that a UN force is a peace force and there is no enemy to be defeated. Therefore, the UN does not mount offensive actions and may never take the initiative in the use of armed force.

This means the use of arms by a United Nations force is permissible only in self-defence and when all peaceful means of persuasion have failed.

It is important to appreciate however what is involved in this right of self-defence. Thus, when forcible attempts are made to compel UN soldiers to withdraw from positions which they occupy under orders from their commanders, or to disarm them, or to prevent them from carrying out their responsibilities, UN troops should be and have been authorized to use force.

What can be done in any situation depends on the mandate given the Force. It is always open to the Security Council or the General Assembly as the case may be to enlarge this mandate and authorize the use of the necessary amount of force to achieve specified objectives. This was done during the Congo operation as the developing situation required, and with the aim of preventing civil war clashes and apprehending mercenaries. The mandate thus determines the extent to which any UN peace-keeping force can employ arms for the discharge of responsibilities which have been clearly assigned to it.

In this lecture I have put forward some modest proposals whereby the United Nations could be better prepared for keeping the peace. There are, however, two large and related issues which make such proposals difficult to carry out. The first is financial. The second, and more important, is political.

We know that for the past few years the United Nations has been teetering on the edge of bankruptcy. There have been heavy burdens assumed in the Middle East and the Congo. A number of member states—including two Great Powers—with full capacity to pay, have failed to assume their share of these burdens and pay their share of the costs. Others have been slow in paying, even when reductions were granted to take into account their relative incapacity to pay.

This is a deplorable, indeed an intolerable situation, for a world Organization established to maintain peace and security. It is especially urgent in view of the growing demands for peace-keeping operations, which have demonstrated not only their worth but their cost. The situation is moving toward a climax this year because a number of states, including the Soviet bloc, now have accumulated arrears of payment which make them subject to Article 19 of the Charter, which provides for the loss of vote in the General Assembly. When it next meets, the Assembly will have to deal with this critical situation, which has far-reaching political and financial implications, unless steps have been taken in the meantime by those in default to liquidate their arrears.

Canada is convinced that the principle of collective responsibility is the only sensible basis for financing peace-keeping operations. We believe that Article 19 was intended to provide, and should provide, the sanction for that principle. We do not seek to force this issue but we are ready to face it if the delinquent states are not prepared to join in a search for a constructive solution. The financial dilemma must be solved.

Even more important is the political conflict which underlies finance and everything else. This conflict has made it all the more necessary to re-define the political basis for United Nations action in the field of peace preservation. It has also made such re-definition more difficult to bring about. The powers and function of the Security Council, the General Assembly and the Secretary-General have to be clarified in an agreed manner. In particular, the Security Council needs to reassert its authority in a way which will be effective when the peace is threatened.

To exert its proper influence, the Council should be enlarged to permit a balanced composition in its membership with equitable representation for all geographical areas. It must be made more capable of preserving the peace. For this, its functions may have to be modified to meet the changing situation in the world.

The United Nations must put its house in order so that it can exercise to the full its responsibility for maintaining peace and security. Stand-by arrangements for peace forces and for the other forms of United Nations presence are part of that process. But this does not embrace the whole responsibility for keeping the peace in our nuclear age.

The World Organization, as such, plays its part but the individual members cannot escape their own responsibility for maintaining peace, for refraining from the use of force in the pursuit of national policy; for leaving aside short-sighted and debilitating manoeuvering, designed for national, regional, or ideological purposes.

The Great Powers have a special responsibility in this regard. The Charter gives them a position of privilege but it also imposes a corresponding obligation to co-operate and show the way in preventing war and securing peace; to strive to avoid major clashes among themselves and to keep clear of minor ones.

The middle powers also have their own position of responsibility. They are and will remain the backbone of the collective effort to keep the peace as long as there is fear and suspicion between the Great Power Blocs. They have a special capacity in this regard which they should be proud to exercise.

Finally there is the particular responsibility of the parties themselves to a dispute. U Thant, the courageous and worthy successor to the Secretary-Generalship, underlined this in his report to the Security Council last week on Cyprus: "It is the parties themselves who alone can remedy the critical situation of Cyprus. The authorities . . . must, with a high sense of responsibility, act urgently to bring completely to an end the fighting in Cyprus, if that Island is to avoid utter disaster." This meant, he added, a voluntary and immediate renunciation of force as the first essential to finding a peaceful solution of the problems of Cyprus.

The United Nations can and will assist the process of peace-making whenever it is given the chance. Its peace forces can restore and have restored the conditions necessary to a peaceful solution of a dispute when they are permitted to operate effectively.

I know that for this purpose and in the long run the political conflicts, and above all the East-West conflict, inside the United Nations must be resolved or at least reduced.

But there is also a growing necessity for planning and preparation so that the machinery for peace-making can operate swiftly and effectively even under present conditions and when required.

To this end, we must do what we can now; and hope that we will soon be able to do more.

In this effort Canada has played and I know will continue to play a good and worthy role.

Appendix C-2

U Thant

UNITED NATIONS PEACE FORCE

An address to the Harvard Alumni Association, delivered in Cambridge, Massachusetts, June 13, 1963, by the Secretary-General of the United Nations, U THANT

The development of an international order, enshrined in an accepted code of world law and guaranteed by an effective world police force, has long been a human aspiration. This dream is based upon the very reasonable idea of projecting the stability and orderliness of a well-governed State onto the relations between nations.

In the history of most nation-States, there came a time when the feuding of a few powerful interests or personages, in disregard of the welfare of the majority, and the ensuing chaos and disaster, became intolerable. From this situation, there was the evolution in due course of a strong central authority, based on popular representation, a sound system of law and a reliable police force. In our world, we reached a similarly intolerable situation many years ago and have twice in this century paid a terrible price for having failed to draw the necessary conclusions.

Most sensible people now agree that some reliable system of ensuring world peace is essential. But, as in most situations involving great and conflicting interests and very large numbers of people, there is all the difference in the world between the need and the practical fulfilment of the need. That fulfilment will be a long and complicated process, requiring a degree of confidence and understanding which we have not yet established in our world.

Few would deny that, if we are to look forward with confidence to the future, we have to take a great step forward in regulating the relations of nations and produce workable institutions for that purpose. One should not, however, underestimate the difficulties of such a step or the inevitable risks which attend it.

Nations and Governments, taking a great step forward, face imponderables and unknown dangers which no research or scientific test can resolve, for these unforeseeable events will be the result of the actions, reactions and interactions of hundreds of millions of human beings, and the human mind and human behavior are still perhaps the most mysterious and awe-inspiring force in our world. Statesmen are wise, therefore, to view the future with caution and to examine proposals for fundamental change with more than usual care.

While we are making this step forward towards a new world order, we need guarantees, we need moderating influences and we need some commonly operated and accepted agency to share the risks and make the necessary tests and experiments, and even mistakes. Certainly we need an agency through which the necessary confidence and contact among nations can be built up and maintained. The United Nations is the nearest thing we have to such an agency, and I believe that it is beginning to play an important role of the kind I have just described.

It is no doubt true that there are certain great problems, such as the struggle between the greatest powers and the related problem of disarmament, which may be with us for a long time and which, perhaps, cannot be tackled head-on by the United Nations. We must, of course, do everything that we can to avoid adding fuel to the great power struggle.

There are, however, a large number of important problems and situations which *can* usefully be tackled and, if this is done, the greatest problems themselves can be isolated, if not resolved. We should, in this process, begin to develop the necessary institutions and practices by which, at a later stage, a more stable world order can be ensured.

I am going to talk today about one particular aspect of our problems, namely, peace-keeping and the use of international peace forces by the United Nations. Due partly to the lack of unanimity among the great powers ever since 1946, and partly to the radical change in the nature of war resulting from the development of atomic and hydrogen weapons, there has been a gradual change in thinking on questions of international security in the United Nations.

There has been a tacit transition from the concept of collective security, as set out in Chapter VII of the United Nations Charter, to a more realistic idea of peace-keeping. The idea that conventional military methods—or, to put it bluntly, war—can be used by or on behalf of the United Nations to counter aggression and secure the peace, seems now to be rather impractical.

There also has been a change in emphasis from the use of the military forces of the great powers, as contemplated in the Charter, to the use, in practice, of the military resources of the smaller powers, which has the advantage of not entangling United Nations actions in the antagonisms of the cold war.

Although there has been one collective action under the aegis of the United Nations—Korea—and although in 1951 the Collective Measures Committee, set up by the General Assembly under the Uniting for Peace resolution, actually published in its report a list of units earmarked by Member States for service with the United Nations in actions to counter aggression, actual developments have in practice been in a rather different direction.

The nature of these developments is sometimes confused, wittingly or unwittingly, by an attempt to relate them to the use of force to counter aggression by the Security Council provided for in Chapter VII of the Charter. In fact, the peace-keeping forces I am about to describe are of a very different kind and have little in common with the forces foreseen in Chapter VII, but their existence is not in conflict with Chapter VII. They are essentially *peace* and not fighting forces and they operate only with the consent of the parties directly concerned.

In this context, it is worth noting that *all* of the permanent members of the Security Council have, at one time or another in the past 15 years, voted in support of the creation of one or other of these forces, and that none of them has in any case gone further than to abstain from voting on them.

Since 1950, the United Nations has been called on to deal with a number of critical situations of varying urgency. The most urgent of these have been what are sometimes called "brush-fire wars," meaning, I take it, small conflagrations which, unless controlled, may all too easily ignite very much larger ones.

If we briefly look through the United Nations experience with this kind of operation, we can see that from small and informal beginnings a useful body of precedent and practice has grown up over the years of using military personnel of Member States on peace-keeping operations. In Greece in 1947, the United Nations Special Committee on the Balkans found that professional military officers were invaluable as an observer group in assessing the highly complicated and fluctuating situation. The Security Council itself set up an observer group of military officers in India and Pakistan to watch over the Kashmir question. This observer group, which was set up in 1948, is still operating.

A much larger use of military observers by the United Nations was made when, in July 1948, the first truce agreements in the Palestine war were supervised on the ground by some 700 United Nations military observers working under the United Nations Mediator and the Chief of Staff. This team developed into the United Nations Truce Supervision Organization after the armistice agreements between Israel and her Arab neighbours were concluded in the period from February to July 1949.

This organization of officers from many countries still plays a vital role in keeping the peace in the Middle East and in reporting on and dealing with incidents which, though small in themselves, might all too easily become the cause of far larger disturbances if not dealt with. Its indefatigable members in their white jeeps are now a familiar and welcome part of the Middle Eastern landscape.

A peace-keeping organization of a different nature made its apperance as a result of the Suez crisis of October 1956. Confronted with a situation of the utmost urgency in which two of the permanent members of the Security Council were directly involved, the General Assembly voted for the urgent creation of a United Nations force. This was essentially *not* a force designed actively to fight against aggression.

It went to Egypt with the express consent of the Egyptian Government and after the other parties concerned had agreed to a cease-fire. It was designed not to fight but rather to allow those involved to disengage without further disturbance. It allowed for the peaceful resolution of one of the most dangerous crises which had faced the world since the Second World War. It also, incidentally, allowed for the clearance by the United Nations of the Suez Canal, which had been blocked during the previous military action.

The United Nations Emergency Force in the Middle East has for six years watched over the borders of Israel with the United Arab Republic in the Gaza Strip and through the Sinai Desert. It also watches over the access to the Gulf of Aqaba and to the Israeli port of Elath. What was once a most troubled and terrorized frontier has become peaceful and prosperous on both sides, and the very presence of the United Nations Force is both an insurance against a resumption of trouble and a good excuse not to engage in it. It presents us with one serious problem. To maintain an army of over 5,000 men costs money, but at present the parties concerned have no wish to see it removed.

In 1958 another very tense situation, with quite different origins, occurred in Lebanon. After the success of UNEF, there were suggestions in many quarters that another United Nations force should be collected and dispatched to that country. Here, however, the problem, though aggravated by external factors, was essentially a domestic one.

The Security Council therefore set up a three-man observer group and left the Secretary-General considerable latitude as to the methods to be employed to make this group effective in watching over the possibilities of infiltration from outside. A highly mobile group of 600 officers was quickly organized to keep watch from ground and air, while the crisis itself was resolved by negotiation and discussion. By the end of 1958, it was possible to withdraw the United Nations Observer Group from the Lebanon altogether.

The greatest and most complex challenge to the United Nations in the peace-keeping field arose a few days after the Congo gained its independence from Belgium on 30 June 1960. The general proportions of this problem are sometimes obscured by a wealth of dramatic detail and are worth restating. Harassed by mutiny, lawlessness and the collapse of public order and services from within, and afflicted by foreign military intervention as well as by ominous threats of other forms of interference from without, the new Government of the Congo appealed to the United Nations for help.

The Security Council committed the United Nations to respond to this appeal and thus made the Organization not only the guarantor of law and order and the protector of the Congo against external interference from any source, but also the adviser and helper of a newly independent State which had virtually no preparation for its independence.

By filling, in the space of a few hours, the very dangerous vacuum which existed in the Congo in July 1960, the urgent danger of a confrontation of the great powers in the heart of Africa was avoided and the territorial integrity of the Congo preserved. The new leaders of the Congo have been given at least a short breathing-spell in which to find their feet. Despite its shortcomings, which must be judged in the light of the fearsome complexity of the problem, the United Nations Operation in the Congo is, in my opinion, a promising and encouraging experiment in international responsibility and action.

The blue helmets of the United Nations Force are known throughout the Congo as the symbol of security. Its soldiers have given protection at one time or another in the last three years to almost every Congolese public figure and almost every group, both African and non-African, when danger and violence threatened them. It is worth noting that, now that the withdrawal of the United Nations Force in the Congo is in sight, the deepest regret, and even alarm, is expressed by the very groups who used to be its most hostile critics and detractors.

In the Force, soldiers from other African countries work side by side in this vast tropical country with those from farther away. Their loyalty to the United Nations, their team spirit and comradeship have been an inspiration to all those who value the peace-keeping role of the United Nations.

I will end my catalogue with two more operations, one of which has already been successfully concluded, and which also involved an unprecedented role for the United Nations. I would like to refer first to the transfer of West Irian from Dutch rule, through a temporary period of United Nations executive authority, backed by a United Nations Security Force, to the administration of Indonesia. This entire operation has taken place with the agreement of the parties concerned, and in consultation with them.

The second is the dispatch to Yemen of an observer team as a basis for the disengagement of the United Arab Republic and Saudi Arabia from the affairs of Yemen. This operation will be paid for by the two parties concerned, and has been undertaken at their request and that of the Government of Yemen.

Although these are peace forces, service in them is hard and can be dangerous. In the Middle East, the United Nations has registered casualties not only from accidents and disease, but from mines. Both there and in West Irian, as also in Yemen, the terrain and the climate are inhospitable. In the Congo, we have had, unfortunately, serious casualties from unwanted fighting as well as from other causes, and I very much hope that we shall have no more.

I have only mentioned here the peace-keeping activities which have involved the use, in one way or another, of military personnel. If I were to mention the many other tense situations in which the United Nations, and my office in particular, have been used as a meeting-ground and as an instrument for mediation and peaceful settlement, the list would be much longer.

To sum up, we have now had experience of three major peace-keeping forces and a variety of military observer and truce supervisory operations. Each of the three forces has been different in composition, nature and task, but they have shared certain common characteristics.

All three were improvised and called into the field at very short notice; all three were severely limited in their right to use force; all three were designed solely for the maintenance of peace and not for fighting in the military sense; all three were recruited from the smaller powers and with special reference to their acceptability in the area in which they were to serve; all three operated with the express consent and co-operation of the States or territories where they were stationed, as well as of any other parties directly concerned in the situation; and all three were under the direction and control of the Secretary-General acting on behalf of the organs of the United Nations.

These facts may now seem commonplace; it is a measure of the progress that has been made that even ten years ago they would have seemed very unusual.

By the standards of an efficient national military establishment, these forces have considerable disadvantages. Obviously, a force put together only after the emergency with which it is to deal is in full swing, will inevitably have some shortcomings. There is difficulty in recruiting at very short notice exactly the right kind of units for the work in hand, and in operating a force whose units and officers meet each other for the first time in the midst of a delicate operation. There are differences not only of language and tradition but of training, equipment and staff procedures. There are differences in pay and emoluments which, if not handled carefully, can cause considerable problems of discipline and morale. Staff-work and command are especially difficult where every decision has important political implications.

Although these contingents from Member States are under the operational control of the United Nations, disciplinary powers are still vested in the national authorities and this could be, although in fact it never has been, the cause of very serious difficulties for the United Nations Force Commander and for the Secretary-General.

The fact that the military establishments of the permanent members of the Security Council cannot be used cuts us off from the most obvious sources of equipment and personnel. The improvised nature of these operations also gives rise to various problems of logistics.

In our experience, these difficulties, which are inherent in the pioneering nature of these operations, have been offset by the enthusiastic co-operation of Member States and by the spirit and comprehension of the officers and men of the contingents which have made up the United Nations forces. It is an encouraging thought that in the military establishments of some 30 or more countries in the world there are now large numbers of officers and men who have served the United Nations with distinction in one or another of these operations and have added thereby a new dimension to their military experience.

The improvised approach also makes it possible on each occasion to make up the United Nations force from the countries which are, politically and in other ways, most suitable for the operation in hand, and at least the United Nations is not afflicted with the age-old problem of having on its hands a standing army with nothing to do.

In my opinion, a permanent United Nations force is not a practical proposition at the present time. I know that many serious people in many countries are enthusiastic about the idea, and I welcome their enthusiasm and the thought they are putting into the evolution of the institution which will eventually and surely emerge. Many difficulties still stand in the way of its evolution.

Personally, I have no doubt that the world should eventually have an international police force which will be accepted as an integral and essential part of life in the same way as national police forces are accepted. Meanwhile, we must be sure that developments are in the right direction and that we can also meet critical situations as and when they occur.

There are a number of reasons why it seems to me that the establishment of a permanent United Nations force would be premature at the present time. I doubt whether many Governments in the world would yet be prepared to accept the political implications of such an institution and, in the light of our current experience with financial problems, I am sure that they would have very serious difficulties in accepting the financial implications.

I believe that we need a number of parallel developments before we can evolve such an institution. We have to go further along the road of codification and acceptance of a workable body of international law. We have to develop a more sophisticated public opinion in the world, which can accept the transition from predominantly national thinking to international thinking.

We shall have to develop a deeper faith in international institutions as such, and a greater confidence in the possibility of a United Nations civil service whose international loyalty and objectivity are generally accepted and above suspicion. We shall have to improve the method of financing international organization. Until these conditions are met, a permanent United Nations force may not be a practical proposition.

But we have already shown that, when the situation demands it, it is possible to use the soldiers of many countries for objectives which are not national ones and that the soldiers respond magnificently to this new challenge. We have also seen that, when the situation is serious enough, Governments are prepared to waive certain of the attributes of national sovereignty in the interest of keeping the peace through the United Nations. We have demonstrated that a loyalty to international service can exist side by side with legitimate national pride.

And, perhaps most important of all, we have shown that there *can* be a practical alternative to the deadly ultimate struggle and that it is an alternative which brings out the good and generous qualities in men rather than their destructive and selfish qualities.

Although it is perhaps too early, for the reasons I have already given, to consider the establishment of a permanent United Nations force, I believe there are a number of measures which could be taken even now to improve on our present capacity for meeting dangerous situations. It would be extremely desirable, for example, if countries would, in their national military planning, make provision for suitable units which could be made available at short notice for United Nations service and thereby decrease the degree of improvisation necessary to an emergency.

I take this opportunity publicly to welcome and express my appreciation for the efforts of the Scandinavian countries in this direction. Denmark, Norway and Sweden have for some time now engaged in joint planning of a stand-by force comprising various essential components to be put at the disposal of the United Nations when necessary. It would be a very welcome development if other countries would consider following the lead of the Scandinavian countries in this matter.

At present, the activities of the United Nations are overshadowed by a very serious financial crisis, a crisis which stems directly from the costs of the special peace-keeping operations in the Middle East and the Congo and from the failure of some Members to pay their assessments for those operations. Although the sums of money involved are small in comparison to the sums spent by many countries on military budgets, they do, nonetheless, present a very serious financial and political challenge to the stability of the United Nations.

The United Nations is the sum of all its Members and, to develop in the right direction, it must maintain this global character. On the other hand, I am convinced that the Organization must maintain and develop its active role in keeping the peace. I therefore view with the gravest concern the prolongation of the financial crisis of the United Nations with its very serious political overtones, and I trust that we may see a solution of the problem before too long.

I am concerned at this financial crisis more particularly because

I see, in the long run, no acceptable alternative method of keeping peace in the world to the steady and sound development of the peace-keeping functions of the United Nations. It is no longer possible to think rationally in terms of countering aggression or keeping the peace by the use of the ultimate weapons.

However improvised and fumbling the United Nations approach may be, we have to develop it to deal with the sudden antagonisms and dangers of our world, until we can evolve more permanent institutions. There has been already a great advance in the world towards co-operation, mutual responsibility and common interest. I have described some of the pioneering co-operative efforts made by the United Nations to keep the peace.

I believe that these efforts constitute vital steps towards a more mature, more acceptable, and more balanced world order. We must have the confidence and the means to sustain them and the determination to develop out of them a reliable and workable system for the future.

I am a firm believer in the organic development of institutions. I also firmly believe that, if the United Nations is to justify the hopes of its founders and of the peoples of the world, it must develop into an active and effective agency for peace and international conciliation by responding to the challenges which face it. May we have the courage, the faith, and the wisdom to make it so.

Appendix C-3

Dag Hammarskjold

UNITED NATIONS EMERGENCY FORCE

Summary study of the experience derived from the establishment and operation of the force. "Concluding Observations and Principles" from the Report of the Secretary-General, DAG HAMMARSKJOLD

A. *Observations*

148. In the preceding pages of this report a summary has been given of the experience of the United Nations derived from the establishment and operation of the United Nations Emergency Force.

In advance of the conclusions, certain observations are called for regarding the specific circumstances in which the experience with UNEF has been gained, since those circumstances definitely limit any detailed application of that experience to the general problem of United Nations operations of this character. It is useful, in this context, also to note and compare the subsequent experience with United Nations operations in relation to Lebanon and Jordan.

149. UNEF was brought into being to meet a particular situation in which a United Nations force could be interposed between regular, national military forces which were subject to a cease-fire agreed to by the opposing parties. UNEF has continued to function along the "dividing line" between the national forces. It follows that in UNEF there has never been any need for rights and responsibilities other than those necessary for such an interposed force under cease-fire conditions. The Force was not used in any way to enforce withdrawals but, in the successive stages of the withdrawals, followed the withdrawing troops to the "dividing line" of each stage. It is also to be noted that the Force has functioned under a clear-cut mandate which has entirely detached it from involvement in any internal or local problems, and also has enabled it to maintain its neutrality in relation to international political issues. The fact that UNEF was designed to meet the needs of this specific situation largely determined its military components, geographical composition, deployment and status, and also its effectiveness.

150. A further factor of significance in the evaluation of the UNEF experience is that in Gaza the Force is in an area having special status under the Armistice Agreement. In Gaza and elsewhere in its area of operations, UNEF has been able to function without any question arising of its presence infringing upon sovereign rights, on the basis that, at the invitation of the Egyptian Government and in accordance with the decision of the General Assembly, the United Nations assists in maintaining quiet on the Armistice Demarcation Line around the Gaza Strip and along the international line to the south. The Government of Egypt has co-operated by taking necessary steps to facilitate the functioning of UNEF in the Gaza area. The same is true of the position of the Egyptian Government in keeping its limited military units in the Sinai Peninsula away from the area in which the UNEF chiefly functions.

151. Obviously, some of the above-mentioned circumstances are of such a nature that it could not reasonably be expected that they

would often be duplicated elsewhere. Nor can it be assumed that they provide a sufficient basis to warrant indiscriminate projection of the UNEF experience in planning for future United Nations operations of this kind. Indeed, the more recent experiences in Lebanon and Jordan serve only to emphasize the uniqueness of the UNEF setting, which, in part at least, explains the success of this pioneer venture. Neither in Lebanon nor in Jordan would it have been possible to interpose a United Nations force between conflicting parties. Nor would it have been possible in either of those situations to preserve a natural distinction between the presence and functions in various areas of any United Nations force and the presence and functions of government troops. In Lebanon, it is unlikely that a United Nations force could have operated without soon becoming a party to the internal conflicts among nationals of the country. In Jordan, the presence of a United Nations force has been regarded by the Government as difficult to reconcile with its own exercise of full sovereignty over the people and territory of the country. United Nations experience with these three Middle East operations justifies the assumption that, in each new conflict situation in which the United Nations might be called upon to intervene with military personnel, the nature of the actual organization required and its paramilitary aspects would be determined by the particular needs of the situation and could not, therefore, be anticipated in advance. Thus, for example, stand-by arrangements for a force designed for a UNEF-type operation would not have been of practical value in either of the situations in Lebanon or Jordan, where conditions required an approach in all relevant aspects quite different from that employed in UNEF.

152. The foregoing leads to the obvious conclusion that, in considering general stand-by arrangements for United Nations operations of the kind envisaged in this report, a course should be followed which would afford a considerable degree of flexibility in approaching the varying needs that may arise. This could be achieved if stand-by arrangements were to consist of an approval of those general conclusions regarding principles which can be reached in the light of the UNEF experience, and which would provide a setting within which, with the necessary variations of approach, personnel in units or otherwise could be recruited and an operation organized without delay and with full adjustment to the specific situation requiring the action.

153. Further support for the position here taken is found in that the type and rank of military personnel required, the need for specialists and for supporting units, as well as the vehicle and equipment demands, as experience has shown, also vary so much from case to case that more far-reaching and firm arrangements—as, for example, the maintenance of a nucleus United Nations force of the type generally envisaged—would be without great practical value and certainly would not warrant the substantial sacrifices involved. By way of illustration of this point UNEF has been able to use enlisted men with short military experience under the command of experienced officers; the recruitment of personnel for the United Nations Observation Group in Lebanon has been limited largely to officers, who, however, with few exceptions, did not have to be rigorously screened for the mission; while the arrangements in relation to Jordan may involve, if any, only a very limited number of military personnel, all of officer rank but individually and carefully chosen for the purpose. Similar differences are apparent as regards the need for matériel with UNEF being adequately served by, in military calculations, a quite modest number of aircraft and vehicles, while UNOGIL has had to operate with a considerably higher ratio of planes and vehicles to the men involved, because of the specific tasks with which it has been entrusted.

B. Basic Principles

154. In view of the impossibility of determining beforehand the specific form of a United Nations presence of the type considered in this report, which would be necessary to meet adequately the requirements of a given situation, a broad decision by the General Assembly should attempt to do no more than endorse certain basic principles and rules which would provide an adaptable framework for later operations that might be found necessary. In a practical sense, it is not feasible in advance of a known situation to do more than to provide for some helpful stand-by arrangements for a force or similar forms of a United Nations presence. In the following paragraphs, certain principles and rules are laid down in the light of the experience gathered in the past years, which, if they were to meet with the approval of the General Assembly, would provide a continuing basis on which useful contacts in a stand-by context might be established with interested Governments, with the aim of being prepared for any requests which might arise from future decisions

by the Assembly on a force or similar arrangement to deal with a specific case.

155. As the arrangements discussed in this report do not cover the type of force envisaged under Chapter VII of the Charter, it follows from international law and the Charter that the United Nations cannot undertake to implement them by stationing units on the territory of a Member State without the consent of the Government concerned. It similarly follows from the Charter that the consent of a Member nation is necessary for the United Nations to use its military personnel or matériel. These basic rules have been observed in the recent United Nations operations in the Middle East. They naturally hold valid for all similar operations in the future.

156. The fact that a United Nations operation of the type envisaged requires the consent of the Government on whose territory it takes place creates a problem, as it is normally difficult for the United Nations to engage in such an operation without guarantees against unilateral actions by the host Government which might put the United Nations in a questionable position, either administratively or in relation to contributing Governments.

157. The formula employed in relation to the Government of Egypt for UNEF seems, in the light of experience, to provide an adequate solution to this problem. The Government of Egypt declared that, when exercising its sovereign right with regard to the presence of the Force, it would be guided by good faith in the interpretation of the purposes of the Force. This declaration was balanced by a declaration by the United Nations to the effect that the maintenance of the Force by the United Nations would be determined by similar good faith in the interpretation of the purposes.

158. The consequence of such a bilateral declaration is that, were either side to act unilaterally in refusing continued presence or deciding on withdrawal, and were the other side to find that such action was contrary to a good faith interpretation of the purposes of the operation, an exchange of views would be called for towards harmonizing the positions. This does not imply any infringement on the sovereign right of the host Government, nor any restriction of the right of the United Nations to decide on termination of its own operation whenever it might see fit to do so. But it does mean a mutual recognition of the fact that the operation, being based on collaboration between the host Government and the United Nations, should be carried on in forms natural to such collaboration, and

especially so with regard to the questions of presence and maintenance.

159. It is unlikely that any Government in the future would be willing to go beyond the declaration of the Government of Egypt with regard to UNEF. Nor, in my view, should the United Nations commit itself beyond the point established for UNEF in relation to the Government of Egypt. In these circumstances, I consider it reasonable to regard the formula mentioned in paragraph 158 above as a valid basis for future arrangements of a similar kind.

160. Another point of principle which arises in relation to the question of consent refers to the composition of United Nations military elements stationed on the territory of a Member country. While the United Nations must reserve for itself the authority to decide on the composition of such elements, it is obvious that the host country, in giving its consent, cannot be indifferent to the composition of those elements. In order to limit the scope of possible difference of opinion, the United Nations in recent operations has followed two principles: not to include units from any of the permanent members of the Security Council; and not to include units from any country which, because of its geographical position or for other reasons, might be considered as possibly having a special interest in the situation which has called for the operation. I believe that these two principles also should be considered as essential to any stand-by arrangements.

161. Given the two principles mentioned in paragraph 160, in actual practice the area within which conflicting views may be expressed will in all probability be so reduced normally as to facilitate the harmonizing of the rights of the United Nations with the interests of the host country. It would seem desirable to accept the formula applied in the case of UNEF, which is to the effect that, while it is for the United Nations alone to decide on the composition of military elements sent to a country, the United Nations should, in deciding on composition, take fully into account the viewpoint of the host Government as one of the most serious factors which should guide the recruitment of the personnel. Usually, this is likely to mean that serious objections by the host country against participation by a specific contributing country in the United Nations operation will determine the action of the Organization. However, were the United Nations for good reasons to find that course inadvisable, it would remain free to pursue its own line, and any result-

ing conflict would have to be resolved on a political rather than on a legal basis. I would recommend that the basis thus laid in the case of UNEF be considered as the formula on composition applicable to similar operations in the future.

162. The principles indicated in the four points discussed above (paragraphs 155-161 inclusive) were either established by the General Assembly itself, elaborated in practice or in negotiations with the Government of Egypt. They have served as the basis for a status Agreement which applies to the United Nations personnel in the Force in Egypt. In its entirety, this status Agreement has stood up well to the test of experience. Its basic principles should be embodied in similar agreements in the future, and their recognition, therefore, would seem necessarily to form part of any stand-by arrangements for a force. The Agreement regarding the presence of UNOGIL in Lebanon, although much less elaborate because of the modest size of the operation and the fact that normal immunity rules could be applied to the bulk of the personnel, also reflects the basic principles I have in mind.

163. The most important principle in the status Agreement ensures that UNEF personnel, when involved in criminal actions, come under the jurisdiction of the criminal courts of their home countries. The establishment of this principle for UNEF, in relation to Egypt, has set a most valuable precedent. Experience shows that this principle is essential to the successful recruitment by the United Nations of military personnel not otherwise under immunity rules, from its Member countries. The position established for UNEF should be maintained in future arrangements.

164. Another principle involved in the UNEF status Agreement, and which should be retained, is that the United Nations activity should have freedom of movement within its area of operations and all such facilities regarding access to that area and communications as are necessary for successful completion of the task. This also obviously involves certain rights of over-flight over the territory of the host country. These principles have been maintained in the case of UNOGIL. Their application requires an agreement on what is to be considered as the area of operations and as to what facilities of access and communications are to be considered necessary. On the assumption that, like UNEF, any similar United Nations operation in the future would be of assistance to the nation on whose territory it is stationed, it is not to be expected that the necessary process

of agreement will give rise to any serious complications in the interpretation of the principle.

165. Apart from the principles thus established in negotiated agreements or formal decisions, a series of basic rules has been developed in practice. Some of these rules would appear to merit general application. This is true especially of the precept that authority granted to the United Nations group cannot be exercised within a given territory either in competition with representatives of the host Government or in co-operation with them on the basis of any joint operation. Thus, a United Nations operation must be separate and distinct from activities by national authorities. UNEF experience indicates how this rule may apply in practice. A right of detention which normally would be exercised only by local authorities is extended to UNEF units. However, this is so only within a limited area where the local authorities voluntarily abstain from exercising similar rights, whether alone or in collaboration with the United Nations. Were the underlying principle of this example not to be applied, United Nations units might run the risk of getting involved in differences with the local authorities or public or in internal conflicts which would be highly detrimental to the effectiveness of the operation and to the relations between the United Nations and the host Government.

166. A rule closely related to the one last-mentioned, and reflecting a basic Charter principle, precludes the employment of United Nations elements in situations of an essentially internal nature. As a matter of course, the United Nations personnel cannot be permitted in any sense to be a party to internal conflicts. Their role must be limited to external aspects of the political situation as, for example, infiltration or other activities affecting international boundaries.

167. Even in the case of UNEF, where the United Nations itself had taken a stand on decisive elements in the situation which gave rise to the creation of the Force, it was explicitly stated that the Force should not be used to enforce any specific political solution of pending problems or to influence the political balance decisive to such a solution. This precept clearly imposes a serious limitation on the possible use of United Nations elements, were it to be given general application to them whenever they are not created under Chapter VII of the Charter. However, I believe its acceptance to be necessary, if the United Nations is to be in a position to draw on

Member countries for contributions in men and matériel to United Nations operations of this kind.

168. Military personnel employed by the United Nations in para-military operations are, of course, not under the same formal obligations in relation to the Organization as staff members of the Secretariat. However, the position must be maintained that the basic rules of the United Nations for international service are applicable also to such personnel, particularly as regards full loyalty to the aims of the Organization and to abstention from acts in relation to their country of origin or to other countries which might deprive the operation of its international character and create a situation of dual loyalty. The observance of this rule is not only vital for good relations with the host country, it is also to the benefit of the contributing countries concerned, as any other attitude might involve them in responsibilities which would be undesirable in the light of national policies pursued.

169. In setting up UNEF, the General Assembly appointed a Commander of the Force with the position of an international civil servant responsible for discharge of his task to the Assembly, but administratively integrated with the United Nations organization, and under instructions from the Secretary-General on the basis of the executive authority for the operation vested in him by the Assembly.

170. A somewhat different procedure was followed in the case of UNOGIL, where the Security Council delegated to the Secretary-General the responsibility for constituting the Observation Group. However, basically the same principle employed in UNEF is applied to UNOGIL, for the Group is responsible for the conduct of its business to the Security Council, while administratively it is under the Secretary-General, who is charged with its organization. A basically similar pattern finds reflection also in the arrangements being made by the United Nations in relation to Jordan.

171. The innovation represented by the constitutional pattern thus followed in recent United Nations field operations has, in experience, proved to be highly practical and, especially, politically of decisive importance, as it has provided for an integration giving the operation all the advantages of administrative co-ordination with the Secretariat and of the fully internationalized status of the Secretariat. As pointed out in my "Second and final report on the Emergency Force," on which the General Assembly based its decision to organize the Force, the appointment by the General Assembly of

a Commander determined the legal status of the Force. The other arrangements, mentioned above, reflect the same basic concept.

172. In full recognition of the wide variety of forms which decisions on a United Nations operation may take in seeking to fit differing situations calling for such an operation, the underlying rule concerning command and authority which has been consistently applied in recent years, as set out above, should, in my view, be maintained for the future. Thus, a United Nations operation should always be under a leadership established by the General Assembly or the Security Council, or on the basis of delegated authority by the Secretary-General, so as to make it directly responsible to one of the main organs of the United Nations, while integrated with the Secretariat in an appropriate form.

173. Were soundings with Member Governments, based on the afore-mentioned legal and political principles and rules and on the regulations regarding financial responsibilities set out below, to show that a number of Governments in their planning would be willing to take into account the possibility of having to provide promptly—on an emergency basis, on specific appeal from the United Nations—men and matériel to a United Nations operation of the kind envisaged in this report, a question arises regarding the conditions under which such a desirable stand-by arrangement could be utilized.

174. Under the Charter, and under the "Uniting for Peace" resolution, a formal decision on a United Nations operation must be taken by the General Assembly or by the Security Council. It must be regarded as excluded that the right to take such a decision, in any general terms, could properly be considered as delegated to the Secretary-General. Short of an explicit decision by the General Assembly or the Security Council with a specific authorization, the Secretary-General, thus, cannot be considered as entitled to appeal to a Member nation for military personnel to be dispatched to another Member country in a United Nations operation.

175. The terms of the delegation in each operation thus far have set the limit of the Secretary-General's authority. Thus, for example, as apparent from the description of the new body, the decision relating to UNEF, which was to be implemented by the Secretary-General, qualified the operation as being one of a paramilitary nature, while the absence of an explicit authorization for the Force to take offensive action excluded the organization by the Secretary-

General of units for such action, and consequently, the units generally were equipped only with weapons necessary for self-defence. Had there been any remaining doubts in this respect, the legal basis on which the General Assembly took its decision would have made this limitation clear.

176. Similarly, the Security Council decision on the United Nations Observation Group in Lebanon qualified the kind of operation that the Secretary-General was authorized to organize by the very name given to the unit to be established. That name excluded the creation of a paramilitary force and imposed, in fact, such limitations on the operation as to call for great restraint regarding the arming of the unit and its right of self-defence.

177. The General Assembly decision concerning the arrangements in relation to Jordan was in such broad terms as to provide possibilities for the organization of any kind of operation, short of one possible only under Chapter VII. In this case, however, as in the case of UNEF, a certain incompleteness in the terminology of the decision was covered by the conclusions following from the legal basis on which the decision was taken.

178. Confirmation by the Assembly of the interpretation of the question of authority given above would be useful. This interpretation would signify that a Member country, in deciding upon contribution of men or matériel to a United Nations operation on the basis of such stand-by understandings as may have been reached, could rely upon the explicit terms of the executive authority delegated to the Secretary-General in determining the use which could be made of the units provided; it being understood, naturally, that in the types of operation with which this report is concerned this could never include combat activity. There will always remain, of course, a certain margin of freedom for judgement, as, for example, on the extent and nature of the arming of the units and of their right to self-defence. In the case of UNEF, such questions of interpretation have been solved in consultation with the contributing Governments and with the host Government. The Advisory Committee on UNEF set up by the General Assembly has in this context proved to be of especially great assistance.

179. In the preceding paragraph I have touched upon the extent to which a right of self-defence may be exercised by United Nations units of the type envisaged. It should be generally recognized that such a right exists. However, in certain cases this right should be

exercised only under strictly defined conditions. A problem arises in this context because of the fact that a wide interpretation of the right of self-defence might well blur the distinction between operations of the character discussed in this report and combat operations, which would require a decision under Chapter VII of the Charter and an explicit, more far-reaching delegation of authority to the Secretary-General than would be required for any of the operations discussed here. A reasonable definition seems to have been established in the case of UNEF, where the rule is applied that men engaged in the operation may never take the initiative in the use of armed force, but are entitled to respond with force to an attack with arms, including attempts to use force to make them withdraw from positions which they occupy under orders from the Commander, acting under the authority of the Assembly and within the scope of its resolutions. The basic element involved is clearly the prohibition against any initiative in the use of armed force. This definition of the limit between self-defence, as permissible for United Nations elements of the kind discussed, and offensive action, which is beyond the competence of such elements, should be approved for future guidance.

180. The clear delimitation of the right to use force which has been set out above as a basic rule for the type of operations discussed in this report should dissipate any objections against the suggested stand-by arrangements which would be based on the view that they go beyond the measures which the Charter permits the General Assembly to take and infringe upon prerogatives of the Security Council. The principles outlined above put UNEF on the same level, constitutionally, as UNOGIL, for example, qualifying it so as to make it an instrument of efforts at mediation and conciliation. It may be noted in this context that UNOGIL has not given rise to any constitutional objections; the fact that the Group was created by the Security Council is in this case irrelevant, as the Council acted entirely within the limits of Chapter VI of the Charter, and as a similar action obviously could have been taken by the General Assembly under Article 22.

181. In the case of UNEF, the General Assembly decided to organize an Advisory Committee under the chairmanship of the Secretary-General, to assist the operation. In practice, this arrangement has proved highly useful. In principle, it should be accepted as a precedent for the future. Extensive operations with serious

political implications, regarding which, for practical reasons, executive authority would need to be delegated to the Secretary-General, require close collaboration with authorized representatives of the General Assembly. However, it would be undesirable for this collaboration to be given such a form as to lead to divided responsibilities or to diminish efficiency in the operation. The method chosen by the General Assembly in the case of UNEF seems the most appropriate one if such risks are to be avoided. The Committee is fully informed by the Secretary-General and his associates. There is a free exchange of views in closed meetings where advice can be sought and given. But ultimate decisions rest with the Secretary-General, as the executive in charge of carrying out the operation. Dissenting views are not registered by vote, but are put on record in the proceedings of the Committee. It is useful for contributing countries to be represented on such an advisory committee, but if the contributing States are numerous the size of the committee might become so large as to make it ineffective. On the other hand, it is obviously excluded that any party to the conflict should be a member. Normally, I believe that the same basic rule regarding permanent members of the Security Council which has been applied to units and men in the recent operations should be applied also in the selection of members for a relevant advisory committee.

182. In the administration of UNEF at Headquarters, certain special arrangements were made on an ad hoc basis to provide expert military guidance. Thus, a senior Military Adviser and three officer assistants were attached to the Executive Office as consultants. The Military Adviser, and the Under-Secretary representing the Secretary-General on current matters relating to the Force, were assisted by a group of military representatives from the countries providing contingents, sitting as an informal military advisory committee. Once the operation was firmly established, these arrangements could be and were reduced and simplified, but in the initial stage they proved to be of great value organizationally and also as an added means of maintaining close contacts with contributing Governments.

183. A parallel arrangement was that by which, for a period, a personal representative of the Secretary-General was stationed in the capital of the host country as a liaison officer directly in contact with the Government.

184. In view of the very great diversity likely to characterize the

experience in practice of using United Nations units within the scope of this report, it is impossible to enunciate any principles for organizational arrangements at Headquarters or in the host country that should be made in anticipation of each case. There will always be developed, as a matter of course, the forms of liaison for which there will be a clear need.

185. The question, however, is of interest in this context, as it has a bearing on the problem whether or not such stand-by arrangements as those for which the principles and rules set out here would provide, would call for any kind of nucleus of military experts at United Nations Headquarters. At some stage, a standing group of a few military experts might be useful in order to keep under review such arrangements as may be made by Member Governments in preparation for meeting possible appeals for an operation. I would consider it premature, however, to take any decision of this kind at the present time, since the foreseeable tasks that might evolve for the Secretariat do not go beyond what it is now able to cope with unassisted by such special measures. Were a more far-reaching understanding than I have indicated to prove possible, the matter obviously would have to be reconsidered and submitted again in appropriate form to the General Assembly, which then might consider the organizational problem. Pending such a development later, the present working rule, in my view, should be that the Secretariat, while undertaking the soundings mentioned above and the necessary continuing contacts with the Governments, should not take any measures beyond keeping the situation under constant review, so as to be able to act expeditiously, if a decision by the General Assembly or the Security Council should call for prompt action.

186. It may be reiterated in passing that the United Nations Secretariat has by now had extensive experience in establishing and maintaining United Nations operations involving military personnel and, without improvising or augmenting unduly, can quickly provide any operation of that nature with efficient communications service in the field and with Headquarters, with transportation and vehicles for local transport, with well-tested administrative and accounting systems and expert personnel to man them, and with effective procurement and security arrangements.

187. The financial obligations of Member countries to the United Nations are of two kinds. On the one hand, there are such obligations as are covered by the scale of contributions established by the

General Assembly; on the other, there are certain voluntary commitments outside that scale, such as United Nations technical assistance or the United Nations Children's Fund. While, of course, contributions from individual Member nations to United Nations units for field operations may always be made on a voluntary basis, thus being lifted outside the scale of contributions, the principle must be that, as flowing from decisions of one of the main organs of the United Nations, such contributions should be subordinated to the normal financial rules. Any other principle would seriously limit the possibility of recruiting the necessary personnel from the most appropriate countries and achieving the best geographical distribution, since most countries are not likely to be in a position to assume the additional financial burdens involved and since, unless otherwise agreed, all contributing countries should be treated on the same basis.

188. In the initial stages of UNEF, Member nations assumed certain additional burdens beyond those which would follow from the application of normal rules governing contributions to the United Nations. Later, financial relations were adjusted so as to be based on full compensation for extra and extraordinary costs, financed under the normal scale of contributions. The underlying rule is that a contributing country, by such action, should not be subjected to financial sacrifices beyond those obligations which would be incurred if it were not contributing directly to the operation. On the other hand, naturally, contributing countries should not shift to the United Nations any costs which, in any case they would have had to meet under their normal domestic policy.

189. I believe that, as part of the stand-by arrangements, it should be established that the costs for United Nations operations of the type in question, based on decisions of the General Assembly or the Security Council, should be allocated in accordance with the normal scale of contributions. The United Nations in this way should assume responsibility for all additional costs incurred by a contributing country because of its participation in the operation, on the basis of a cost assessment which, on the other hand, would not transfer to the United Nations any costs which would otherwise have been incurred by a contributing Government under its regular national policy.

190. With relation to the men engaged in one of its operations, the United Nations should naturally assume all responsibilities neces-

sary to safeguard the normal interest of those so employed. Thus, they should be fully compensated by the United Nations for any losses of earning power or social benefits which may be suffered because of their service with the United Nations. In view of the great variety of regulations applied by various countries, it is impossible to go beyond this general statement of principle; the details would have to be worked out with each contributing Government, as appropriate.

191. With relation to a host Government, it should be the rule that as the United Nations units are dispatched to the country in the interest and with the consent and co-operation of the host Government, that Government should provide all necessary facilities for the operation. This, in principle, should be done without any compensation, in cases where such facilities are in the possession of the host Government itself. Thus, for example, contributions of government services or government-owned property placed at the disposal of the United Nations for its operation should not be subject to compensation.

192. Concerning the claims of private citizens in the host country, the applicable rule is that the United Nations should pay compensation for the use of their property or services, whenever the host Government would have been obligated to pay for similar services or uses. The question whether the United Nations, in its turn, should be reimbursed by the host Government for such outlays would properly be settled through negotiation, in the light of the circumstances in each separate case.

193. The approach indicated in this chapter suggests a way in which the United Nations, within the limits of the Charter, may seek the most practical method of mustering and using, as necessary, the resources—both of nations and its own—required for operations involving military personnel which may be conceived in response to the needs of specific conflict situations. The national resources likely to be available for such purposes, if our limited experience is a gauge, are no doubt substantial, but they cannot now be calculated or even estimated, and even their availability at any particular time would probably be subject to considerable fluctuation, for political and other reasons. Formalizing the principles and rules outlined above, however, would afford a strengthened basis on which to expedite the mobilization of voluntary aid towards meeting urgent need. Their approval by the Assembly, thus

clarifying and regularizing important legal and practical issues, would also ensure a more efficient use of any aid extended to the Organization, were it again to have to appeal to Member nations for such assistance.

Appendix D

List of 11 United Nations peace-keeping operations

Appendix D-1

List of nations whose troops or military personnel have served under UN flag 1945-1965

Argentina
Afghanistan
Australia
Austria
Brazil
Belgium
Burma
Canada
Chile
Ceylon
Colombia
Congo (Leopoldville)
Denmark
Ecuador
Ethiopia
Finland
France
Ghana
Greece
Guinea
India
Ireland
Italy
Indonesia
Iran
Liberia
Luxembourg
Malaya
Mali
Mexico
Morocco
Nepal
Netherlands
New Zealand
Norway
Nigeria
Pakistan
Philippines
Peru
Portugal

Republic of Korea (non-member)	Tunisia
Sudan	Turkey
Sierra Leone	United Kingdom
Sweden	United States
South Africa	United Arab Republic
Thailand	Yugoslavia

Appendix D-2

Cyprus 1964—present (UNFICYP)

When violence between Greek and Turkish Cypriotes broke out in 1964, the UN was asked to send a police force to the easternmost island of the Mediterranean to maintain law and order and also act as an observer group. Called United Nations in Cyprus (UNFICYP), this force of seven thousand men is charged with keeping the peace. The force is only good for three month periods because Archbishop Makarios won't permit any long-term UN force.

Austria	Sweden
Canada	New Zealand
Denmark	Australia
Finland	India
Ireland	United Kingdom

Appendix D-3

Congo 1960-1964 (ONUC)

At the request of the new government of the Democratic Republic of the Congo, the United Nations ultimately placed a police force of 35 countries in the Congo and called it Operation des Nations Unies au Congo (*ONUC*). *ONUC was responsible for restoring law and order.*

Argentina	Guinea	Netherlands
Australia	India	Norway
Austria	Indonesia	Pakistan
Brazil	Iran	Philippines
Burma	Ireland	Sierra Leone
Canada	Italy	Sudan
Ceylon	Liberia	Sweden
Denmark	Malaya	Switzerland
Ecuador	Mali	Tunisia
Ethiopia	Morocco	United Arab Republic
Ghana	New Zealand	Yugoslavia
Greece	Nigeria	

Appendix D-4

Yemen 1962-1963 (UNYOM)

The United Nations Observation Mission to Yemen (UNYOM) was sent to the turbulent kingdom to keep the peace by notifying the lawful government of any incursions from hostile forces armed and paid by Egypt and by Saudi Arabia.

Australia	Italy
Austria	Netherlands
Canada	New Zealand
Denmark	Norway
Ghana	Pakistan
India	Sweden

Appendix D-5

Lebanon 1958 (UNOGIL)

The United Nations Observation Group in Lebanon (UNOGIL) was established as strictly an observer group to provide mobile teams to determine if the small eastern Mediterranean country was threatened by hostile external forces.

Afghanistan
Argentina
Burma
Canada
Ceylon
Chile
Denmark
Ecuador
Finland
India
Indonesia
Ireland
Italy
Nepal
Netherlands
New Zealand
Norway
Peru
Portugal
Sweden
Thailand

Appendix D-6

Gaza-Sinai 1956—present (UNEF)

The United Nations Emergency Force (UNEF) is still keeping the peace in the Gaza Strip separating Israel and Egypt. UNEF was organized in 1956 following the ceasefire between Egypt on the one hand and Britain, France and Israel on the other. The UN police force was installed between Egypt and Israel in an effort to maintain the peace and prevent a resumption of hostilities. Observer teams continue to move in the demarcation zone between both countries.

Brazil
Canada
Colombia
Denmark
Finland
India
Indonesia
Norway
Sweden
Yugoslavia

Appendix D-7

West Irian 1962-1963 (UNTEA)

The UN Temporary Executive Authority in West New Guinea (UNTEA) consisted of military observers and a fifteen-hundred-man police force to keep the peace and maintain law and order during the transition to Indonesian control.

Brazil	Nigeria
Canada	Pakistan
Ceylon	Philippines
India	Sweden
Ireland	United States

Appendix D-8

Korea 1950—present (UNC)

Shortly after the outbreak of hostilities on June 25, 1950, Korea became the only case of the application of UN military sanctions to suppress aggression. The United States, acting as "agent" for the United Nations, organized a United Nations Command (UNC) and supervised the military campaign. However, this was not a true UN military operation in that all decisions were made by the United States without consultation with the United Nations. Since the armistice of July 27, 1953 a total of 600,000 U.S. and 750,000 additional Republic of Korea troops have served in Korea under the United Nations Command.

	MEDICAL UNITS
Australia	Sweden
Belgium	India
Canada	Italy
Colombia	Denmark
England	Norway
Ethiopia	
France	
Greece	
Luxembourg	
Netherlands	
New Zealand	
Philippines	
Republic of Korea	
Thailand	
Turkey	
South Africa	
United States	

Appendix D-9

Palestine-Israel 1949—present (UNTSO)

Military observer group called United Nations Truce Supervision Organization (UNTSO) serves as watchdog along troubled borders common between Israel and neighboring Arab countries.

Australia	Italy
Belgium	Netherlands
Canada	New Zealand
Denmark	Norway
France	Sweden
Ireland	United States

Appendix D-10

Indonesia 1948-1949

An observer group called the United Nations Commission for Indonesia was charged with supervising the transfer of the former Dutch colony to the new government of Indonesia.

Australia	United Kingdom
Belgium	United States
France	

Appendix D-11

Kashmir 1948—present (UNMOGIP)

Originally called United Nations Commission India-Pakistan (UNCIP), this group of military observers has since changed its name to United Nation Military Observer Group India-Pakistan (UNMOGIP) and is charged with patrolling to insure that neither of the two nations involved intrudes in the territory under dispute.

Australia	Italy
Belgium	Mexico
Canada	New Zealand
Chile	Norway
Denmark	Sweden
Ecuador	United States
Finland	

Appendix D-12

Greece 1948 (UNSCOB)

The first UN peacekeeping operation was in Greece, beginning in January, 1948, and was known as the United Nations Special Committee on the Balkans (UNSCOB). Swedish military observers later followed.

Australia:	Lt. Col. W. R. Hodgson
Brazil:	Casco T. L. da Cunha
China:	Sih Kwang-tsien
France:	Emil Charveriat
Mexico:	General Tomas Sanchez Hernandez
Netherlands:	Colonel J. J. A. Keuchenius
Pakistan:	Colonel R. S. Chhatari
United Kingdom:	Brigadier J. C. Saunders-Jacobs
United States:	Admiral Alan G. Kirk, chairman of the Mission

Selected Bibliography

Bloomfield, Lincoln P., ed., *International Military Forces:* Boston: Little, Brown and Co., 1964.

Burns, Arthur Lee and Heathcote, Nina. *Peace-Keeping by U. N. Forces: From Suez to the Congo.* New York: Praeger, 1963.

Caidin, Martin. *The Long Arm of America.* New York: Dutton, 1964.

Frye, William R. *A United Nations Peace Force.* New York: Oceana Publications, 1957.

Goodrich, Leland M. *Korea: A Study of U. S. Policy in the United Nations.* New York: Council on Foreign Relations, 1956.

Gordon, King. *The U. N. in the Congo: A Quest for Peace.* New York: Carnegie Endowment for International Peace, 1962.

Hempstone, Smith. *Rebels, Mercenaries and Dividends: The Katanga Story.* New York: Praeger, 1962.

Hennessy, Maurice N. *The Congo: A Brief History and Appraisal.* New York: Praeger, 1961.

Lash, Joseph P. *Dag Hammarskjold: Custodian of the Brushfire Peace.* Garden City: Doubleday, 1961.

Lawson, Richard. *Strange Soldiering.* London: Hodder and Stoughton, 1963.

Lefever, Ernest W. *Crisis in the Congo: A U. N. Force in Action.* Washington, D. C.: The Brookings Institution, 1965.

Lie, Trygve. *In the Cause of Peace.* New York: Macmillan, 1954.

Murphy, Robert. *Diplomat Among Warriors.* New York: Doubleday, 1964.

O'Brien, Conor Cruise. *To Katanga and Back: A UN Case History.* New York: Simon and Schuster, 1962.

Rees, David. *Korea: The Limited War.* New York: St. Martin's Press, 1964.

Ritner, Peter. *The Death of Africa.* New York: Macmillan, 1960.

Rosner, Gabriella. *The United Nations Emergency Force.* New York: Columbia University Press, 1963.

Russell, Ruth B. *United Nations Experience with Military Forces: Political and Legal Aspects.* Washington: Brookings Institution Staff Paper, 1964.

Truman, Harry S. *Memoirs.* Garden City: Doubleday, 1955.

United Nations. *The United Nations and the Congo: Some Salient Facts.* New York: United Nations, 1963.

United Nations. *Everyman's United Nations: The Structure, Functions and Work of the Organization and Its Related Agencies During the Years 1945-1963.* New York: United Nations (seventh edition), October, 1964.

U. S. Army. *Area Handbook for the Republic of the Congo (Leopoldville).* Washington U. S. Government Printing Office, 1962.

U. S. Department of State. *The Elements in Our Congo Policy.* (Based on an address by Undersecretary of State George W. Ball, December 19, 1961.) Pub. No. 7326, African Series 25, December 1961.

Vleurinck, T., Ed., *46 Angry Men: U.N.O. Violations in Katanga.* Brussels: Printing Establissement E. Guyot, s.a., 1962.

Armstrong, Hamilton Fish. "The U. N. Experience in Gaza," *Foreign Affairs,* Vol. 35, No. 4, July 1957, pp. 600-19.

Haekkerup, Per. "Scandinavia's Peace-Keeping Forces for U. N.," *Foreign Affairs,* Vol. 42, July 1964, pp. 675-81.

Larson, Arthur and Don R. "A Plan for Peace in Vietnam," *Saturday Review,* April 24, 1965, pp. 21-24.

Pearson, Lester B. "Force for the U. N.," *Foreign Affairs,* Vol. 35, No. 3, April 1957, pp. 395-404.

Sterling, Claire. "Can the Congo Go It Alone?" *The Reporter,* June 18, 1964, pp. 27-31.

Watkins, Tarleton H. "The Congo Airlift," Air University Quarterly Review, Vol. 13, No. 1 (Summer 1961), pp. 19-33.

Index